# Guide to the Essentials of *American History*

Prentice Hall

Needham, Massachusetts
Upper Saddle River, New Jersey
Glenview, Illinois

## To the Teacher

The *Guide to the Essentials of American History* is designed to provide students with the most essential content in their high school American history course in an easy-to-follow format. The text summaries and graphic organizers will help students organize key information. Vocabulary terms are highlighted and defined in the text narrative, as well as in the glossary. A chapter test at the end of each chapter checks students' understanding of the basic content.

You may wish to use the *Guide to the Essentials* as a preview or review of the textbook chapters covered in the course, or as a summary of textbook chapters that cannot be studied in detail because of time considerations.

## Content Consultants


**Andrew Cayton**
Professor of History
Miami University
Oxford, Ohio

**Linda Reed**
Director
African American Studies Program
University of Houston
Houston, TX

**Elisabeth Israels Perry**
Professor of History
Saint Louis University
St. Louis, Missouri

**Allan Winkler**
Professor of History
Miami University
Oxford, OH


## Reading Consultant


**Bonnie Armbruster**
Professor of Education
University of Illinois at Urbana-Champaign
Urbana, IL





ISBN 0-13-062930-8
1 2 3 4 5 6 7 8 9 10 06 05 04 03 02

Prentice Hall

# Contents

## UNIT 7 Boom Times to Hard Times (1920–1938)



## UNIT 8 Hot and Cold War (1931–1960)



## UNIT 9 A Period of Turmoil and Change (1950–1975)



## UNIT 10 Continuity and Change (1969 to the Present)

# The Atlantic World, to 1600

CHAPTER 1

SECTION 1

## The Native American World

### TEXT SUMMARY

Experts conclude that the first Americans came from Asia thousands of years ago. In a great **migration,** a movement of people to settle in a new place, these people crossed over a land bridge, now known as the Bering Strait, that once connected Asia and Alaska.

The Native Americans adapted to the varying environments in which they settled. To the far North lived the Inuit and the Aleut. In the Northwest lived the Coos, Coast Salish, and Maka. On the Pacific Coast lived the Cumash and Yurok. On the Plateau lived the Chinook and the Cayuse. On the Great Basin lived the Paiute, Ute, and Shoshoni. In the Southwest lived the Hopi and the Zuñi, along with the Anasazi, who are descendants of the Pueblo people. On the Plains lived the Mandans, Wichita, and Pawnee, and in the Northeast lived the matrilineal groups the Seneca and the Lanape. Also in this area were the Iroquois, five groups of similar language and culture. They formed this group to end constant warfare among their tribes. In the Southeast lived the Hopewell or "mound builders."

Although ways of life varied, most Native Americans shared social structures based on **kinship,** family relationships, and organized their societies into **clans,** groups of families descended from a common ancestor. They shared common religious beliefs and passed customs and traditions down through **oral histories.**

**Barter,** or trade, was also a shared tradition. Trade routes followed by Native Americans crisscrossed North America. One thing that was never traded was land, for Native Americans believed that no one person or group owned the land, and it could not be bought and sold.

**THE BIG IDEA**

**Over thousands of years, Native Americans in North America developed different ways of life with many shared traditions.**

### GRAPHIC SUMMARY: *Native American Societies*

| SIMILARITIES | DIFFERENCES |
|---|---|
| • Social structure based on families and clans<br>• Religious ceremonies recognized powerful spiritual forces in world<br>• Economic life depended on barter<br>• Belief that land could not be owned | • Way of life adapted to environment<br>• Some farmed; some hunted and fished; some were nomads<br>• Many different cultural groups existed |

**Although Native Americans developed different ways of life, they shared a number of customs and beliefs.**

### REVIEW QUESTIONS

1. How did the first people arrive in the Americas?
2. **Chart Skills** How did Native Americans feel about land?

# SECTION 2 THE EUROPEAN WORLD

## TEXT SUMMARY

In the **Middle Ages** (around A.D. 500 to 1300), life was organized around **feudalism.** Under this system, peasants, called serfs, farmed a lord's land and gave their lord a portion of the harvest. Europe's foreign trade all but stopped. About the only educated people were the clergy of the Roman Catholic Church, which had great power.

> **THE BIG IDEA**
>
> **As the Middle Ages gave way to the Renaissance, Europeans began to explore the larger world.**

Around the year 1000, new farming methods produced more food and populations grew. New trade ties developed as a result of the **Crusades,** military campaigns by Christians to take Jerusalem from the Muslims. Trade led to the growth of cities and the rise of a **middle class** of merchants, traders, and artisans. Feudalism weakened, and **monarchs,** rulers of a territory or state, gained power. Monarchs clashed with nobles, and in 1215 England's weak King John was forced to sign the **Magna Carta,** a document granting nobles various legal rights and the basis for the English parliamentary system.

Beginning in 1300 was a period of great creativity and change called the **Renaissance**. Scholars, artists, and writers sought knowledge in nearly every field of study. Martin Luther, a German monk, revolted against the power of the Church and began a new religion called Protestantism, based on the Bible, not the clergy, as the true authority. His revolt began what was known as the **Reformation.**

With expanded knowledge, the power of the Church declined, and monarchs became more powerful, forming nation-states, which soon began competing for trade with Asia. Two powerful nations, Spain and Portugal, challenged each other to open sea routes to Asia.

## GRAPHIC SUMMARY: *From the Middle Ages to the Renaissance*

| EARLY MIDDLE AGES (500–1000) | LATE MIDDLE AGES (1000–1300) | RENAISSANCE (1300–1500) |
|---|---|---|
| • Isolation of Europe<br>• Feudalism<br>• Powerful Roman Catholic Church | • Crusades<br>• Trade with Asia<br>• Growth of cities<br>• Rise of monarchs<br>• Rise of universities | • Pursuit of learning<br>• Invention of printing press<br>• Formation of new Protestant churches<br>• Development of seafaring technology<br>• Competition among nations |

**As Europe moved from the Middle Ages to the Renaissance, interest in the outside world increased.**

## REVIEW QUESTIONS

1. Which groups were powerful in Europe during the Early Middle Ages?
2. **Chart Skills** In which period did trade become important to Europe?

# SECTION 3 THE WORLD OF THE WEST AFRICANS

## TEXT SUMMARY

In the 1400s West Africa had three distinct vegetation regions that affected the way people lived their lives. In rain forests along the coast, people hunted, fished, mined, and farmed. Farther north, in the drier areas of grasslands, the **savanna,** nomadic people hunted and raised livestock. Even farther north lay the desert, which remained largely uninhabited.

West African cultures were organized along kinship lines, tracing their origins to a common ancestor, a system called **lineage.** Lineage groups formed the ruling classes and kingdoms.

West Africans' ideas about land differed from those of Europeans. In Europe land was **scarce,** in short supply, so Europeans counted wealth and power in the amount of land they owned. Land in West Africa was plentiful, and labor was valued more than land. Kings were powerful because of the number of people they could rule, which included many slaves to work the land.

West Africans' ideas of slavery also differed from those of Europeans. Slaves in West Africa were war captives, criminals, orphans, and people captured from rival lineage groups. African slaves could be adopted into a new lineage and were sometimes given high positions in society or government. By the 1500s Portugal and Spain were exchanging goods and technology with these kingdoms for African slaves. As the Americas developed, Europeans demanded more and more slaves and conducted bloody slave raids.

**THE BIG IDEA**

**At the time of European contact, West African rulers had built wealthy kingdoms with distinct cultures.**

## GRAPHIC SUMMARY: *West African Societies, 1400s*

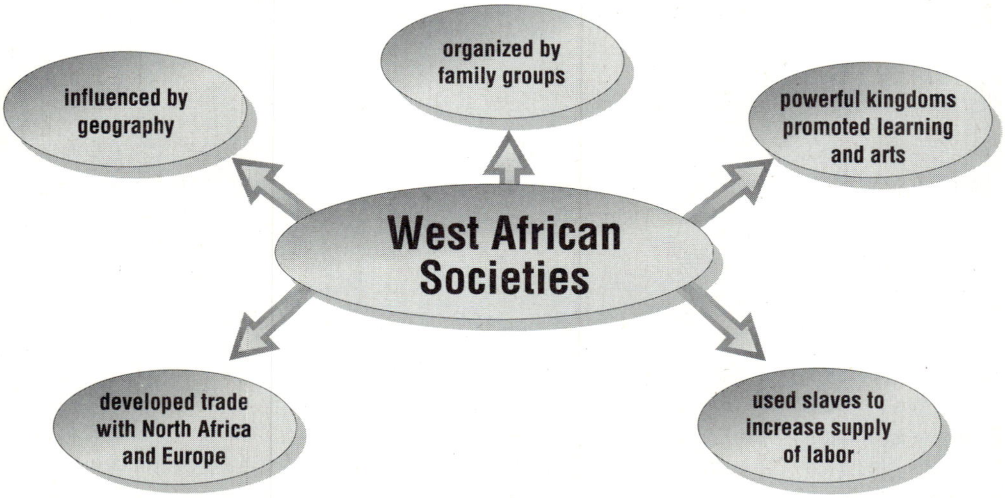


In the 1400s West African kingdoms had complex societies.

## REVIEW QUESTIONS

1. What three geographic regions existed in West Africa and how did these environments affect life in each area?
2. **Chart Skills** Identify three characteristics of West African societies.

SECTION 4

# THE ATLANTIC WORLD IS BORN

## TEXT SUMMARY

**THE BIG IDEA**

**Columbus's voyage to the Americas led to a reshaping of American, European, and African history.**

When Christopher Columbus set sail from Spain in 1492, he was searching for a western trade route to Asia. He sought glory, honor, and fame. His patrons, the monarchs of Spain, sought to spread Christianity, but more importantly to find the trade route in order to compete with the Portuguese, who had already sailed around Africa east to India. After a difficult voyage, Columbus finally reached land, but it was not India. He had arrived in the Americas. Columbus met with Native Americans who offered him gifts, which Columbus took back to Spain.

The historic first voyage of Columbus and his three later trips led Europeans to realize that a new continent lay to the west. Columbus's voyages and those of explorers who followed him resulted in a new era of transatlantic trade known as the **Columbian Exchange.** Ships carried new products like tomatoes, potatoes, and cocoa to Europe, and Europeans introduced grains such as wheat, animals such as cattle and horses, and technologies such as firearms and the wheel to the Americas. However, Europeans also brought diseases, such as smallpox, that devastated Native American populations.

Europeans gained immense wealth from the gold and silver they took from the Americas as well as agricultural products they demanded. To supply Europe, Spain and Portugal built **plantations,** huge farms that produced **cash crops,** crops that were not for their own use but to sell in Europe. Because huge numbers of workers were required to work these plantations, and so many Native Americans died from disease, the Europeans turned to the West African slave trade to fill this need. Over two centuries, some six million Africans were taken from West Africa and enslaved into a system in which they became the lifetime property of their owners.

## GRAPHIC SUMMARY: *Columbus's Voyage*

**CAUSES**

- Quest for knowledge of the world
- Wish to bring Christianity to other lands and peoples
- Desire for new trade routes to the East
- Rivalry with Portugal
- Desire for wealth

**Columbus's Voyage** →

**EFFECTS**

- Columbian Exchange
- Conquest of Native Americans and establishment of European empires in the Americas
- Deaths of many Native Americans from disease
- Enslavement of Africans
- Blending of cultures in America

## REVIEW QUESTIONS

1. Why did Columbus's Spanish patrons support the voyage?
2. **Chart Skills** List two causes and two effects of Columbus's voyage.

Name ______________________ Class ______________ Date __________

# CHAPTER 1 Test

## IDENTIFYING MAIN IDEAS

Write the letter of the correct answer in the blank provided. (10 points each)

____ **1.** Native Americans' way of life was influenced by their
- **A.** history.
- **B.** wealth.
- **C.** religion.
- **D.** environment.

____ **2.** The social structure of Native American groups was often based on
- **A.** family and clan.
- **B.** location.
- **C.** the environment.
- **D.** individualism.

____ **3.** Native American trading networks were
- **A.** extensive.
- **B.** limited.
- **C.** locally based.
- **D.** nonexistent.

____ **4.** During the Early Middle Ages, Europeans
- **A.** were isolated from the rest of the world.
- **B.** traded widely with the rest of the world.
- **C.** were constantly at war with outsiders.
- **D.** were able to maintain high levels of learning.

____ **5.** Which of the following declined during the Renaissance?
- **A.** the power of individual monarchs
- **B.** the power of the church
- **C.** the number of large cities
- **D.** the number of explorers

____ **6.** The increase in trade caused European monarchs
- **A.** to be weakened.
- **B.** to cooperate with one another.
- **C.** to compete with one another.
- **D.** to turn to the church for help.

____ **7.** At first, Europeans and West Africans developed a relationship based on
- **A.** slavery.
- **B.** war.
- **C.** religion.
- **D.** trade.

____ **8.** One way African slavery differed from the way Europeans began to practice it was that
- **A.** persons enslaved by Europeans performed physical labor.
- **B.** persons enslaved in Europe could become free by becoming soldiers.
- **C.** persons enslaved in Africa could leave slavery.
- **D.** the children of those enslaved by Europeans did not automatically become slaves.

____ **9.** One reason the rulers of Spain supported Columbus's journey was
- **A.** to win an advantage over their European rivals.
- **B.** to increase their trade in African slaves.
- **C.** to make contact with the natives of the Americas.
- **D.** to find a source of new types of food for their people.

____ **10.** The Spanish began bringing African slaves to the Americas
- **A.** to fight against Native American rebels.
- **B.** as a new source of labor.
- **C.** immediately after settling their first colonies.
- **D.** to work alongside Native Americans on plantations.

CHAPTER 2

# European Colonization of the Americas (1492–1752)

SECTION 1

## SPANISH EXPLORERS AND COLONIES

### TEXT SUMMARY

After Columbus, more Spanish explorers, such as Ponce de León, Balboa, and Magellan, expanded European knowledge of lands and seas from Florida to the Pacific and around the globe. Spain established **colonies,** areas settled by immigrants who continue to be ruled by the parent country. Soon, Spanish **conquistadors,** or conquerors, such as Cortés and Pizarro, who wanted to spread Christianity and gain fame and riches, arrived and conquered the empires of the Aztecs in Mexico and the Incas in Peru. The conquistadors built more colonies, and Spain gained great wealth from gold and silver mines and vast ranches and farms worked by Native Americans under the *encomienda* system.

**THE BIG IDEA**

**After 1492 the Spanish built an empire that stretched from South America to the Southwest and Southeast of North America.**

Spanish explorers pushed north into the present-day southeastern United States. They established **presidios,** or forts to protect ships carrying gold and silver to Spain. Spain also pushed into what is now California. The Spanish hoped to expand their mining industry into the Southwest and establish trade routes across the Pacific from California.

The Spanish also established many **missions,** settlements of Catholic priests to preach, teach, and convert Native Americans to Christianity. But some Native Americans resisted, and in the late 1600s, revolts, such as the **Pueblo Revolt of 1680** in which Native Americans drove the Spanish out of Santa Fe, New Mexico, destroyed many Spanish missions and weakened Spain's control in those areas.

### GRAPHIC SUMMARY: *The Spanish in the Americas*

THE SPANISH IN THE AMERICAS

- Spanish conquistadors explore the Americas, conquering Native American peoples and starting colonies.
- The Spanish force Native Americans to work on farms and in mines, producing great riches for Spain.
- In North America the Spanish build missions, where priests attempt to convert Native Americans to Christianity and have them adopt European customs.

**Spain conquered Native Americans and started colonies in the Americas that brought it great wealth.**

### REVIEW QUESTIONS

1. How did Spain gain great riches from its colonies?
2. **Chart Skills** What was the purpose of the Spanish missions?

# SECTION 2 JAMESTOWN

## TEXT SUMMARY

English explorers sailed along the North Atlantic Coast in search of the Northwest Passage, a route through North America to Asia, while English adventurers, called **privateers,** attacked and pirated Spanish ships.

Attempts by England in the late 1580s to build colonies had failed, most notably the Roanoke Island colony started by Sir Walter Raleigh. In 1607 a group of investors formed a **joint-stock company,** received a **charter,** and founded the colony of Jamestown in Virginia. The colony almost failed due to conflict with Native Americans, unrealistic expectations, location, starvation, and poor leadership. Jamestown was governed by a **legislature,** a lawmaking assembly of representatives from the colony known as the **House of Burgesses.** Virginia was a **royal colony** whose governor was appointed by the king. The colony started to thrive when colonists began growing and shipping tobacco to England. Many workers were needed to grow this profitable crop, and landowners brought **indentured servants** from England, who worked for a period of time in exchange for payment of their passage.

As more settlers arrived in Jamestown, some became discontented with the colonial government. In 1676 Nathaniel Bacon led **Bacon's Rebellion.** Bacon and his supporters attacked and burned Jamestown, and although he held much of Virginia for a time, the rebellion crumbled when he died suddenly. Bacon's Rebellion showed that the frontier settlers were frustrated with the government.

**THE BIG IDEA**

**The English overcame hunger, disease, and conflicts with Native Americans to establish a successful colony in Virginia.**

## GRAPHIC SUMMARY: *The First English Colonies*

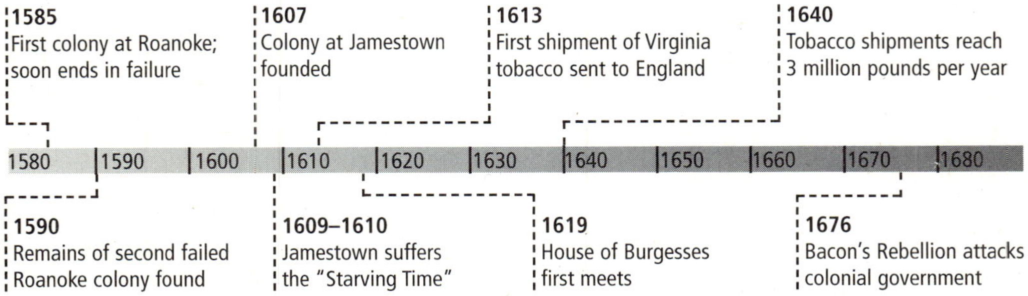


**After a failed attempt at Roanoke, the English slowly built a successful colony at Jamestown.**

## REVIEW QUESTIONS

1. What was the cause of Bacon's Rebellion?
2. **Time Line Skills** How many years after Jamestown was founded did the House of Burgesses first meet?

# SECTION 3 THE NEW ENGLAND COLONIES

## TEXT SUMMARY

Like Spain and England, France sent explorers to North America and they established a colony along the St. Lawrence River called New France. New France stretched to the Great Lakes and was built on a successful fur trade with Native Americans.

**THE BIG IDEA**

**During the early 1600s the French and English established colonies on land that is now Canada and the northeastern United States.**

While the French were expanding their fur trade, the English were building the **New England Colonies** along the northeastern Atlantic coast. The founders were called **Puritans** because they wanted a "purer" religion. They had been **persecuted** in England and wanted to worship freely. In 1620 Puritans, known as Pilgrims, founded the Plymouth Colony and drew up the **Mayflower Compact,** agreeing to obey rules to govern their colony. Ten years later, another group of Puritans founded the Massachusetts Bay Colony, which grew quickly during the **Great Migration** to a community of small towns, farms, and the city of Boston.

As the population expanded and farmland grew scarce, some Puritans left Massachusetts to set up other colonies. Conflict with Puritan authorities who did not believe in **religious tolerance,** that people of different religious beliefs could live together in peace, also drove some to found the colony of Rhode Island.

The expansion of New England pushed Native Americans off their lands, and they rebelled. In the **Pequot War,** Connecticut settlers defeated and wiped out most of the Pequot people. In **King Philip's War,** Native Americans destroyed many English towns and farms, but were finally overwhelmed. By 1676 English settlers had conquered most of the region.

## GRAPHIC SUMMARY: *The New England Colonies*

| Colony | Settled In | Reason for Settlement | Economic Activities |
|---|---|---|---|
| Massachusetts | | | |
| Plymouth | 1620 | Escape religious persecution | Fishing, lumber, shipbuilding, whaling, trade |
| Massachusetts Bay | 1630 | Establish a Puritan society | |
| New Hampshire | 1623 | Escape religious persecution; profit from trade and fishing | Trade, fishing |
| Connecticut | 1636 | Establish a Puritan settlement; establish a fur trade route | Fur trade |
| Rhode Island | 1636 | Escape religious intolerence of Massachusetts Bay | Shipping, farming |

**Many settlers came to New England in search of religious freedom.**

## REVIEW QUESTIONS

1. Why were the first New England settlers called Puritans?
2. **Chart Skills** What was the reason for the settlement of Rhode Island?

# SECTION 4 THE MIDDLE AND SOUTHERN COLONIES

## TEXT SUMMARY

England also established the **Middle Colonies** of New York, Pennsylvania, New Jersey, and Delaware. These colonies were places of great **diversity,** or variety, of people. The original Dutch colony of New Netherland contained the first **synagogue,** or house of Jewish worship, in North America. This colony was taken over by the English in 1664 and became New York as a **proprietary colony,** one granted by a monarch to an individual or group to govern.

William Penn, a **Quaker**, founded Pennsylvania as a **haven,** or safe place for people of different backgrounds to settle. Swedish settlers started a colony in Delaware. It became part of the English colony of Pennsylvania. New Jersey was split between two English noblemen but eventually became one colony. All the Middle Colonies were proprietary colonies until the 1700s, when they became royal colonies whose governors were appointed by the king.

The Southern Colonies included Virginia, Maryland, the Carolinas, and Georgia. Maryland was founded as a safe place for Roman Catholics. The Carolinas were given by the king to a group of noblemen and split into North and South Carolina. Georgia was founded as a refuge for people who had been jailed in England because they could not pay their debts. Georgia was ruled by **trustees,** people who look after a business.

**THE BIG IDEA**

**Settlers came to the Middle and Southern Colonies in search of religious freedom and economic opportunities.**

## GRAPHIC SUMMARY: *The Middle and Southern Colonies*

| The Middle Colonies | Date | Reason for Settlement | Economic Activities |
|---|---|---|---|
| New York | 1625 | Expansion | Trade, farming, lumber, furs, shipbuilding |
| Delaware | 1638 | Trade | Trade, farming |
| New Jersey | 1664 | Trade; haven for Quakers | Trade, farming |
| Pennsylvania | 1637 | Haven for Quakers; religious tolerance | Trade, farming |
| **The Southern Colonies** | | | |
| Virginia | 1607 | Search for gold | Tobacco |
| Maryland | 1632 | Haven for Catholics; religious tolerance | Tobacco |
| The Carolinas | 1663 | Land wealth; home for small farmers | Rice, indigo, tobacco |
| Georgia | 1732 | Haven for debtors; buffer Carolinas from Spain | Rice, indigo, lumber, trade |

**The Middle and Southern Colonies were founded for a variety of reasons, and colonists there pursued varied economic activities.**

## REVIEW QUESTIONS

1. Why did William Penn found Pennsylvania?
2. **Chart Skills** What were the main economic activities in the Middle Colonies?

Name ________________________________ Class ____________________ Date __________

# CHAPTER 2 Test

## IDENTIFYING MAIN IDEAS

Write the letter of the correct answer in the blank provided. (10 points each)

____ **1.** The Spanish conquistadors conquered the Mexican empire of the
**A.** Incas.
**B.** Aztecs.
**C.** Mayans.
**D.** Pueblo.

____ **2.** At missions, Spanish priests worked to
**A.** explore the Americas.
**B.** convert Native Americans to Christianity.
**C.** search for gold.
**D.** encourage religious freedom.

____ **3.** In the Pueblo Revolt of 1680,
**A.** Spanish priests took over the missions.
**B.** Spanish farmers rebelled against the conquistadors.
**C.** Native Americans drove the Spanish out of Santa Fe, New Mexico.
**D.** Native Americans in New Mexico fought the Spanish and lost.

____ **4.** The House of Burgesses was significant because
**A.** it worked closely with Spanish explorers.
**B.** it solved problems between English settlers and Native Americans.
**C.** it was an important step toward self-government in the English colonies.
**D.** it was run by poorer colonists.

____ **5.** The growing of tobacco
**A.** was impossible at Jamestown.
**B.** ensured the failure of Jamestown.
**C.** ensured the success of Jamestown.
**D.** made life more difficult at Jamestown.

____ **6.** The French in North America established
**A.** colonies without contact with Native Americans.
**B.** large cities.
**C.** extensive agricultural settlements.
**D.** a fur trade with the Native Americans.

____ **7.** The New England Colonies were founded by people who wished to
**A.** explore Canada.
**B.** escape religious persecution.
**C.** search for gold.
**D.** convert the Native Americans.

____ **8.** During King Philip's War
**A.** rival English groups fought over religion.
**B.** Native Americans resisted the growth of English colonies.
**C.** the French and English fought over North America.
**D.** the English and Native Americans fought Spanish raiders.

____ **9.** The Middle Colonies were all
**A.** founded by the Dutch.
**B.** havens for Quakers.
**C.** tobacco-growing regions.
**D.** proprietary colonies granted by the king.

____ **10.** People jailed for debt in England could find a haven in
**A.** Pennsylvania.
**B.** Georgia.
**C.** New York.
**D.** Delaware.

# Growth of the American Colonies (1689–1754)

CHAPTER 3

## SECTION 1 AN EMPIRE AND ITS COLONIES

### TEXT SUMMARY

By the end of the 1600s many nations of Europe supported **mercantilism,** the theory that a nation should obtain as much bullion, gold and silver, as possible. Nations could gain bullion through a **balance of trade,** or the difference in value between imports and exports. To help its balance of trade, England passed the Navigation Act. It placed a **duty,** or tax, on goods colonists sold to other nations. This law made England the main recipient of colonial goods. It also angered the colonists.

However, the monarchs followed a policy of **salutary neglect,** under which they did not strictly enforce their trade regulations and allowed the colonies a great deal of self-government. Both England and the colonies prospered from the arrangement.

Colonial economies were diverse. In the Southern Colonies, **staple crops,** those always in demand, were harvested by slave labor on large plantations. There were few towns and cities. In the Middle Colonies, the economy was a mixture of farming and commerce.

The New England Colonies consisted of small towns and farms. Atlantic traders' ships carried goods from England to the Caribbean where they traded for sugar, which was turned into rum back in New England. The rum was then carried to Africa and exchanged for slaves, who were taken back to the Caribbean to work on the plantations. The system was called **triangular trade.**

**THE BIG IDEA**

**During the mid-1600s and early 1700s, the American colonies grew and prospered with little interference from England.**

### GRAPHIC SUMMARY: *Triangular Trade*

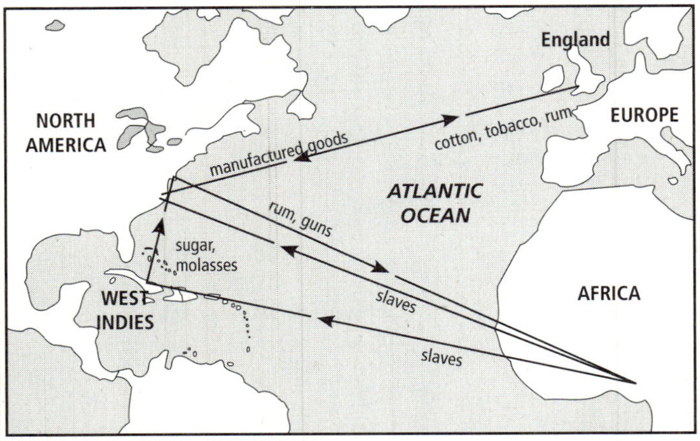


American merchants profited from trade with England, Africa, and the West Indies.

### REVIEW QUESTIONS

1. Describe the theory of mercantilism.
2. **Map Skills** What was shipped from England to the British colonies in triangular trade?

# SECTION 2 LIFE IN COLONIAL AMERICA

## TEXT SUMMARY

**THE BIG IDEA**

**In colonial society, groups had different roles and ways of living.**

Most colonists believed that the wealthy and powerful were superior members of society, and people were divided into different social ranks. At the top were the **gentry,** the wealthy who set themselves apart as large landowners and displayed their status through their manners, expensive clothes, and elaborate homes.

However, those from other walks of life had opportunities to develop specialized skills and trades. Boys from most families became **apprentices,** people placed under legal contract to work for another person in exchange for learning a trade. Artisans created furniture, glassware, silver items, tinware, and pottery. Colonial printers collected and circulated news and information. Farmers provided food, and coastal settlers hauled abundant fish from the sea. Indentured servants were often harshly treated, but they could hope for their freedom after a number of years.

Colonial women were under the control of their husbands and had no political or legal standing. Nevertheless, women's work managing the home, caring for children, cooking, weaving, and making clothing contributed to the well-being of the entire community. Colonial households were mostly **self-sufficient,** being able to make what they needed to maintain themselves. Colonists worked hard, but they lived better than most of their European counterparts.

Although school attendance was not required, the New England Colonies were early leaders in developing public education through grammar schools. Outside New England, if no public schools existed, children were taught at home.

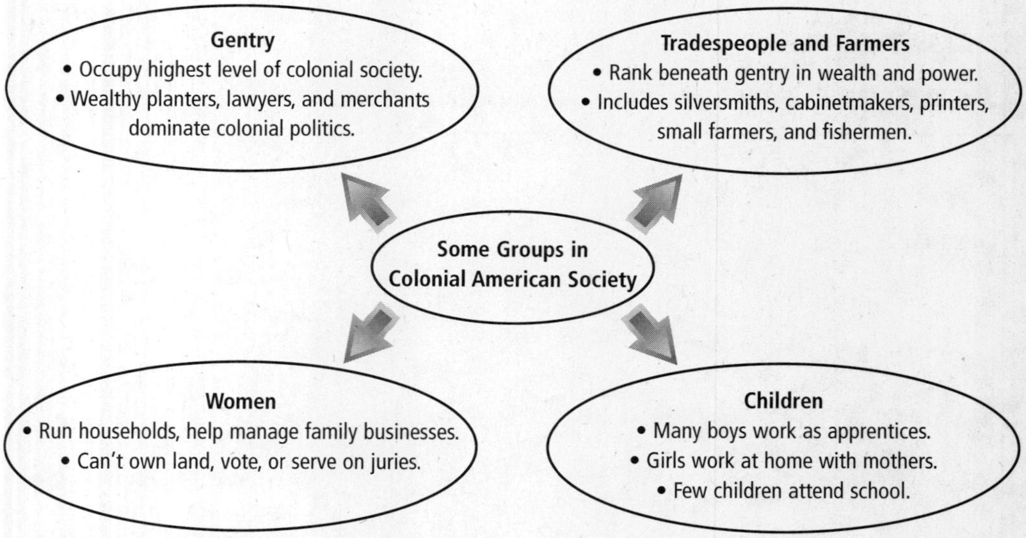


The American colonies developed diverse societies in which people had different rights and responsibilities.

## REVIEW QUESTIONS

1. How did boys learn a trade in colonial times?
2. **Diagram Skills** Which group was at the highest level of colonial society?

SECTION 3

# AFRICAN AMERICANS IN THE COLONIES

## TEXT SUMMARY

Enslaved Africans were carried from Africa to the Americas across the Atlantic Ocean on a voyage called the **Middle Passage.** Chained and crowded together, it is estimated that up to 40 percent died in the crossing. Some led **mutinies,** or revolts, but most were unsuccessful.

The lives of enslaved Africans varied from region to region. In the Carolinas and Georgia, where slaves were the majority, conditions in the plantation fields were brutal, as heat and disease took a terrible toll. These Africans were isolated from Europeans, allowing them to preserve some of their cultural traditions.

In Virginia and Maryland, Africans were not in the majority, relatively few came from Africa, and they were allowed to perform other work. They had more regular contact with Europeans, leading to an integration of culture.

In the Middle and New England Colonies, slave labor was not needed as much. Enslaved Africans here did other jobs, including fishing and trading.

A small free black population existed at this time. Free Africans performed much of the same kind of work as slaves, but they faced poor economic conditions and severe discrimination.

Whites passed harsh laws to restrict the movement of slaves and enacted severe punishments for minor offenses. Rebellion was difficult since slaves in one area had limited contact with slaves in another. Nevertheless, several slave revolts, such as the **Stono Rebellion** in South Carolina, occurred in the 1700s.

**THE BIG IDEA**

**Africans, brought to America as slaves, helped build the colonies while enduring harsh and brutal treatment.**

## GRAPHIC SUMMARY: *African American Population*

| Year | New England Colonies | Middle Colonies | Southern Colonies |
|---|---|---|---|
| 1690 | 905 | 2,472 | 13,307 |
| 1700 | 1,680 | 3,361 | 22,476 |
| 1710 | 2,585 | 6,218 | 36,063 |
| 1720 | 3,956 | 10,825 | 54,058 |
| 1730 | 6,118 | 11,683 | 73,220 |
| 1740 | 8,541 | 16,452 | 125,031 |
| 1750 | 10,982 | 20,736 | 204,702 |

Source: *Historical Statistics of the United States, Colonial Times to 1970*

The African American population grew rapidly during the early 1700s.

## REVIEW QUESTIONS

1. Describe the conditions of the Middle Passage.
2. **Chart Skills** Which region had the largest population of African Americans in 1750?

# SECTION 4 EMERGING TENSIONS

## TEXT SUMMARY

Because of a rising birth rate and the influx of **immigrants,** people who enter a new country to settle, the colonial population grew rapidly in the mid-1700s. Land on the eastern coast was shrinking, and settlers looked to the interior. Many began to **migrate,** or move, west.

As settlers moved, they took over Native American lands, causing conflicts. Colonists migrating west also clashed with French settlers, who were disturbed because the British were building trading posts in the Ohio Valley, an area claimed by France. Tensions increased along the western frontier when Virginia and Pennsylvania colonists confronted the French and Native Americans over control of the area around the forks of the Ohio River.

Religious tensions increased in the 1730s and 1740s when the **Great Awakening** swept through the colonies. This religious movement was meant to revive religious feelings and renew people's religious commitments. **Itinerant,** or traveling, ministers toured the colonies, preaching that rich or poor, young or old, men or women could have a personal relationship with God. This idea attracted many ordinary people and led to growing feelings of equality among colonists. Many split from traditional churches, and others joined new churches, which were often more tolerant of **dissent,** or differences of opinion, than traditional churches.

### THE BIG IDEA

**During the mid-1700s, the American colonies grew quickly and experienced a new religious movement.**

## GRAPHIC SUMMARY: *Colonists Move West*

### Causes

- Population of colonies increases quickly due to high birth rate and immigration.
- Colonists begin to feel crowded.
- Many colonies lack enough fertile land for growing population.

**Colonists Move West**

### Effects

- Settlers take over Native American lands.
- Native Americans forced onto land already occupied by other Indian groups.
- British build trading posts in areas claimed by France.
- France responds by preparing for war.

In the mid-1700s, English colonists began moving west.

## REVIEW QUESTIONS

1. What caused the population of the colonies to grow in the mid-1700s?
2. **Chart Skills** How did the French respond to the westward movement of English settlers?

Name ______________________ Class ______________ Date __________

# CHAPTER 3 Test

## IDENTIFYING MAIN IDEAS

Write the letter of the correct answer in the blank provided. (10 points each)

____ **1.** During the mid-1600s, England
**A.** directly interfered with the colonial economy.
**B.** allowed the colonies a great deal of freedom.
**C.** shipped raw materials to the colonies.
**D.** did not benefit from the colonies.

____ **2.** The economy of the Middle Colonies was based on
**A.** commerce.
**B.** farming.
**C.** both farming and commerce.
**D.** large plantations.

____ **3.** Triangular trade involved trade between
**A.** Africa, England, and the Americas.
**B.** Africa and the West Indies.
**C.** New England, the Middle Colonies, and England.
**D.** New England, the Middle Colonies, and the South.

____ **4.** In colonial America, the gentry
**A.** could not hire others to work for them.
**B.** had no legal rights.
**C.** had power and wealth.
**D.** worked as apprentices.

____ **5.** In colonial society, boys from many families
**A.** went to public school.
**B.** worked on plantations.
**C.** worked as apprentices.
**D.** worked at home with their mothers.

____ **6.** In the English colonies, women
**A.** had few legal rights.
**B.** were equal to men.
**C.** ran most farms and businesses.
**D.** made no contributions to society.

____ **7.** In the Southern Colonies, slaves
**A.** worked under especially harsh conditions.
**B.** worked mostly on small farms.
**C.** could travel without written permission.
**D.** were an unimportant part of the farming economy.

____ **8.** In the Middle Colonies and New England Colonies most slaves lived
**A.** on ships.
**B.** on plantations.
**C.** in cities.
**D.** on small farms.

____ **9.** Colonists moved west in the mid-1700s
**A.** in search of land of their own.
**B.** because Native Americans were pushing them west.
**C.** because the French were building forts on the frontier.
**D.** to escape the Great Awakening.

____ **10.** The Great Awakening was the name for
**A.** a religious movement.
**B.** a time of economic success.
**C.** an increase in the number of immigrants.
**D.** the movement west of British settlers.

CHAPTER 4

# The Road to Independence (1753–1783)

## SECTION 1 THE FRENCH AND INDIAN WAR

### TEXT SUMMARY

**THE BIG IDEA**

**The French and Indian War brought about increased tensions between American colonists and Great Britain.**

The **French and Indian War,** between the British and their colonies and the French and their Indian allies, began in 1754 and was the result of the struggle among the British, French, and Native Americans for control of North American lands.

As the war began, a group of delegates from seven northern colonies met in Albany, New York, to try to form a union of the colonies for the war effort. Called the **Albany Plan of Union,** it was rejected by all the colonies because they did not want too much power in a central government. However, the plan was a model for the future U.S. government.

After early defeats, the British and the colonial **militia,** armed citizens who serve as soldiers in an emergency, began to win. The tide of war turned as the British sent better-prepared and better-led soldiers. Seizing most French forts along the St. Lawrence River, the British finally laid siege to the city of Quebec. British troops surrounded the city and its defenders surrendered. In the **Treaty of Paris (1763),** the French turned over Canada to the British and surrendered its claims to almost all lands in North America.

The war strained relations between the British, who thought the colonists had not contributed enough, and the colonists, who thought British military power was weak. The colonists also felt the British had not treated them with enough respect, and now that the French were gone from the west, the colonists wanted to move onto these lands and prosper without British restraints.

### GRAPHIC SUMMARY: *Land Claims after the French and Indian War, 1763*

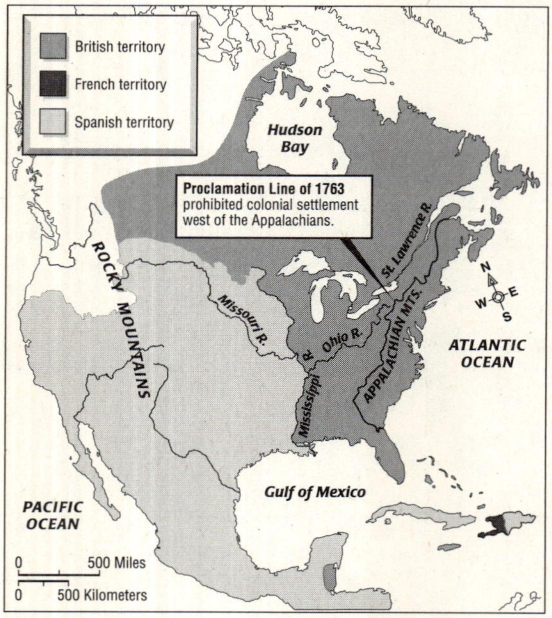


After the French and Indian War, France was no longer a major power in North America.

### REVIEW QUESTIONS

1. How did the Treaty of Paris affect French power in North America?
2. **Map Skills** Which European country claimed Canada after the French and Indian War?

SECTION 2

# ISSUES BEHIND THE REVOLUTION

## TEXT SUMMARY

Britain was left with debts from the French and Indian War, and money was needed to defend and govern its colonies. In addition, a Native American revolt, **Pontiac's Rebellion,** erupted in the Ohio Valley. When a number of British forts were seized and settlers killed, Britain issued the **Proclamation of 1763,** closing land west of the Appalachian Mountains to settlement.

To raise money, Britain passed a series of new taxes. The Sugar Act taxed molasses, hurting colonial trade, and the Quartering Act forced colonists to provide housing and supplies to British troops in the colonies.

The **Stamp Act,** which placed a tax on all printed materials, such as newspapers, pamphlets, and legal documents, especially angered colonists because it affected nearly everyone. Some colonists protested with a **boycott** of British goods, refusing to buy products.

Still insisting it had the right to tax the colonies, Britain placed further duties on imported goods. More boycotts limited some of Britain's laws, but many colonists remained angry. In Boston a protest erupted into violence and British soldiers killed five colonists. This event became known as the **Boston Massacre.**

In 1773 Parliament passed the Tea Act, and a group of angry colonists participated in the **Boston Tea Party** by dumping a shipload of British tea into the harbor. Colonists formed the **First Continental Congress** to decide what to do about the situation. The Congress advised the colonies to begin forming militias and storing weapons. In 1775, when the British decided to finally end this resistance, fighting broke out. The first shots were fired in Massachusetts at the **Battles of Lexington and Concord** between British troops and militia. The **Revolutionary War** for American independence had begun.

**THE BIG IDEA**

**British attempts to tax American colonists caused tensions that finally led to the American Revolution.**

## GRAPHIC SUMMARY: *The Road to Revolution*

| | |
|---|---|
| **1765** | • British pass Stamp Act<br>• Colonists protest, boycott British goods. |
| **1766–1767** | • British repeal Stamp Act.<br>• British pass Townshend Acts, a new series of taxes on imports. |
| **1770** | • In Boston Massacre, British soldiers fire on American protesters, killing five. |
| **1773** | • British pass Tea Act, placing new tax on imported tea.<br>• In protest, colonists hold Boston Tea Party, dumping British tea in harbor. |
| **1774** | • British pass Intolerable Acts to punish colonists.<br>• Colonial leaders meet at First Continental Congress. Colonial militias begin storing weapons. |
| **1775** | • Revolutionary War begins with battles of Lexington and Concord. |

**A long series of events led to the outbreak of the Revolutionary War.**

## REVIEW QUESTIONS

1. Why did the Stamp Act anger the colonists?
2. **Diagram Skills** How did colonists respond to the Tea Act?

# SECTION 3 IDEAS BEHIND THE REVOLUTION

## TEXT SUMMARY

**THE BIG IDEA**

**New ideas that people were born equal and could rule themselves helped inspire the American Revolution.**

At the beginning of the Revolutionary War, many Americans still hoped for a peaceful settlement. Others were convinced by a pamphlet called ***Common Sense.*** Written by Thomas Paine, it argued in forceful and easily understood terms that complete independence was needed.

To discuss the issue, delegates from the colonies met in Philadelphia in the summer of 1775 at the **Second Continental Congress.** When their **Olive Branch Petition,** a statement to the king that the colonists were loyal subjects and only wanted peace, was rejected by Britain, the delegates took another course. Deciding finally that it was time for complete independence, the delegates adopted the **Declaration of Independence,** written by Thomas Jefferson. Jefferson was influenced by the **Enlightenment,** a European intellectual movement that emphasized science and reason as the key to improving society.

The first section of the Declaration of Independence, the **preamble,** or introduction, explained the purpose of the document and was followed by a section explaining that people have **natural rights,** which belong to them because they are human beings. The third section listed the wrongs the colonists believed the British king had committed. Under a **rule of law,** Jefferson wrote that public officials must make decisions based on law, not on their personal wishes. The fourth section declared the colonies the independent United States of America. The Declaration was adopted on July 4, 1776.

## GRAPHIC SUMMARY: *The Declaration of Independence*

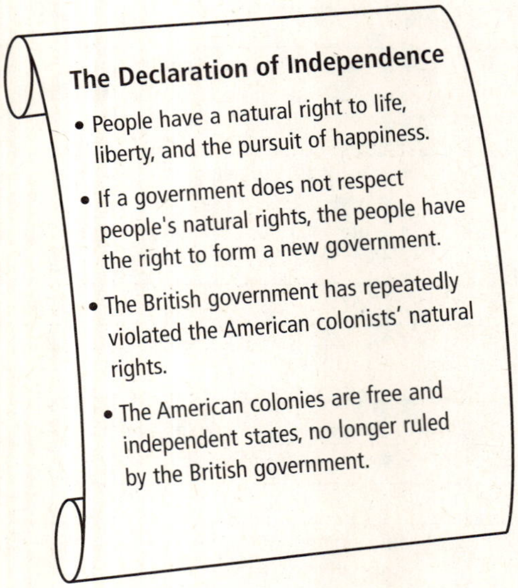


**Jefferson argued that Americans had the right to form their own government.**

## REVIEW QUESTIONS

1. What was rule of law?
2. **Chart Skills** List three natural rights given in the Declaration of Independence.

## SECTION 4 *FIGHTING FOR INDEPENDENCE*

### TEXT SUMMARY

In June 1775 the British won the first major battle of the war, the **Battle of Bunker Hill,** outside Boston. Although **casualties,** or persons killed, wounded, or missing, were high on both sides, the British felt they could easily defeat the Patriots. However, the Americans rallied and, with cannons taken from the British in northern New York, drove the British from Boston.

Both sides had strengths and weaknesses. Britain had a well-trained and well-supplied army, and its navy ruled the seas. Many **Loyalists,** colonists still loyal to Britain, also fought with the British, and they could count on Native American allies. However, the war was unpopular in Great Britain, and getting soldiers and supplies across the ocean took time. The British also hired **mercenaries,** foreign soldiers who fight for pay.

The Patriots had the advantage of fighting on their own land, and they had learned tactics from fighting in the French and Indian War. They also had a superb military leader in George Washington. Their disadvantage was the lack of a well-supplied, stable, and effective body of soldiers. Patriot troops often headed home when their term of service was over.

Leaving Boston, British forces attacked New York City, forcing Washington to retreat to New Jersey where he fought and won the **Battle of Trenton,** and gained a victory at Princeton. Defeats Washington suffered in Pennsylvania were offset by a great victory of Patriot forces in New York. At the **Battle of Saratoga,** Americans surrounded and cut off a large British force, which surrendered. The battle was a turning point in the war because it brought the French into the war on the side of the Patriots with supplies, loans, and fighting forces.

**THE BIG IDEA**

**After early defeats, the American army won key battles against the British in 1776 and 1777.**

### GRAPHIC SUMMARY: *Major battles of the Revolution, 1775–1777*

| BATTLE | YEAR | RESULTS |
|---|---|---|
| Bunker Hill | 1775 | British drive Patriots from hill overlooking Boston, but suffer terrible losses. Patriots show they will not be easily defeated. |
| Long Island | 1776 | British drive Washington's army out of New York. |
| Trenton | 1776 | Washington's troops cross Delaware River at night, surprising British and winning an inspiring victory. |
| Saratoga | 1777 | Patriots defeat British in northern New York, leading French to join war on American side. The battle is the turning point of the war. |

**Despite important weaknesses, the Patriots proved they would not be easily defeated.**

### REVIEW QUESTIONS

1. What strengths did the British have as the war began?
2. **Chart Skills** Which battle was the turning point of the war?

SECTION 5

# WINNING INDEPENDENCE

## TEXT SUMMARY

Americans endured many hardships during the war. The army suffered from a lack of support by the Continental Congress, which could not force the states to raise money or provide troops. Civilians suffered from a British **blockade** of Atlantic ports, which cut off overseas supplies. Even when goods were available, **inflation,** a steady increase of prices over time, limited the colonists' ability to buy necessities.

Victories in the West helped morale when the Patriot militia captured an important British fort and persuaded Native Americans to leave their British allies. In the South, fighting was vicious as many Loyalists fought their Patriot brothers. British and Patriot forces also clashed in the South, with victories and defeats on both sides. When a British army marched into Virginia, it faced combined American and French forces. Defeated at the **Battle of Yorktown** in Virginia in 1781, Britain surrendered.

The **Treaty of Paris (1783)** finally ended the war. Among its provisions were British recognition of American independence, British withdrawal from United States territory, and extension of United States territory to the Mississippi River.

The American Revolution inspired **patriotism,** or love of country. For women, the Revolution challenged some of the traditional ideas about women. However, for African Americans, the effect was mixed. Most northern states had abolished slavery, but these states passed new laws limiting the rights of African Americans. For Native Americans, the Revolution was a disaster, with most tribes losing all power and being pushed farther west. But the greatest effect was to spread the idea of liberty, both at home and abroad.

**THE BIG IDEA**

**The United States won its independence by defeating the British in a long and costly war that had important consequences.**

## GRAPHIC SUMMARY: *Effects of the American Revolution*

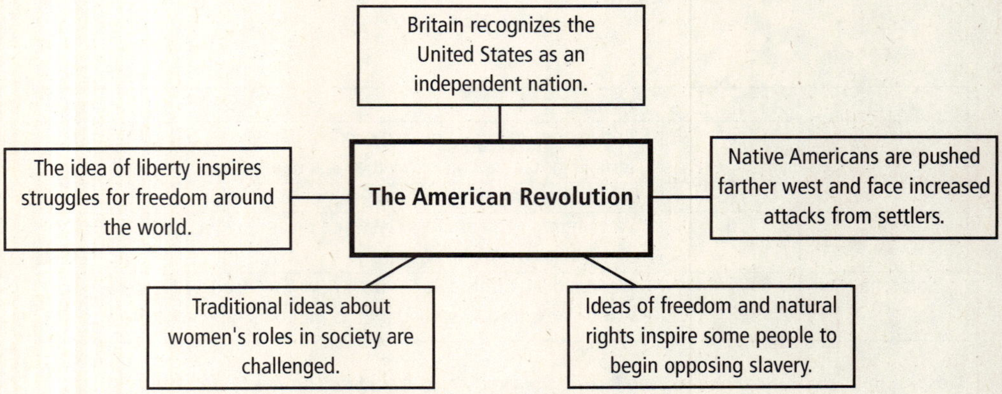


**The Revolution had important consequences for many groups of people.**

## REVIEW QUESTIONS

1. What effect did the British blockade have on Americans?
2. **Diagram Skills** What hardships did Native Americans face after the American Revolution?

Name ______________________ Class ______________ Date __________

# CHAPTER 4 Test

## IDENTIFYING MAIN IDEAS

Write the letter of the correct answer in the blank provided. (10 points each)

____ **1.** One cause of the French and Indian War was the movement of
**A.** French colonists east.
**B.** British colonists west.
**C.** British colonists into Canada.
**D.** Native Americans north from Florida.

____ **2.** During the French and Indian War, British troops and colonial militia fought
**A.** side by side.
**B.** against one another.
**C.** in completely different areas.
**D.** the French and Indians separately.

____ **3.** After the French and Indian War, the British decided to
**A.** listen more closely to advice from colonial leaders.
**B.** allow the colonies to expand by themselves.
**C.** leave the colonies alone.
**D.** raise more money from the colonies.

____ **4.** Colonists protested the Stamp Act because they felt
**A.** the British had no right to tax them.
**B.** the tax was too low.
**C.** there should not be a tax on tea.
**D.** it was unfair to Native Americans.

____ **5.** The pamphlet *Common Sense* called for
**A.** colonial leaders to be represented in Parliament.
**B.** the king to visit the colonies.
**C.** keeping ties with Great Britain.
**D.** independence from Great Britain.

____ **6.** The Declaration of Independence was based on the idea of natural rights, or rights that
**A.** are granted if people are mistreated by their rulers.
**B.** belong to people who have earned them in war.
**C.** belong to all human beings.
**D.** are granted to people by kings.

____ **7.** British strengths at the beginning of the war for independence included
**A.** British commanders' knowledge of the colonies.
**B.** Great Britain's well-trained army and large navy.
**C.** the Americans' dependence on Native American allies.
**D.** the popularity of the war among the British people.

____ **8.** The Battle of Saratoga resulted in
**A.** American control of the city of Boston.
**B.** France's entry into the war on the side of the Americans.
**C.** France's entry into the war on the side of the British.
**D.** British control of the city of Philadelphia.

____ **9.** Which of these was an effect of the British blockade of American ports?
**A.** Trade was disrupted.
**B.** Food prices dropped.
**C.** Markets were filled with French goods.
**D.** American exports increased.

____ **10.** After the American Revolution, many Native Americans were
**A.** forced to work on plantations.
**B.** forced farther west.
**C.** given jobs in American cities.
**D.** accepted as American citizens.

CHAPTER 5

# The Constitution of the United States (1776–1800)

SECTION 1

## GOVERNMENT BY THE STATES

### TEXT SUMMARY

During the war, the United States was governed under a set of laws called the **Articles of Confederation** and a limited national government. Each state had its own **constitution,** or plan of government, which gave the states more power than the national government.

**THE BIG IDEA**

**Under the Articles of Confederation, the states had most of the power while the national government was weak.**

Americans generally agreed that the new nation was a **democracy,** and that the United States should become a **republic,** a government run by people through their representatives. However, many leaders feared that a weak national government could not maintain order. The huge debt from fighting the war also caused economic problems. Each state owed money but found it nearly impossible to pay its debts.

Leaders like George Washington, James Madison, and Alexander Hamilton became part of a group called Nationalists, who favored a strong central government. In 1786 they met at the Annapolis Convention to try to resolve the problems. The convention had little success but did agree to meet again in 1787.

Meanwhile, in Massachusetts, a revolt called **Shays' Rebellion** bolstered the Nationalist cause. Led by Daniel Shays, farmers gathered an army and revolted against a state tax that severely hurt their farms. The national Congress was helpless, and the rebellion was finally put down by the state government. Shays' Rebellion showed many Americans that a stronger national government was necessary to prevent civil and social upheaval.

### GRAPHIC SUMMARY: *The Case for a New Constitution*

**Reasons for a New Constitution**

| National Government Is Weak | States Don't Work Together | Nationalists Fear Nation Will Fail | Shays' Rebellion |
|---|---|---|---|
| • No power to collect taxes<br>• No executive branch<br>• No national courts | • Each state prints its own money<br>• States fight over trade and other issues | • Warn of dangers of weak government<br>• Want the United States to be a model for the world | • Shows the disorder occurring under weak government |

**By 1787, many Americans agreed on the need for a new constitution.**

### REVIEW QUESTIONS

1. What were Shays and his followers rebelling against?
2. **Chart Skills** What were two reasons that people wanted a new constitution?

# SECTION 2 THE CONSTITUTIONAL CONVENTION

## TEXT SUMMARY

In 1787 delegates from almost all the states met in Philadelphia at the **Constitutional Convention** to revise the national government. Some wanted to **amend,** or revise, the Articles of Confederation and others wanted a whole new plan. Two plans arose, the Virginia Plan and the New Jersey Plan, which differed over the issue of representation. It was settled by the **Great Compromise** that there would be a bicameral legislature. The House of Representatives would have representatives based on state population. The Senate would have two senators from each state. The delegates also settled on the **Three-fifths Compromise,** which allowed three fifths of a state's slave population to be counted toward representation.

The Constitution created a **federal system of government** in which states and the national government share powers. The Constitution called for a **separation of powers** among the legislative, executive, and judicial branches. Each branch has its own area of authority, but no branch has complete control. A system of **checks and balances** also gives one branch of government the authority to stop, or check, the other branches.

The Constitution also created the office of the President with the power to **veto,** or prohibit, an act of Congress from becoming law. The President would be elected by the **Electoral College.** The Constitution also provided for a Supreme Court.

**THE BIG IDEA**

**During the summer of 1787, delegates to the Constitutional Convention wrote the United States Constitution.**

## GRAPHIC SUMMARY: *The Three Branches of Government*

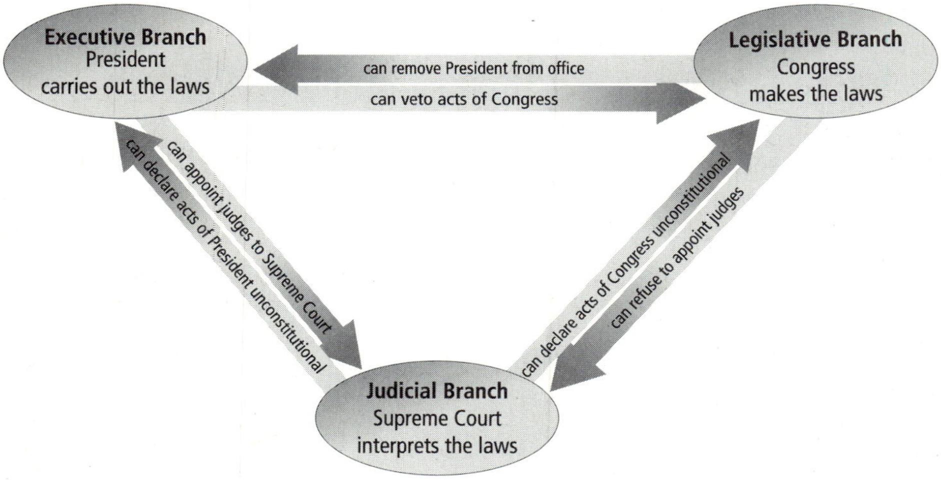


The system of checks and balances keeps any one branch from becoming too powerful.

## REVIEW QUESTIONS

1. How did the Great Compromise resolve the issue of representation?
2. **Diagram Skills** How can the President limit the power of Congress?

SECTION 3

# RATIFYING THE CONSTITUTION

## TEXT SUMMARY

For the Constitution to take effect, 9 of 13 states had to **ratify,** or approve, the document. **Federalists** wanted a strong national government, and strongly supported the Constitution. They argued that even though the federal government was supreme over state governments, the states still had powers reserved for them in the Constitution. **Anti-Federalists** feared the power of the national government and argued that the Constitution was a threat to the rights of individuals.

THE **BIG** IDEA

**All thirteen states approved the new Constitution, later adding the Bill of Rights to protect individual liberties.**

To promote the Constitution, Hamilton, Madison, and John Jay of New York published essays called *The Federalist.* Considered the best explanation of the American political system, *The Federalist* essays defended the Constitution and explained the role of government. Madison also tried to quell the fears of those who thought that one powerful **faction,** or group with a special interest, could control the government.

Well organized, united behind the Constitution, and having the support of George Washington, the Federalists won. The voting was close, and an important factor in winning was the Federalists' willingness to include a **Bill of Rights,** or the first 10 amendments to the Constitution. The Bill of Rights guaranteed many important freedoms, including freedom of speech and religion, the right to a jury trial, and protection against cruel and unusual punishment.

Most Federalists saw this Bill of Rights as unnecessary, but conceded to the anti-Federalists on this point to get the Constitution ratified.

## GRAPHIC SUMMARY: *Should the Constitution Be Ratified?*

| Anti-Federalist Concern | | Federalist Response |
|---|---|---|
| Constitution will give national government too much power. | → | Constitution will give national government enough power to solve the country's problems. |
| President will be just like a king. | → | System of checks and balances will limit President's power. |
| Individual liberties will be threatened by a powerful government. | → | Bill of Rights will protect citizens' freedom. |
| Federal government could come under control of one powerful faction. | → | Country is too big to be dominated by any one faction. |

**The Federalists and anti-Federalists both had strong arguments.**

## REVIEW QUESTIONS

**1.** What did *The Federalist* essays do?

**2.** **Chart Skills** Give two reasons the anti-Federalists opposed the Constitution.

# SECTION 4 THE NEW GOVERNMENT

## TEXT SUMMARY

George Washington had been elected the first President in 1789. Following his **inauguration,** the official swearing-in ceremony, he selected his **Cabinet,** officials to head departments of the executive branch. Two crucial posts were filled by Alexander Hamilton, as Secretary of the Treasury, and Thomas Jefferson, as Secretary of State.

Jefferson was more concerned with **domestic affairs,** a nation's internal matters, than with foreign affairs. He did not fully trust the government, resigned in 1793, and eventually became a harsh critic of Washington. Hamilton was a staunch Federalist who believed in strong government power to get things done.

During his first **administration,** or term of office, Washington and his officials established **precedents,** or rules, examples, or traditions to be followed by others. Aware he would be doing this, Washington worked to establish a tone of dignity, and even though he was often surrounded by elaborate ceremonies, he remained a very popular figure.

In the years of Washington's presidency, New York City and Philadelphia both served as the nation's capital. In 1790 it was decided that a new city should be built on the Potomac River at the border of Virginia and Maryland in a federally ruled District of Columbia. Designed by a French architect, Pierre-Charles L'Enfant, the White House and the Capitol building were not yet completed when the Congress moved to the new capital of Washington, D.C., in 1800.

**THE BIG IDEA**

**As the country's first President, George Washington worked to earn respect for the new government of the United States.**

## GRAPHIC SUMMARY: *The First Cabinet*

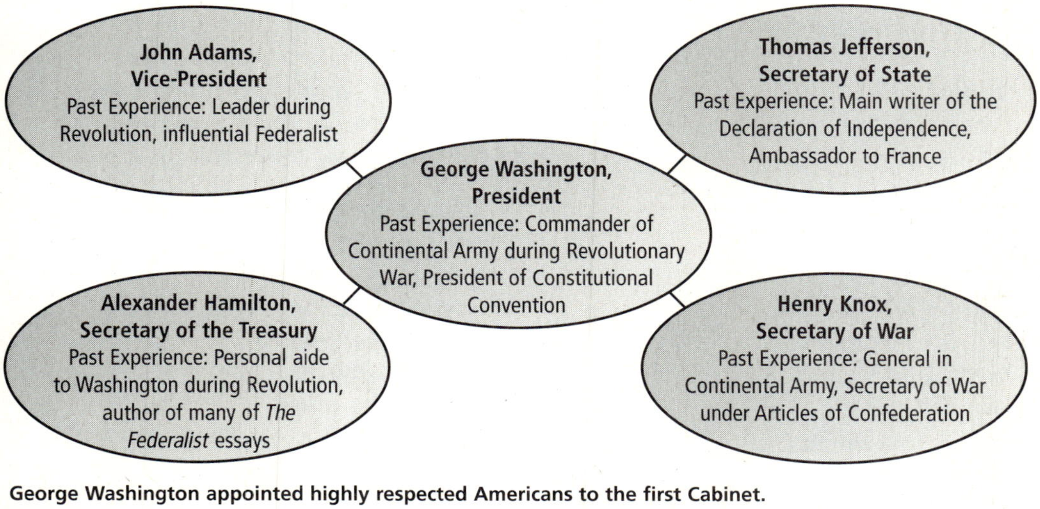


**George Washington appointed highly respected Americans to the first Cabinet.**

## REVIEW QUESTIONS

1. List the three cities that have served as capital of the United States.
2. **Chart Skills** What was Hamilton's role during the American Revolution?

Name ______________________ Class ______________ Date ________

# CHAPTER 5 Test

## IDENTIFYING MAIN IDEAS

Write the letter of the correct answer in the blank provided. (10 points each)

____ **1.** The Articles of Confederation created a
**A.** powerful President.
**B.** limited national government.
**C.** Supreme Court.
**D.** strong national government.

____ **2.** The Nationalists believed the United States needed
**A.** a weaker national government.
**B.** stronger state governments.
**C.** a stronger national government.
**D.** a king.

____ **3.** Shays' Rebellion convinced many prominent Americans that
**A.** rebellions were good for the country.
**B.** the Articles of Confederation were working.
**C.** taxes should be lowered.
**D.** it was time to strengthen the national government.

____ **4.** The Great Compromise resolved the issue of
**A.** representation in the legislature.
**B.** the power of the executive branch.
**C.** the power of the Supreme Court.
**D.** who would be the first President.

____ **5.** In order to keep one branch of government from becoming too powerful, the Constitution called for
**A.** a veto of members of Congress.
**B.** a system of checks and balances.
**C.** the impeachment of the President.
**D.** a federal system of government.

____ **6.** The executive branch of the United States government is led by the
**A.** House of Representatives.
**B.** President.
**C.** Senate.
**D.** Supreme Court.

____ **7.** The Federalists argued that the Constitution
**A.** was a betrayal of the American Revolution.
**B.** should be rejected by the states.
**C.** should be ratified by the states.
**D.** gave the President too much power.

____ **8.** The Bill of Rights was added to the Constitution to
**A.** protect citizens' liberties.
**B.** make the Federalists happy.
**C.** strengthen the national government.
**D.** restrict personal freedom.

____ **9.** As President, Washington tried to
**A.** act like an ordinary citizen.
**B.** set good examples for future Presidents.
**C.** ignore the opinion of foreign leaders.
**D.** hire only close friends as advisors.

____ **10.** Which member of the first Cabinet resigned and became a critic of Washington?
**A.** Henry Knox
**B.** Alexander Hamilton
**C.** Thomas Jefferson
**D.** Edmund Randolph

# The Origins of American Politics (1789–1820)

CHAPTER 6

## SECTION 1 LIBERTY VERSUS ORDER IN THE 1790S

### TEXT SUMMARY

When Secretary of the Treasury Alexander Hamilton persuaded Congress to assume the war debts of the states, he strengthened the power of the national government. To raise money, Hamilton placed a **tariff,** or tax on imported goods, on whiskey.

Opponents, such as Thomas Jefferson, favored a less active central government. Jefferson believed in **strict construction** of the Constitution—that the national government could not do anything unless it was specifically stated in the Constitution. Hamilton favored **loose construction** of the Constitution—that the government could do anything not specifically forbidden in the Constitution.

Americans' ideas on foreign policy were also split. Some people supported the radical French Revolution. Others opposed it as too violent. When France and Britain went to war, the United States remained **neutral,** not taking either side. However, to remain friendly with Britain, Washington sent John Jay to England, and he negotiated **Jay's Treaty.** The treaty called for the British to leave forts in the Northwest Territory in exchange for expanded trade. Many Americans felt it was a betrayal of revolutionary ideals.

Meanwhile, in western Pennsylvania, a group of farmers revolted in protest of the whiskey tariff. Washington sent an army to put down the **Whiskey Rebellion,** showing the American citizens and the world that the national government was committed to enforcing its laws. Critics, including Jefferson, formed a new **political party,** a group of people who seek to be elected to office. These Jeffersonian Republicans made Jefferson their presidential candidate in the 1796 election. Jefferson lost to the Federalist candidate, John Adams.

**THE BIG IDEA**

**During the 1790s, Americans became divided over how much power should be held by the federal government.**

### GRAPHIC SUMMARY: *Federalists versus Jeffersonian Republicans*

| FEDERALISTS | JEFFERSONIAN REPUBLICANS |
|---|---|
| • Led by Washington and Hamilton | • Led by Jefferson |
| • Favor strong central government | • Favor weak central government |
| • Support new taxes and tariffs | • Oppose new taxes and tariffs |
| • Support more powerful army and navy | • Against large army and navy |
| • Pro-British | • Pro-French |
| • Pro-business | • Pro-agriculture |

**By the 1790s the first two political parties had formed.**

### REVIEW QUESTIONS

**1.** What was the Whiskey Rebellion a protest against?

**2. Chart Skills** Which party supported business interests?

# SECTION 2 THE ELECTION OF 1800

## TEXT SUMMARY

**THE BIG IDEA**

**Jefferson's election in 1800 represented the nation's first transition of power from one political party to another.**

Like Washington, John Adams was a Federalist, and he faced the challenge of leading a nation that was politically divided. Conflicts with France, such as the **XYZ affair,** helped the Federalists expand the power of government. They increased the size of the army and imposed higher taxes. They also passed the **Alien and Sedition Acts** in 1798, under which the President could imprison or deport aliens and fine or imprison Americans who criticized the government.

Jeffersonian Republicans declared these acts unconstitutional, claiming that the acts violated freedom of speech. They promoted their views in the **Virginia and Kentucky Resolutions,** which said that the states, not the federal government, could decide what laws were constitutional. Virginia and Kentucky proposed the idea of nullification, that if a state declared a federal law unconstitutional, they could also declare that law as "null and void" within the state.

As tensions increased, President Adams became unpopular with his own party for making peace with France. Many people also viewed the Alien and Sedition Acts as unjustifiable. The election of 1800 was a smear campaign in which each party brutally insulted the opposition's candidate. The outcome was that Jefferson defeated Adams. More important, however, was the fact that power was peacefully transferred from one political party to another.

## GRAPHIC SUMMARY: *The Election of 1800*

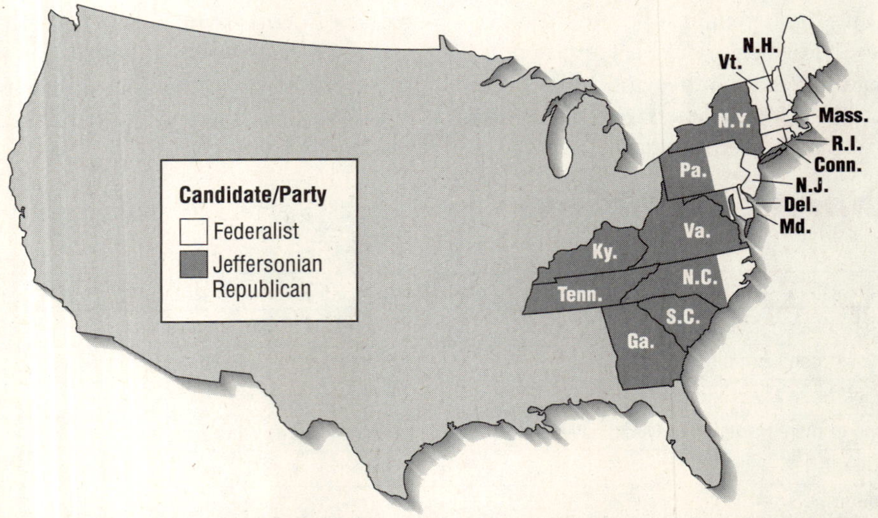


The election of 1800 showed that the nation's voters were divided between two political parties.

## REVIEW QUESTIONS

1. What were the Alien and Sedition Acts and why were they opposed?
2. **Map Skills** Which political party did most southern voters support in the election of 1800?

# SECTION 3 THE JEFFERSON ADMINISTRATION

## TEXT SUMMARY

As President, Jefferson set out to limit the power of the government. He reduced the size of the **bureaucracy,** the departments and workers that make up the federal government, and reduced taxes. He also supported the Supreme Court decision in the case *Marbury* v. *Madison*. This decision established the principle of **judicial review,** that is, the power of the Supreme Court to decide whether laws passed by Congress are constitutional.

Although Jefferson opposed the development of a strong central government, he used the government's power and money to further his policies. He encouraged Americans to buy land in the West, and he approved a western land deal with France called the **Louisiana Purchase,** which dramatically increased the size of the United States. Jefferson sent the Lewis and Clark Expedition to explore the new area and learn about its resources.

Jefferson's policies were popular, and he had kept peace with Europe. In the 1804 election, Jefferson's only true rival, Alexander Hamilton, was killed in a duel and Jefferson won a landslide victory. In his second term, however, he faced growing conflict with Britain and France over their seizure of American ships. In 1807 Jefferson imposed an **embargo,** or restriction of trade with Britain and France. The embargo did not hurt those nations, but it did hurt American merchants and traders. In the 1808 election James Madison, a Jeffersonian Republican, became President, and Jefferson retired as an unpopular figure.

**THE BIG IDEA**

**As President, Jefferson reduced the power of government, yet increased the country's size with the Louisiana Purchase.**

## GRAPHIC SUMMARY: *The Louisiana Purchase, 1803*

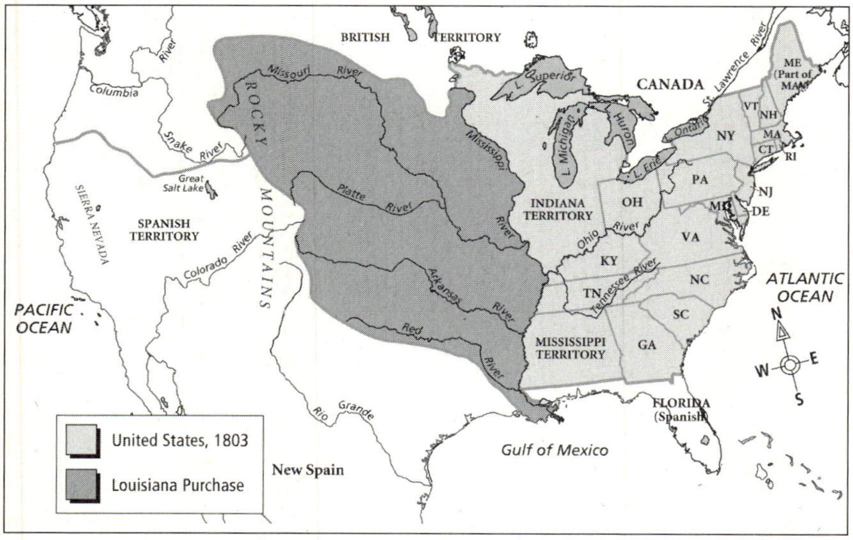


The Louisiana Purchase greatly increased the size of the United States.

## REVIEW QUESTIONS

1. Why was the case of *Marbury* v. *Madison* important?
2. **Map Skills** Which river formed the western boundary of the United States before the Louisiana Purchase?

SECTION 4

# NATIVE AMERICAN RESISTANCE

## TEXT SUMMARY

In the 1790s conflict along the frontier in the Old Northwest occurred between settlers and Native Americans over the United States' increasing westward expansion. In 1794, at the **Battle of Fallen Timbers,** American soldiers defeated Native American tribes and forced them to accept the **Treaty of Greenville,** which gave most Native American land in Ohio to the United States.

**THE BIG IDEA**

**Native Americans responded in different ways as the United States expanded onto their lands.**

In the early 1800s several Native American leaders proposed different ways to deal with the United States. Little Turtle, a leader of the Miami people, had lived on a **reservation,** an area that the federal government set aside for Native Americans who had lost their homelands. He encouraged Native Americans to accept white culture and live peacefully with settlers. Others, like Handsome Lake, a Seneca leader, called for his people to revive some of their traditional customs that would blend with white culture.

Two Shawnee leaders disagreed with these views. Tenskwatawa opposed **assimilation,** or the merging of one culture into another, and called for war. His brother, Tecumseh, a skilled war chief, urged the Native Americans to unite to resist American expansion. When the United States and Native American forces clashed at the **Battle of Tippecanoe** in 1811, neither side won, but Native American morale was shattered. Tecumseh then joined the British Army in Canada, and in the War of 1812 between Britain and the United States, he was killed in battle.

## GRAPHIC SUMMARY: *Native American Responses to United States Expansion*

| LEADER | PEOPLE | RESPONSE |
|---|---|---|
| Little Turtle | Miami | Accept white culture; live in peace |
| Handsome Lake | Seneca | Blend Indian and American cultures |
| Tenskwatawa | Shawnee | Reject white culture; return to Indian traditions |
| Tecumseh | Shawnee | Take military action against American expansion |

**Native American leaders suggested a variety of responses to United States expansion onto their lands.**

## REVIEW QUESTIONS

1. What did Tecumseh believe was Native Americans' only hope?
2. **Chart Skills** Which response was proposed by Little Turtle?

# SECTION 5 THE WAR OF 1812

## TEXT SUMMARY

One cause of the **War of 1812** between Britain and the United States was Americans' belief that Britain encouraged Native American attacks. Another cause was Britain's practice of **impressment,** stopping American ships at sea and forcing sailors into the British navy.

The Americans had some victories and some defeats on land and at sea. However, the British blockaded American ports and managed to burn Washington, D.C. The war ended with the **Treaty of Ghent** in 1814, which was signed just before the **Battle of New Orleans,** at which American General Andrew Jackson won a remarkable victory over superior forces. Jackson became a hero, and Americans felt a new sense of national pride.

After the war, the United States entered a period of growth and prosperity. Encouraged by credit from banks and newt land laws, Americans were rapidly moving westward. Then, in 1819, a **depression,** or economic downturn, struck when banks demanded repayment of loans from people who had borrowed in times of prosperity.

The depression ended, but another problem arose over whether Missouri would be admitted to the Union as a slave or free state. Northerners feared a slave state would increase southern power in the Senate. The South argued that the federal government could not tell states whether they could be free or slave. After bitter debate, Congress reached the **Missouri Compromise** in 1820. Slavery would be permitted in Missouri, and Maine would be admitted as a free state, keeping the balance of power.

**THE BIG IDEA**

**Americans gained increased national pride from the fighting of the War of 1812, but conflict over slavery was intensifying.**

## GRAPHIC SUMMARY: *The Missouri Compromise, 1820*

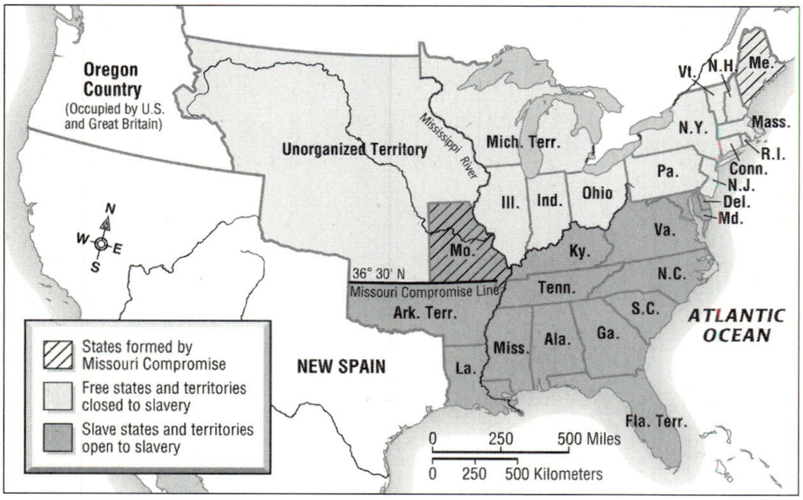


## REVIEW QUESTIONS

1. Name one cause of the War of 1812.

2. **Map Skills** What states were admitted to the United States under the Missouri Compromise?

Name ______________________ Class ______________ Date ________

# CHAPTER 6 Test

## IDENTIFYING MAIN IDEAS

Write the letter of the correct answer in the blank provided. (10 points each)

____ **1.** Which of these did Alexander Hamilton support?
- **A.** Low tariffs
- **B.** Strong central government
- **C.** The French Revolution
- **D.** The Whisky Rebellion

____ **2.** The Whiskey Rebellion was a revolt against
- **A.** the price of imported whiskey.
- **B.** laws against drinking whiskey.
- **C.** laws against making whiskey.
- **D.** a tax on whiskey.

____ **3.** People opposed the Alien and Sedition Acts because they
- **A.** violated people's right to freedom of speech.
- **B.** were unfair to immigrants.
- **C.** decreased the power of government.
- **D.** made President Adams too popular.

____ **4.** The election of 1800 proved that
- **A.** Adams could be reelected.
- **B.** the Federalists were very popular.
- **C.** political power could be transferred peacefully.
- **D.** most people in New England supported Jefferson.

____ **5.** Jefferson's main goal as President was to
- **A.** increase the power and size of government.
- **B.** raise taxes and tariffs.
- **C.** decrease the power and size of government.
- **D.** increase the size of the United States.

____ **6.** The goal of the Lewis and Clark expedition was to
- **A.** force Britain to stop attacking United States ships.
- **B.** explore the land of the Louisiana Purchase.
- **C.** make contact with French settlers in the west.
- **D.** establish new power for the Supreme Court.

____ **7.** Tecumseh believed Native Americans should
- **A.** abandon Native American traditions.
- **B.** blend Indian and American cultures.
- **C.** move onto reservations.
- **D.** join together and fight American expansion.

____ **8.** One cause of the War of 1812 was that the
- **A.** British were encouraging Native Americans to resist the expansion of the United States.
- **B.** French were attacking American ships.
- **C.** Americans wanted the British to leave the Louisiana Territory.
- **D.** British were encouraging slaves to revolt.

____ **9.** Andrew Jackson became a national hero after his victory
- **A.** in the election of 1816.
- **B.** at the Battle of New Orleans.
- **C.** at the Battle of Tippecanoe.
- **D.** in signing the Treaty of Ghent.

____ **10.** The main goal of the Missouri Compromise was to
- **A.** maintain the same number of free states and slave states.
- **B.** expand onto Native American lands.
- **C.** expand slavery into northern states.
- **D.** end the War of 1812.

# Life in the New Nation (1783–1850)

CHAPTER 7

## SECTION 1 Cultural, Social, and Religious Life

### TEXT SUMMARY

With independence from Great Britain, Americans gained the right to determine their own destiny. An increasing number of people begin to devote time to scholarship and the arts. The nation also began to focus on the importance of learning. Many Americans hoped to develop character by promoting **republican virtues,** such as self-reliance, hard work, frugality, harmony, and sacrifice for the community.

A rapidly growing population brought crowding along the Atlantic seaboard, and the United States became a **mobile society,** one in which people continually move from place to place. Being mobile also meant the ability to move upward in society. Although women still had a supporting role in society, they had more freedom to choose a partner and were more cautious about marriage.

Women were also active in the **Second Great Awakening,** a powerful Protestant religious movement of the early 1800s along the western frontier. It was an **evangelical** movement that stressed the importance of the **congregation,** or the members of the church, over the ministers. One common feature was the **revival,** where people are brought back to religious life by listening to preaching. Several Protestant **denominations,** or religious subgroups, experienced rapid growth. African Americans turned also to this type of worship and formed the African Methodist Episcopal (AME) Church.

**THE BIG IDEA**

**As the American population grew and moved west, society changed as well, causing people to find new rules and religious ideas to guide their lives.**

### GRAPHIC SUMMARY: *Second Great Awakening Ideas*

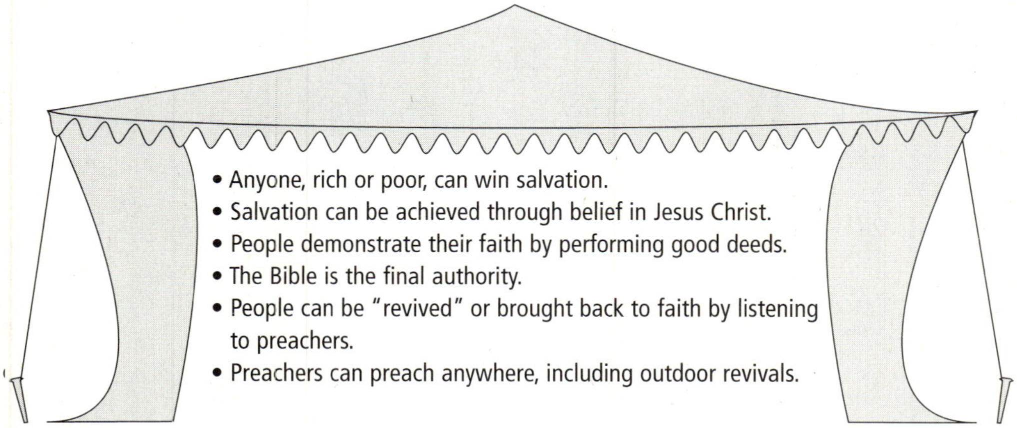


Revivals, often held in tents, helped spread the ideas of the Second Great Awakening.

### REVIEW QUESTIONS

1. Give two characteristics of American mobile society in the early 1800s.
2. **Chart Skills** What was the role of the Bible in the Second Great Awakening?

# SECTION 2 *TRAILS TO THE WEST*

## TEXT SUMMARY

Americans on the move were attracted by **trans-Appalachia,** the area west of the Appalachian Mountains. Following several roads west, thousands of Americans settled in the Ohio Valley to farm, build homes, and found towns. Entering Native American lands, settlers pushed them farther and farther west. By 1840 most eastern Native American groups had been moved onto reservations west of the Mississippi River.

**THE BIG IDEA**

**As the American population grew larger and younger, people began moving west.**

Many Americans also headed south into Spanish Florida, where Seminole Indians also lived. In the Seminole wars, the U.S. Army under General Andrew Jackson overcame the Seminoles. Through the **Adams-Onís Treaty,** Spain agreed to **cede,** or give up, Florida to the United States.

Following the idea of **manifest destiny,** that the United States had a divine mission to spread across the continent, Americans set out for the Oregon Country on the Pacific Coast. Beginning in 1843, on a long and difficult journey, hundreds of wagon trains pushed along the **Oregon Trail,** the main route across the Plains and the Rockies. Others took the **Santa Fe Trail,** which veered southwest into New Mexico. One group that migrated across the country was the Mormons. Seeking shelter from religious persecution, they finally settled in Salt Lake City in Utah Territory.

When gold was discovered in California in 1848, the California Gold Rush attracted thousands of miners, settlers, and merchants. By 1852 California's population had jumped to around 200,000 people, and San Francisco was a major city. However, most mining communities had short lives and soon turned into **ghost towns.**

## GRAPHIC SUMMARY: *U.S. Population Growth, 1780–1830*

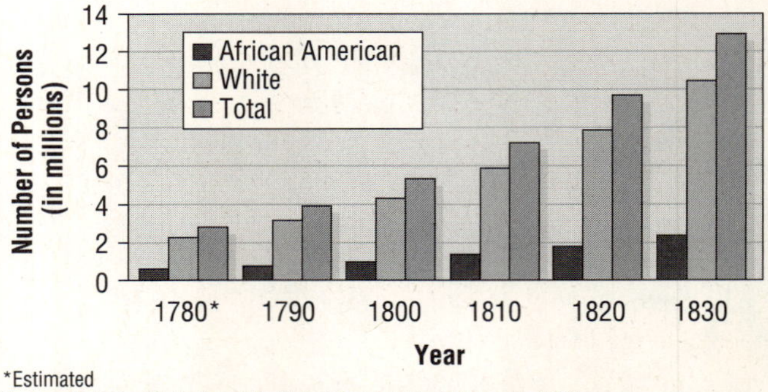


*Estimated
Source: *Historical Statistics of the United States, Colonial Times to 1970*

**During the first part of the 1800s, the United States had the fastest growing population of any nation in the world.**

## REVIEW QUESTIONS

1. What territory did the United States gain from the Adams-Onís Treaty?
2. **Graph Skills** What was the population of the United States in 1800?

# SECTION 3 THE GREAT PLAINS AND THE SOUTHWEST

## TEXT SUMMARY

In the 1840s thousands of settlers crossed the **Great Plains,** the vast grassland between the Mississippi River and the Rockies. However, few settled on the plains, which were considered unfit for farming and were also home to the Plains Indians. These people were **nomadic,** people who migrate from place to place. The introduction of the horse to North America allowed western Plains Indians to hunt buffalo and carry their possessions using horses. In the eastern part of the plains, Native Americans hunted, but also lived in settled villages and farmed. The expansion of settlers into the West pushed tribes like the Sioux and Cheyenne onto the western plains, where they developed a warrior culture. Some village tribes, like the Mandan, did not move, and diseases brought by settlers wiped out village after village.

In California, Spain held onto its territory by building **presidios,** or forts, and establishing missions. These were Spanish settlements until 1821, when Mexico won its independence from Spain and took over Spanish lands in North America. American merchants now benefited from trade with California, New Mexico, and Texas.

Many settlers looked for opportunities in Texas, and Mexico granted land to American immigrants. However, conflict erupted when Texas settlers wanted more political control and Mexico refused to grant them self-government. In 1835 the **Texas War for Independence** began. At the **Battle of the Alamo,** a few Texans held out for 13 days, but were finally overcome by thousands of Mexican troops. However, the Texans would not give up. Under the leadership of Sam Houston, the Texans finally defeated the Mexican Army, declaring Texas an independent republic. The loss of Texas would bring future conflict between Mexico and the United States.

**THE BIG IDEA**

**The migration of Spaniards from central Mexico and settlers from the United States into the Southwest led to economic and political changes.**

## GRAPHIC SUMMARY: *Impact of American Settlement on the Southwest*

| Native American Life | Hispanic North America | Texas |
|---|---|---|
| Introduction of the horse improves hunting and transportation. | Spanish build presidios and missions to protect their lands. | American settlers are allowed into Mexican-owned Texas. |
| Settlers push more eastern Native American tribes west, causing conflict. | Mexico wins independence from Spain. | Texans fight a war with Mexico and gain independence. |
| Native American village life declines. | | |

**American settlement in the Southwest impacted the lives of the people already living there.**

## REVIEW QUESTIONS

1. At what battle did Texans' hope for independence seem lost?
2. **Chart Skills** What effect did American settlement have on Native American village life?

Name ______________________ Class ______________ Date __________

# CHAPTER 7 Test

## IDENTIFYING MAIN IDEAS

Write the letter of the correct answer in the blank provided. (10 points each)

____ **1.** To encourage an American national character, educators, artists, and scientists promoted
**A.** moving west.
**B.** more freedom for women.
**C.** religion.
**D.** republican virtues.

____ **2.** Which best describes a society in which people move from place to place?
**A.** conservative
**B.** traditional
**C.** mobile
**D.** improved

____ **3.** Which kind of movement was the Second Great Awakening?
**A.** economic
**B.** political
**C.** religious
**D.** artistic

____ **4.** In the early 1800s thousands of settlers were moving
**A.** to the Pacific coast.
**B.** into the Ohio Valley.
**C.** north into Canada.
**D.** south into Mexico.

____ **5.** The Adams-Onís Treaty gave the United States the territory of
**A.** California.
**B.** New Mexico.
**C.** Florida.
**D.** Texas.

____ **6.** What was a major reason for Americans to move west to the Oregon Country?
**A.** new inventions
**B.** a religious awakening
**C.** manifest destiny
**D.** new trails and routes

____ **7.** California experienced a population explosion because of
**A.** improved transportation.
**B.** the gold rush.
**C.** Mormon migrations.
**D.** the rise of ghost towns.

____ **8.** Which of the following had the greatest impact on the lives of Plains Indians?
**A.** Spanish settlers
**B.** acquiring horses
**C.** herds of buffalo
**D.** trade with settlers

____ **9.** In the early 1800s, which Spanish settlement in North America gained its independence?
**A.** Florida
**B.** California
**C.** Mexico
**D.** New Mexico

____ **10.** Which best describes the reason Texas fought Mexico?
**A.** to gain independence
**B.** to gain land in California
**C.** to abolish slavery
**D.** to join the United States

# The Growth of a National Economy (1790–1850)

CHAPTER 8

## SECTION 1 *INVENTIONS AND INNOVATIONS*

### TEXT SUMMARY

Inventions grew out of the **Industrial Revolution,** the increase in production using new technologies. Eli Whitney created **interchangeable parts,** which revolutionized industry, and the cotton gin, which separates the seeds and fibers. Whitney obtained a **patent,** a government grant giving the inventor of a product the sole right to make, use, and sell it. The cotton gin caused cotton profits to soar, plantations to rely on cotton, and the enslaved population to double. Transportation and communication expanded with new roads, canals, and steam-powered railroads.

Americans began buying and selling goods, creating the **Market Revolution.** In the Northeast, **manufacturing,** the production of goods by machinery, expanded. In 1813 came the world's first truly **centralized** textile factory—a single facility where all the tasks to make a product were carried out. The Market Revolution was created within the **free enterprise system,** in which private companies compete for profit. These factories used **specialization,** a worker performing one task.

Another important business was banking. Banks made money by charging interest on loans, many as **investment capital,** money a business spends to grow. Banks also issued **bank notes,** but as they were not backed by gold or silver, they caused the value of money to fluctuate.

**THE BIG IDEA**

**An American spirit of improvement led to new inventions and advances in education and transportation.**

### GRAPHIC SUMMARY: *The Transportation Revolution*

**Changes in Transportation**

**Steam Power**
- In 1807, Robert Fulton's *Clermont* steams up the Hudson River.
- Steamships help farmers ship their goods to markets around the world.

**Canals**
- Erie Canal connects Lake Erie to New York City in 1825.
- By 1840, 3,000 miles of canals are in use.

**Roads**
- By 1833, the Cumberland Road runs from Maryland to Ohio.
- New roads of stone and gravel help Americans move west.

**Railroads**
- In 1828, the B & O railroad line becomes the nation's first railroad.
- By 1840, U.S. has more miles of railroad track than any other country in the world.

**Inventions and new technologies changed the way Americans traveled and transported goods.**

### REVIEW QUESTIONS

1. What was the Industrial Revolution?
2. **Diagram Skills** Name the first railroad line in the United States.

# SECTION 2 *THE NORTHERN SECTION*

## TEXT SUMMARY

In the early 1800s the northern United States was made up of two distinct regions, or **sections.** The Old Northwest, the section north and west of the Ohio River, was fertile land where farmers grew corn and wheat and raised livestock. With newly invented farm machinery, fewer workers were needed, and farming became very profitable. New businesses, such as slaughterhouses, shipping companies, and banks arose to process, ship, and sell farm products of the Old Northwest.

**THE BIG IDEA**

**Northern cities and industries grew quickly between 1800 and 1850, bringing new wealth and new problems.**

The Northeast was becoming an industrial section as more and more people left **rural** areas of farms and the countryside to work in cities, or **urban** areas. **Industrialization,** the development of industry, increased rapidly.

Northeast cities filled with people looking for work in industries. As the population expanded, a growing number of urban poor lived in cheap, rundown **tenements,** crowded apartments that lacked sanitation, safety, and comfort. With primitive sewage systems and contaminated water, many of the poor died of disease.

In addition, factory workers labored long hours in dangerous conditions for low pay. Workers sometimes called a **strike,** or work stoppage, and formed **labor unions** to negotiate better pay and working conditions. Early unions soon died out because factory owners would obtain court rulings against them and financial panics caused increased unemployment, so workers could not afford to lose their jobs.

## GRAPHIC SUMMARY: *Urban and Rural Populations, 1800–1850*

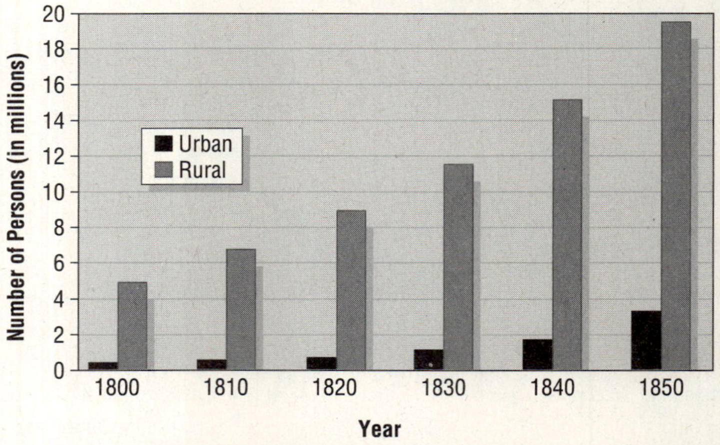


Source: *Historical Statistics of the United States, Colonial Times to 1970*

**Both urban and rural populations grew rapidly in the early 1800s. By 1850, 12 percent of the total population lived in urban areas.**

## REVIEW QUESTIONS

1. Why did many people move to urban areas?
2. **Graph Skills** About how many people lived in urban areas in 1850?

# SECTION 3 THE SOUTHERN SECTION

## TEXT SUMMARY

While the northern sections of the nation built urban industries, the economy of the South was based mainly on one agricultural crop, cotton. By 1850 the South's **cotton belt,** the area from South Carolina to Texas, had produced a billion pounds of cotton.

The South remained mostly rural, with a few major cities. Southern geography, with its fertile soil, warm weather, and plentiful rainfall, favored farming. Large cotton plantations used hundreds of enslaved Africans to work in the fields. On smaller farms, which grew most of their own food and cash crops, there were only a few slaves.

As cotton became more profitable, the population of enslaved Africans increased, and by 1850 some 2 million enslaved Africans labored in the South, mostly on large cotton plantations. Most southerners considered slaves as property that performed labor for their owners; therefore, they were bought and sold at will.

On these large plantations, conditions were generally harsh and cruel. Few slaves managed to escape or win their freedom, but rebellions did occur. In 1834, in **Turner's Rebellion,** a black preacher named Nat Turner led a violent uprising in Virginia, in which slaves raided plantations and killed more than 50 white people. Turner was caught and hanged, but alarmed southerners tightened restrictions on slave movements and meetings.

**THE BIG IDEA**

**As cotton farming grew, so did the slave trade, leading to several slave revolts.**

## GRAPHIC SUMMARY: *The Growth of "King Cotton"*

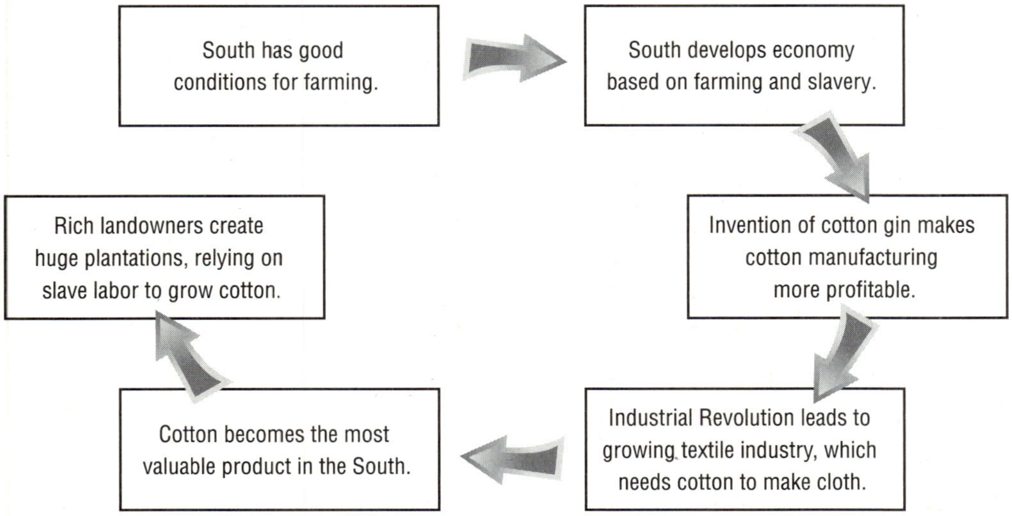


In the early 1800s cotton became the South's most important crop.

## REVIEW QUESTIONS

1. In 1850, on what kind of farms did most slaves live?
2. **Diagram Skills** Which invention caused the demand for cotton to increase?

SECTION 4

# THE GROWTH OF NATIONALISM

## TEXT SUMMARY

**THE BIG IDEA**

**Rising nationalism in the 1820s led to new developments in foreign policy and the beginning of new political parties.**

By the 1820s Americans were thinking of themselves not just as members of their local community or state, but also as citizens of the United States. To help resolve economic problems and disputes Americans adopted new nationalist policies. Domestically, Congress passed a new tariff on foreign goods to encourage the purchase of American goods. Supreme Court decisions helped protect businesses from state regulation, supported the national bank, and regulated commerce.

While the Supreme Court was strengthening federal authority, President James Monroe was strengthening the nation's foreign policy. He established America's foreign policy in the **Monroe Doctrine.** It stated that the United States would not intervene in European affairs and prohibited further Western Hemisphere colonization.

By 1824 political conflict had signaled an end to the Era of Good Feelings as key political leaders competed for power. The controversial 1824 presidential election, which Andrew Jackson supporters labeled the "corrupt bargain," led to the formation of two new political parties. Supporters of John Quincy Adams and Henry Clay called themselves National Republicans and favored an active federal government. Jackson supporters were Jacksonian Democrats, who argued for limited government. Andrew Jackson, a national hero, won the 1828 presidential election by a large majority.

## GRAPHIC SUMMARY: *The Election of 1828*

| | Adams | Jackson |
|---|---|---|
| Party | National Republicans (also known as Whigs) | Democrats (also known as Jacksonian Democrats) |
| Slavery | Against | For |
| Bank of the United States | For | Against |
| Voting rights for propertyless workers | Against | For |
| Spending federal government money on roads and bridges | For | Against |

**In the election of 1828, voters had a choice between two very different leaders and political parties.**

## REVIEW QUESTIONS

1. How did President Monroe change American foreign policy?
2. **Chart Skills** Compare the views of Adams and Jackson on using federal funds to build transportation improvements.

# SECTION 5 THE AGE OF JACKSON

## TEXT SUMMARY

Under Jackson, **patronage,** the system of giving government jobs to friends and supporters, became an official policy. He argued that any intelligent person could be a government official. His policy made him a champion of the common man.

Jackson believed in limited government, but he used its power when he felt it was necessary. In 1832 South Carolina **nullified,** or rejected, the **Tariff of 1828** as unconstitutional and threatened to **secede,** or withdraw, from the Union if it was not repealed. When Jackson threatened to send federal troops to enforce the law, a compromise was worked out.

In 1830 Jackson supported the **Indian Removal Act,** which allowed the government to remove thousands of Cherokees from their homelands. When the Cherokee took their case to the Supreme Court and won, Jackson ignored the ruling, and sent the Cherokee west. Jackson also sent the U.S. Army to put down Native American uprisings in Illinois and Florida.

Jackson also waged war on the Bank of the United States, arguing it was controlled by wealthy easterners. Popular support was behind him, and he won reelection in 1832. Because of poor health, Jackson did not seek a third term. In 1836 Martin Van Buren, Jackson's Vice President, was elected. He had a rocky four years with several bank panics. William Henry Harrison soundly defeated Van Buren in 1840, but he died one month after taking office. His Vice President, John Tyler, took over. He, too, blocked the revival of a national bank, and experienced four years of political deadlock.

**THE BIG IDEA**

**Jackson's election strengthened the power of the voters and led to a more limited federal government.**

## GRAPHIC SUMMARY: *The Presidency of Andrew Jackson*

| President Andrew Jackson |
|---|
| Fires over 2,000 government workers and replaces them with his own supporters. |
| Vetoes more acts of Congress than all six previous Presidents combined. |
| Closes Bank of the United States. |
| Threatens to send huge army to South Carolina to force the state to obey tariff laws. |
| Uses Indian Removal Act to force 100,000 Native Americans from their homelands. |

**Jackson's forceful actions earned him both strong support and angry opposition throughout the country.**

## REVIEW QUESTIONS

1. What argument did Jackson use against the Bank of the United States?
2. **Chart Skills** How did Jackson limit the power of Congress?

Name ______________________ Class ______________ Date ________

# CHAPTER 8 Test

## IDENTIFYING MAIN IDEAS

Write the letter of the correct answer in the blank provided. (10 points each)

____ **1.** Which invention led to an increase of enslaved Africans?
**A.** the steam engine
**B.** the cotton gin
**C.** the textile mill
**D.** canals

____ **2.** What key role did banks play in the Market Revolution?
**A.** They helped create a household economy.
**B.** They collected tariffs.
**C.** They provided businesses with investment capital.
**D.** They encouraged the growth of labor unions.

____ **3.** In the early 1800s, the manufacturing center of the country was
**A.** the Northeast.
**B.** the South.
**C.** the West.
**D.** the Old Northwest.

____ **4.** Labor unions struggled for
**A.** a lower minimum wage.
**B.** better conditions for factory owners.
**C.** longer hours for workers.
**D.** higher pay and better conditions for workers.

____ **5.** During the first half of the 1800s the South's most valuable crop was
**A.** tobacco.
**B.** cotton.
**C.** rice.
**D.** sugar.

____ **6.** What led to the revolt of Nat Turner?
**A.** high tariffs
**B.** tobacco tax
**C.** laws against labor unions
**D.** cruel treatment of slaves

____ **7.** The Monroe Doctrine warned European powers to
**A.** end the slave trade.
**B.** give up their colonies in Asia.
**C.** stay out of the Western Hemisphere.
**D.** stop attacking American ships.

____ **8.** Jackson supporters labeled the 1824 election a
**A.** fair deal.
**B.** corrupt bargain.
**C.** nasty ratrace.
**D.** just bargain.

____ **9.** President Andrew Jackson's closing of the Bank of the United States was an example of his desire to
**A.** spend more money on roads and bridges.
**B.** ask Congress to create a new bank.
**C.** give more money to Native Americans.
**D.** limit the power of the federal government.

____ **10.** Jackson used the Indian Removal Act to
**A.** clear Native Americans from the Louisiana Purchase.
**B.** force Native Americans to leave their homelands in southeastern states.
**C.** encourage Native Americans to grow cotton.
**D.** return Native Americans to their homelands.

# Religion and Reform (1815–1855)

CHAPTER 9

## SECTION 1 Reforming Society

### TEXT SUMMARY

The problems of poverty, ill health, alcoholism, poor housing, and declining moral values in the growing northern cities fueled reform movements in the 1830s and 1840s. Some of the movements were based in religion, as Protestant reformers, such as Charles Grandison Finney and Lyman Beecher, preached that God allowed people to control their own destinies, and that individuals could reform themselves through hard work. Other movements were inspired by **transcendentalism,** a philosophy that people could find truth through spiritual discovery rather than reason.

To fight alcoholism, the **temperance movement** sought to eliminate alcohol consumption by urging people to pledge not to drink. The movement pointed out the social, moral, and health values of **abstinence,** refraining from doing something. Due to the efforts of the temperance movement, alcohol consumption between 1830 and 1860 dropped dramatically.

Some reformers also focused on improving education, promoting better public schools. A leader in this movement was Horace Mann. However, most girls and African Americans were still denied a better education.

Dorothea Dix, another social reformer, focused her efforts on improving conditions in prisons, persuading the state of Massachusetts to build facilities for the mentally ill.

Some reformers tried to create their own perfect societies through **utopian communities** where people lived together in equality and harmony.

**THE BIG IDEA**

**Inspired by religion and new ideas, reform movements began battling the country's growing social problems.**

### GRAPHIC SUMMARY: *Reform Movements of the 1830s and 1840s*

| Reform Movement | Goal | Impact |
|---|---|---|
| Temperance movement | End alcohol consumption | During mid-1800s, alcohol consumption drops sharply |
| Educational reform | Improve public education | By 1850s most northern states have free public elementary schools |
| Prison reform | Improve prison conditions | Many states improve prison conditions and build special hospitals for the mentally ill |

**Reform-minded Americans worked to improve society and help those in need.**

### REVIEW QUESTIONS

1. What did Protestant reformers encourage people to do?
2. **Chart Skills** What was the goal of the educational reform movement?

SECTION 2

# THE ANTISLAVERY MOVEMENT

## TEXT SUMMARY

**THE BIG IDEA**

**Free African Americans and whites began a small but committed movement against slavery in the early 1800s.**

Many reformers joined the **abolitionist movement** to end slavery. Most favored the gradual **emancipation,** or freeing, of enslaved Africans by stopping the spread of slavery. Some abolitionists promoted establishing a nation in West Africa for freed slaves. This plan offended most African Americans because they considered themselves to be Americans. Boston's abolitionist William Lloyd Garrison sought full equality for African Americans. Frederick Douglass, a former slave, opposed violence but demanded action.

Abolitionists often disagreed. Some wanted to exclude women. Some black abolitionists thought whites believed them inferior. Some thought passing laws was useless, while others argued for legal action.

Some abolitionists worked on the **Underground Railroad,** a network of secret routes and hiding places for escaping slaves. Conductors, or guides, led them along the dangerous routes. The most famous conductor was Harriet Tubman, who rescued about 300 slaves.

Many people in both the North and the South strongly opposed the abolitionist movement. Northern white workers feared for their jobs, and many believed blacks were inferior. The majority of white southerners were determined to defend slavery. Southerners pushed through a **gag rule** prohibiting antislavery petitions from being read or acted on in the House of Representatives.

## GRAPHIC SUMMARY: *The Underground Railroad*

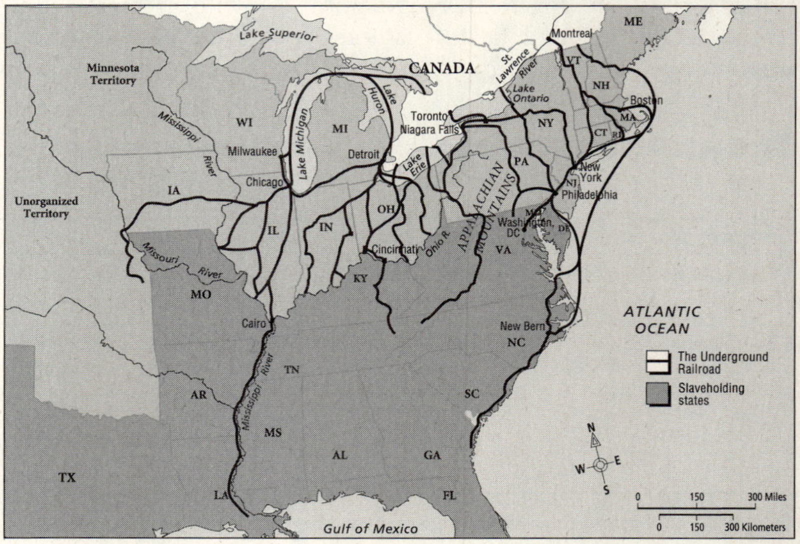


The Underground Railroad helped thousands of people escape slavery.

## REVIEW QUESTIONS

1. Why was Harriet Tubman famous?
2. **Map Skills** To what country did many Underground Railroad routes lead?

SECTION 3

# THE MOVEMENT FOR WOMEN'S RIGHTS

## TEXT SUMMARY

In the early 1800s most Americans believed women's place was in the home. They were expected to manage their homes and raise and educate their children. Reformist educator Catharine Beecher believed women should be proud of these roles and that they could improve society by teaching their children to be good citizens.

Not all women agreed with this view, however. A small number of women were working outside the home, helping to lead reform movements, and beginning to become politically active. Leading the struggle for improving women's rights were abolitionists Lucretia Mott and Elizabeth Cady Stanton. After Mott and Stanton were prohibited from taking part in an antislavery conference, they began organizing a convention to further women's rights. In July 1848 they and other women met at the **Seneca Falls Convention,** the first women's rights convention in the nation. Delegates signed a declaration protesting women's lack of legal and political rights and called for women's **suffrage,** or the right to vote. Although the convention did not persuade a great many Americans to support their cause, it was the beginning of the organized movement in the United States for women's rights, including the right to vote.

**THE BIG IDEA**

**Women's active role in reform movements led to a women's rights movement in the 1840s.**

## GRAPHIC SUMMARY: *Leading Women Reformers*

| | |
|---|---|
| **Harriet Beecher Stowe**<br>Author of famous abolitionist novel *Uncle Tom's Cabin* | **Sojourner Truth**<br>Travels the nation preaching against slavery and for women's rights |
| **Catharine Beecher**<br>Teaches women to improve society through their roles as wives, mothers, and teachers | **Elizabeth Cady Stanton**<br>Leads the Seneca Falls Convention, the first women's rights convention in U.S. history |
| **Dorothea Dix**<br>Leads campaign to improve prison conditions and build hospitals for the mentally ill | **Harriet Tubman**<br>Leads over 300 slaves to freedom as the most famous conductor of the Underground Railroad |

## REVIEW QUESTIONS

**1.** The Seneca Falls Convention marked the beginning of what struggle?

**2. Chart Skills** What was a contribution of Elizabeth Cady Stanton?

## SECTION 4 *GROWING DIVISIONS*

### TEXT SUMMARY

**THE BIG IDEA**

**Immigration and the growing differences between North and South increased tensions throughout the United States during the mid-1800s.**

In the early 1800s American society was becoming more culturally diverse. The gap between the working class and the middle class was widening, and rapidly rising immigration brought people of several cultures into the United States. The North and the South were growing into distinct regions.

In the 1840s hundreds of thousands of Irish people fled the **Irish Potato Famine,** when disease ruined their potato crop and caused massive starvation. Most settled in northern cities, filling jobs as laborers on canals and railroads and as factory workers. Most Irish became Democrats and were a strong voting bloc in the Democratic party. Many German immigrants came to the United States at this time, seeking political freedom and settling in cities. Both groups brought their own traditions, language, and religion to the nation. Both groups faced **discrimination,** unequal treatment because of race, nationality, sex, or religion. Native-born Americans feared that the newcomers would take their jobs, and they often disapproved of immigrant cultures and religions.

Tensions between the North and South were also growing. Southerners bitterly resented the abolitionist movement as well as reformers' ideas about public education and improved women's rights. A region of plantations and farms, most of the South was untouched by industrialization and urbanization and saw no need for social reform. They thought any new social reforms would destroy their way of life. Tensions between the North and the South were becoming more and more difficult to resolve with compromise.

### GRAPHIC SUMMARY: *Immigration to the United States, 1821–1860*

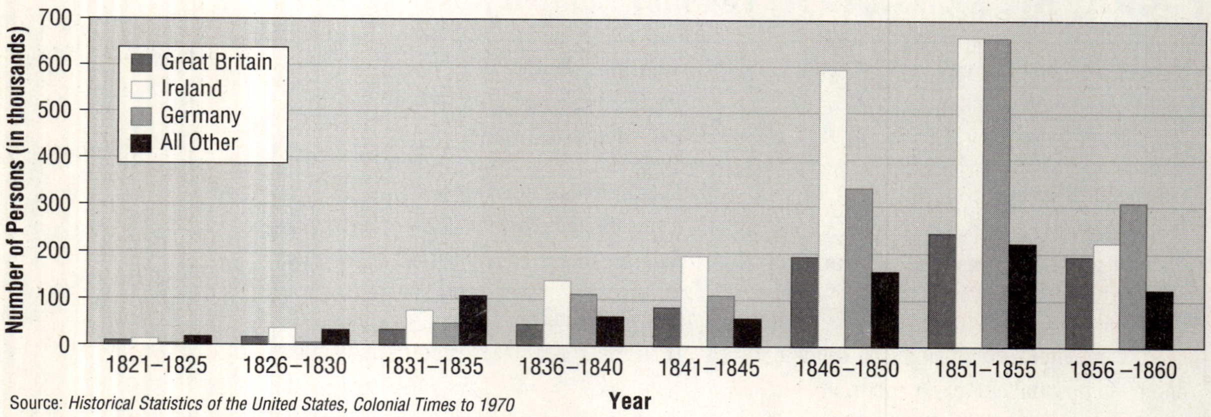


Source: *Historical Statistics of the United States, Colonial Times to 1970*

**Immigration increased sharply in the mid-1800s.**

### REVIEW QUESTIONS

1. What caused many Irish immigrants to come to the United States?

2. **Graph Skills** From where did most immigrants come in 1846–1850? In 1856–1860?

Name ______________________________ Class ______________ Date __________

# CHAPTER 9 Test

## IDENTIFYING MAIN IDEAS

Write the letter of the correct answer in the blank provided. (10 points each)

____ **1.** Transcendentalists encouraged people to
- **A.** follow religious laws.
- **B.** find truth through spiritual means.
- **C.** support slavery.
- **D.** care only about the material world.

____ **2.** The temperance movement wanted people to avoid
- **A.** going on strike.
- **B.** drinking alcohol.
- **C.** abusing slaves.
- **D.** an imperfect society.

____ **3.** Horace Mann was known for defending
- **A.** prison reforms.
- **B.** the right to immigrate.
- **C.** public education.
- **D.** revival meetings.

____ **4.** The abolitionist movement was started by
- **A.** the government.
- **B.** slave owners.
- **C.** free African Americans and whites.
- **D.** factory workers.

____ **5.** What was the goal of the Underground Railroad?
- **A.** to smuggle cotton to the North
- **B.** to help free slaves return to Africa
- **C.** to help capture escaped slaves
- **D.** to help people escape slavery

____ **6.** Which of these groups did NOT oppose the abolitionists?
- **A.** southern plantation owners
- **B.** northern merchants
- **C.** free African Americans
- **D.** northern workers

____ **7.** In the early 1800s most women were expected to work
- **A.** at home.
- **B.** in factories.
- **C.** on plantations.
- **D.** for reform movements.

____ **8.** The Seneca Falls Convention marked the beginning of the struggle for
- **A.** women's suffrage.
- **B.** emancipation of the slaves.
- **C.** new utopian communities.
- **D.** the establishment of public schools.

____ **9.** In the early 1800s, the number of immigrants coming to the United States
- **A.** increased slowly.
- **B.** increased quickly.
- **C.** decreased quickly.
- **D.** remained steady.

____ **10.** What was one result of the growing differences between the North and South?
- **A.** The regions ignored each other.
- **B.** There was faster reform in the South.
- **C.** There were increased tensions between the regions.
- **D.** The regions enjoyed improved relations.

CHAPTER 10

# The Coming of the Civil War (1846–1861)

## SECTION 1 TWO NATIONS

### TEXT SUMMARY

In 1861 North and South began a Civil War. The outcome would determine if the **Union,** the unified states of the nation, could survive. Some historians believe that the United States could have avoided the Civil War. They argue that if Americans had elected better leaders and established stronger political institutions, extremists on both sides could not have pushed the nation into war. Others say that war was inevitable, because society was deeply divided geographically, politically, and socially.

**THE BIG IDEA**

**By the 1850s the North and the South had developed into regions with very different economies, societies, and views on slavery.**

The basic issue dividing the North and South was slavery. By the 1850s many Northerners believed slavery was wrong, among them the writer Harriet Beecher Stowe, whose book *Uncle Tom's Cabin* starkly pointed out the horrors of slavery. The book convinced many people that slavery had to end. Southerners were outraged by the book and claimed that slavery was not a terrible evil, arguing that most plantation owners took good care of enslaved Africans.

Other important differences in trade and communication separated the North and South. Railroads had made canals **obsolete,** or outdated, and thousands of miles of railroad track were laid, almost all in the North. Railroads created northern centers of trade like Chicago, and although Atlanta, Georgia, grew from railroads, the South still used mostly canals for transport. Communications technologies like the telegraph, whose wires connected northern towns and cities, also advanced more rapidly in the North.

### GRAPHIC SUMMARY: *Differences between North and South*

| | NORTHERN STATES | SOUTHERN STATES |
|---|---|---|
| Population | 21.5 million | 9 million |
| Number of Factories | 110,100 | 20,600 |
| Miles of Railroad | 21,700 | 9,000 |
| Bank Deposits | $207 million | $47 million |
| Cotton Production | 4 thousand bales | 5 million bales |

During the 1850s differences between the North and South continued to grow.

### REVIEW QUESTIONS

1. What was the impact of the novel *Uncle Tom's Cabin*?
2. **Chart Skills** Which region had a larger population? Which had more factories?

# SECTION 2 THE MEXICAN WAR AND SLAVERY EXTENSION

## TEXT SUMMARY

Migration into western territories soared in the 1830s and 1840s as Americans carried out **manifest destiny,** the theory that the United States should spread its ideals from coast to coast. In Texas, where settlers had won their independence from Mexico, the people voted to be **annexed,** or joined, to the United States. Annexation was controversial. Most southerners and Democrats supported it, hoping to gain another slave state. Northerners feared another slave state would give the South more political power. Many in the North also worried that annexing Texas could cause conflict with Mexico.

Congress approved annexation of Texas in 1845, and the United States and Mexico disagreed over where the boundary was between the two nations. President James Polk wanted Texas as well as all the territory between Texas and the Pacific Ocean. Negotiations with Mexico failed, and the Mexican War was declared in May 1846. At the same time, settlers in California and New Mexico, aided by the U.S. Army, rebelled and took over the two territories.

The U.S. Army invaded northern Mexico and, after several hard-fought battles, conquered the region. Under General Winfield Scott, U.S. forces marched to Mexico City and captured it, ending the war. The **Treaty of Guadalupe Hidalgo,** signed in February 1848, gave the United States the territories of Texas, New Mexico, and California and paid Mexico $15 million. Only three years later, Mexico sold land that is now part of southern New Mexico and Arizona to the United States for $10 million in a deal called the **Gadsden Purchase.**

Acquiring these territories resurfaced the issue of slavery and whether it would be allowed to extend into the West. A measure in Congress called the **Wilmot Proviso,** asking not to allow slavery in any western territories, was consistently defeated by Congress.

**THE BIG IDEA**

**The annexation of Texas and the Mexican War extended the boundaries of the United States across the continent.**

## GRAPHIC SUMMARY: *Events in the Mexican War*

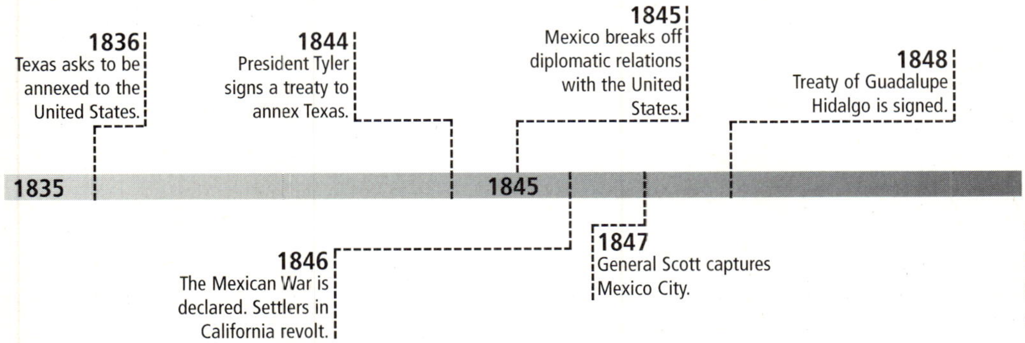


**From 1836 to 1848 the Mexican War is fought between the United States and Mexico.**

## REVIEW QUESTIONS

1. What territory did the United States acquire in the Treaty of Guadalupe Hidalgo? the Gadsden Purchase?
2. **Time Line Skills** In what year did General Scott capture Mexico City?

# SECTION 3 NEW POLITICAL PARTIES

## TEXT SUMMARY

**THE BIG IDEA**

**Congress failed to settle the issue of slavery in the West, leading to the formation of new political parties.**

The debate about allowing slavery in western territories was settled for a time with the Missouri Compromise of 1820. After the Mexican War the issue of slavery arose once more when California asked to join the Union as a free state. This would upset the balance between free and slave states. Congress attempted to settle the issue with the **Compromise of 1850,** which gave the people of the territories the right to decide for themselves. The compromise also included the **Fugitive Slave Act,** which ordered all citizens to assist in the capture of runaway slaves.

The compromise was hotly debated in Congress. The compromise was finally approved, but it did not settle the issue of slavery.

Tensions in the 1850s created new political parties, including the Northern Republican party, which bitterly opposed slavery. Nativists, people who believe in **nativism,** that native-born Americans received better treatment than immigrants, created a new political party called the American Party, which many people nicknamed the "Know-Nothings."

The slavery issue resurfaced again when Kansas and Nebraska asked to join the Union. Another compromise was reached in the **Kansas-Nebraska Act,** which supported the idea of **popular sovereignty,** stating that a territory could decide whether to become a free or slave state. This infuriated northerners while pleasing southerners. Northerners launched a new Republican Party, direct ancestors of today's Republican Party. It vowed to fight slavery in the new territories.

## GRAPHIC SUMMARY: *The Compromise of 1850*

**THE BACKGROUND**

- California applies for statehood as a free state.
- Equal balance between slave states and free states is threatened.

**THE COMPROMISE OF 1850**

- California admitted as a free state.
- In territories won from Mexico, voters will decide slavery issue for themselves.
- Sale of enslaved people outlawed in Washington, D.C.
- Fugitive Slave Act requires all citizens to help return escaped enslaved persons.

**THE EFFECTS**

- Compromise is only temporary: issue of slavery in territories not resolved.
- Neither southerners nor northerners satisfied.

**The Compromise of 1850 brought a period of calm to the nation but did not really settle the issue of slavery in the West.**

## REVIEW QUESTIONS

1. To what purpose was the new Republican party dedicated?

2. **Diagram Skills** According to the Compromise of 1850, how would the question of slavery be decided in the territories won from Mexico?

## SECTION 4 *THE SYSTEM FAILS*

### TEXT SUMMARY

Northerners were determined that Kansas would be a free state and vowed to send **free soilers,** people who would fight slavery, into Kansas. Violence soon erupted as proslavery forces in Missouri were organized. In 1856 proslavery forces attacked and looted Lawrence, Kansas, setting off raids and counter-raids that gave Kansas the label "bleeding Kansas."

Hatred escalated in the presidential election of 1856 as Democrats won solidly in the South, electing James Buchanan, who wanted the Supreme Court to resolve the slavery issue.

Instead, in 1857, in the ***Dred Scott* v. *Sandford*** decision, the Supreme Court ruled against Dred Scott, a slave who once lived in free territory and declared he should be free. The Supreme Court ruled he was not a citizen but was the property of his owner. It was a major victory for slave owners.

As tensions mounted, Republican Abraham Lincoln, who was seeking a Senate seat, debated Stephen Douglas in the **Lincoln-Douglas Debates** in 1858 over popular sovereignty. Douglas argued that the majority of people should make the decisions. Lincoln opposed the spread of slavery and believed that a majority of people did not have the right to deny freedoms to a minority.

Lincoln did not win a Senate seat, but his eloquence and moral commitment won him a following. A year after the debates, John Brown attacked the federal **arsenal,** a place where weapons were stored, in Harpers Ferry, Virginia.

Brown's dream of a slave uprising alarmed southerners, while many northerners hailed him as a hero. Captured and hanged, Brown became a symbol of antislavery forces.

**THE BIG IDEA**

**A series of violent clashes in the 1850s deepened the distrust and anger between North and South.**

### GRAPHIC SUMMARY: *Slavery Issue Dominates the Nation*

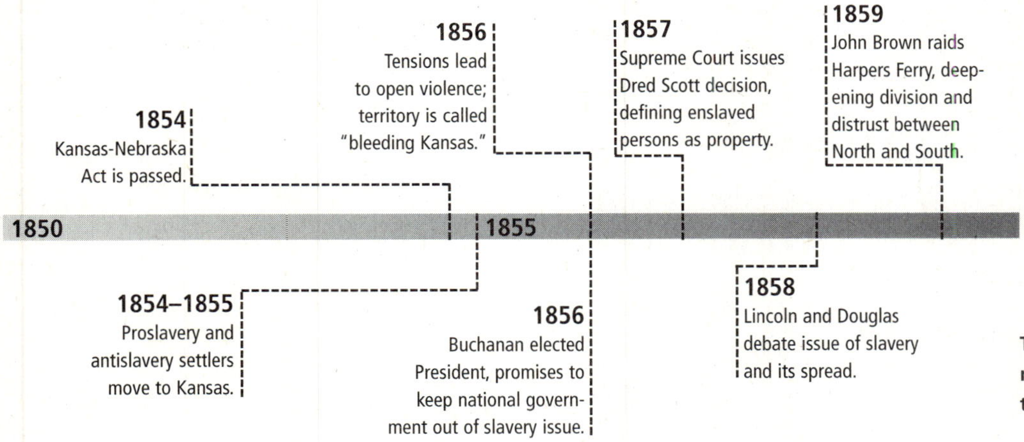


The issue of slavery dominated national politics throughout the 1850s.

### REVIEW QUESTIONS

1. Why was the Dred Scott decision a victory for slave owners?
2. **Time Line Skills** When was Buchanan elected President and what promise did he make?

# SECTION 5 A NATION DIVIDED

## TEXT SUMMARY

**THE BIG IDEA**

**After Lincoln was elected President, southern states began to leave the Union and the Civil War began.**

As the election of 1860 approached, the nation was divided. It was clear that southerners would not accept a northern president. However, some moderate southerners from the **Border States** of Delaware, Maryland, Kentucky, and Missouri met and formed the Constitutional Union party and nominated their own candidate. Abraham Lincoln was nominated by the Republican party. John Breckinridge was supported by the states of the **Lower South**—Texas, Louisiana, Mississippi, Alabama, Florida, Georgia, and South Carolina. This split among the candidates gave Lincoln the election, although he did not win a single vote in the South.

Outraged southerners believed they could no longer expect fairness from the national government and called for the South to withdraw from the Union. These **secessionists,** those who wanted to secede, said they had the right to leave the Union voluntarily. South Carolina seceded in late 1860, and in early 1861 delegates from seven southern states met and declared themselves the **Confederate States of America,** naming Jefferson Davis as their President.

Lincoln refused to recognize the Confederate States and vowed to preserve the Union, but he hoped war could be avoided. Compromise failed, and in April 1861, Confederate troops fired on the federal **Fort Sumter** in the harbor of Charleston, South Carolina. Firing on the fort was an act of rebellion, and Lincoln responded with a call for volunteers to fight. At that, states of the **Upper South**—Virginia, North Carolina, Tennessee, and Arkansas—left the Union, and the Civil War began.

## GRAPHIC SUMMARY: *The Union and the Confederacy, 1861*

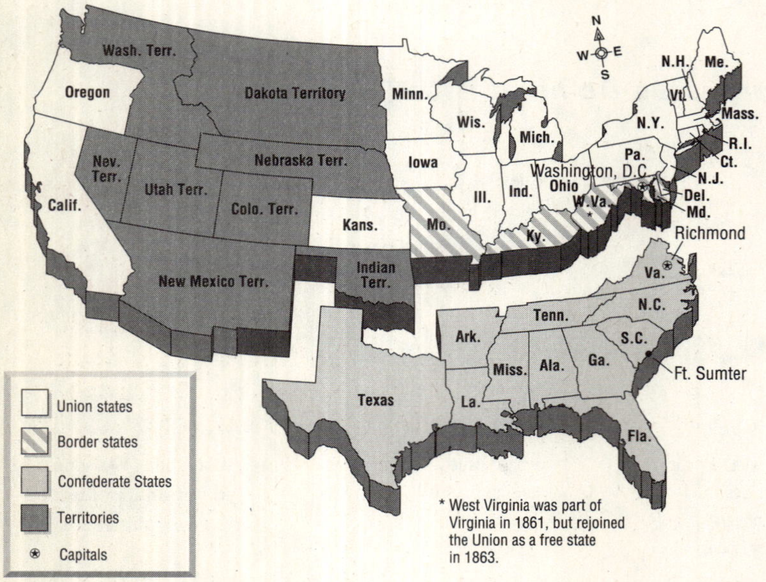


The Civil War divided the United States into two nations.

## REVIEW QUESTIONS

1. Why did Lincoln's election upset many southerners?
2. **Map Skills** How many states were there in the Confederacy?

Name ______________________________ Class ________________ Date __________

# CHAPTER 10 Test

## IDENTIFYING MAIN IDEAS

Write the letter of the correct answer in the blank provided. (10 points each)

____ **1.** *Uncle Tom's Cabin* convinced many northerners that
- **A.** slaves were treated better than factory workers.
- **B.** slavery was necessary.
- **C.** slavery was wrong.
- **D.** slaves were well treated.

____ **2.** The Compromise of 1850 was designed to settle the issue of
- **A.** popular sovereignty.
- **B.** the war with Mexico.
- **C.** slavery in the territories won from Mexico.
- **D.** the Kansas-Nebraska Act.

____ **3.** Which best describes the result of the Mexican War?
- **A.** the annexation of Texas
- **B.** expansion of the United States from the Atlantic to the Pacific
- **C.** United States gains California
- **D.** Mexico loses New Mexico

____ **4.** A main goal of the new Republican party was to
- **A.** prevent slavery from spreading into the western territories.
- **B.** promote the policy of popular sovereignty.
- **C.** slow the pace of immigration.
- **D.** keep the federal government out of the slavery debate.

____ **5.** Under popular sovereignty, the question of whether to allow slavery in a territory was to be decided by
- **A.** the people of the surrounding states.
- **B.** the people of the territory itself.
- **C.** the Congress of the United States.
- **D.** voters in a national election.

____ **6.** The Kansas-Nebraska Act led to
- **A.** violence between proslavery and antislavery groups.
- **B.** an end to the debate over slavery in the West.
- **C.** peaceful elections in Kansas and Nebraska.
- **D.** the admission of Kansas to the United States as a slave state.

____ **7.** In the Dred Scott decision, the Supreme Court declared that slaves were
- **A.** citizens of the United States.
- **B.** free if they are moved to the western territories.
- **C.** free if Congress banned slavery.
- **D.** the property of their masters.

____ **8.** Abraham Lincoln believed that slavery should be
- **A.** outlawed everywhere.
- **B.** allowed to spread.
- **C.** prevented from spreading.
- **D.** allowed only in the territories.

____ **9.** One result of Lincoln's victory in the election of 1860 was that
- **A.** the Democrats took over the government.
- **B.** the Republican party was founded.
- **C.** Lincoln could claim strong support from all regions of the United States.
- **D.** the states of the South began seceding from the Union.

____ **10.** The fighting at Fort Sumter in April 1861 was significant because it
- **A.** led to the creation of the Confederate States of America.
- **B.** helped Lincoln win the Presidential election.
- **C.** was the first battle of the Civil War.
- **D.** was the first major southern defeat.

CHAPTER 11

# The Civil War (1861–1865)

## SECTION 1 FROM BULL RUN TO ANTIETAM

### TEXT SUMMARY

In April 1861 Confederate guns fired on Fort Sumter, South Carolina, and the **Civil War** began.

In July a poorly prepared Union army marched on Richmond, Virginia, the new Confederate capital. They met Confederate troops in the **First Battle of Bull Run.** Due to the Union troops' lack of training and Confederate General Thomas "Stonewall" Jackson, the Union army was defeated.

**THE BIG IDEA**

**The bloody battles of 1861 and 1862 proved to both sides that the Civil War would be long and difficult.**

The North had clear advantages over the South. They had twice as much railroad, which allowed faster transport of troops and supplies; a large population and a large number of factories, which allowed people to fight and to produce military supplies; a balanced economy; and patriotism. However, the South had more experienced military leaders, and the belief that they were fighting to preserve their way of life and their right to self-government.

The Union's strategy was to cut off the South's cotton supply to Europe and to invade the South from the West and cut it in half. The South's strategy was to wage a defensive **war of attrition** in which it would continually inflict losses on the North and wear them down.

In the West, General Ulysses S. Grant won important Union victories on the Mississippi River at Forts Henry and Donelson and at the **Battle of Shiloh.**

In the East, a naval battle raged between two ironclad warships, the *Merrimack* and the *Monitor.* On land, Union forces threatened Richmond, but Confederate general Robert E. Lee was victorious at the Second Battle of Bull Run. In 1862 Lee invaded the North and fought at the Battle of Antietam, the bloodiest one-day battle of the war.

### GRAPHIC SUMMARY: *Preparing for War*

**NORTH**

Strengths
- More railroad track
- Larger population could provide more soldiers and workers
- More factories to produce supplies

Strategies
- Use naval blockade to prevent South from trading
- Gain control of the Mississippi River
- Capture Confederate capital of Richmond, Virginia

**SOUTH**

Strengths
- Experienced military commanders
- Fighting for a strong belief in self-government and their way of life
- Needed only to defend territory, not to attack

Strategies
- Prepare and wait, hoping Union will not pursue war
- Inflict losses and wear down North (war of attrition)
- Gain support of European countries

The North and South began the war with different strengths and different strategies for victory.

### REVIEW QUESTIONS

1. How did the North's larger population give it an advantage?
2. **Chart Skills** Which side had more experienced military leaders?

# SECTION 2 *LIFE BEHIND THE LINES*

## TEXT SUMMARY

Both the North and South experienced political difficulties during the Civil War. Both governments enforced a **draft** requiring men to serve in the military, and opposition was widespread. Southerners believed so strongly in states' rights that Confederate President Jefferson Davis had trouble getting local authorities to carry out the draft and many other economic measures to help the South. The South turned to Europe for help, but was denied.

In the North, Congress passed improvements, tariffs, and income taxes to help the war effort and the nation. Congress also created the nation's first official currency, **greenbacks.** However, President Lincoln did have some opposition. Democrats called **Copperheads** tried to hinder the war effort. Lincoln also had trouble with the border states and took emergency measures such as **martial law,** emergency rule by the military, and suspending the **writ of habeas corpus,** the legal right to a trial, to silence dissent.

Lincoln was also being pressured to make the end of slavery a goal of the war. Despite opposition, on January 1, 1863, Lincoln issued the **Emancipation Proclamation,** which freed slaves only in areas still under Confederate control. It had little direct impact, but it inspired abolitionists, slaves, and many northern African Americans, who enlisted in the Union army.

Meanwhile, Southerners faced food shortages and inflation. Northerners' stronger economy helped them solve these problems. In some cases, Northern industry flourished. But soldiers on both sides suffered from unsanitary conditions and disease. Although women on both sides worked in hospitals, more Civil War soldiers died from disease than from wounds.

**THE BIG IDEA**

**The Civil War brought political and economic changes to the North and South, including the first steps toward abolishing slavery.**

## GRAPHIC SUMMARY: *The North and South in Wartime*

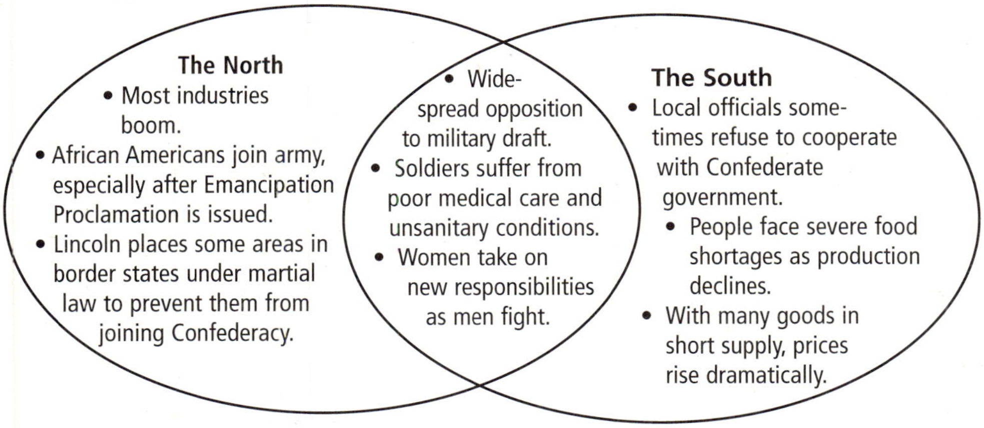


Soldiers and ordinary people in the North and South alike faced a variety of hardships during the war.

## REVIEW QUESTIONS

1. Describe the effects of the Emancipation Proclamation.
2. **Diagram Skills** What problems did both the North and South face during wartime?

## SECTION 3 THE TIDE OF WAR TURNS

### TEXT SUMMARY

**THE BIG IDEA**

**In 1862 and 1863 the Confederates won important battles in Virginia, but Union victories at Gettysburg and Vicksburg were the turning points of the war.**

During late 1862 and early 1863, General Lee's army won major victories at the **Battle of Fredericksburg** and the **Battle of Chancellorsville** in Virginia. It was a low point for the North, and some Northern leaders began to consider making peace with the Confederacy.

In June 1863 Lee invaded Pennsylvania, hoping a victory on Union soil would push the North into giving up the war. At the three-day **Battle of Gettysburg,** the bloodiest battle of the war, Lee lost a third of his army and was forced to retreat to Virginia. The Confederacy never again attempted to invade the North.

Meanwhile, in the West, General Grant had made several unsuccessful attempts to capture Vicksburg, the last city on the Mississippi River still held by Confederate troops. Finally, he laid **siege** to Vicksburg by surrounding the city and starving it into surrendering. Grant's victory gave the North complete control of the Mississippi River, cutting the Confederacy in half. Both the Battle of Gettysburg and the fall of Vicksburg were turning points in the war.

To honor the soldiers who died at Gettysburg, Lincoln dedicated a Pennsylvania cemetery. In his **Gettysburg Address,** Lincoln explained that the Union's purpose in the Civil War was to protect and expand freedom. He proclaimed that the nation would have "a new birth of freedom—and that government of the people, by the people, and for the people, shall not perish from the earth."

### GRAPHIC SUMMARY: *The Gettysburg Address*

| THE GETTYSBURG ADDRESS |
| --- |
| **Date:** November 19, 1863 |
| **Purpose:** Dedication of cemetery to honor Union soldiers who died in Battle of Gettysburg |
| **Length:** 2 minutes |
| **Important Points of Speech:**<br>• Reminded people that the United States was founded on the principles of liberty and equality<br>• Argued that the purpose of the Civil War was to protect these principles<br>• Proclaimed that the United States would have a "new birth of freedom" |

**The Gettysburg Address has become one of the most important speeches in American history.**

### REVIEW QUESTIONS

1. What was the importance of the Union victory at Vicksburg?
2. **Chart Skills** In the Gettysburg Address, what did Lincoln declare was the purpose of the Civil War?

SECTION 4

# DEVASTATION AND NEW FREEDOM

## TEXT SUMMARY

In March 1864 Lincoln appointed General Grant commander of the Union army. Grant's strategy was to wear down the Confederacy at any cost. Fighting in the East, he threw his troops into three brutal battles in Virginia, the **Battle of the Wilderness,** the **Battle of Spotsylvania,** and the **Battle of Cold Harbor,** forcing Lee to retreat toward Richmond. Grant then laid siege to the city of Petersburg and cut off supply to the Confederate troops from the Shenandoah Valley, hoping to starve Lee out of Richmond.

In the West, Union General William Tecumseh Sherman moved south from Tennessee, invaded Georgia, and captured Atlanta, an important railroad town. From Atlanta, Sherman marched across Georgia to Savannah. He set fire to the whole city of Atlanta before he left. His forces also burned homes, destroyed food stores, and tore up railroad tracks on his way to Savannah. Sherman captured Savannah on December 21, 1863.

Lincoln needed these victories to gain reelection in 1864. He used them to convince Northerners that the end of the war was near. Lincoln won the election, which showed that his actions opposing slavery had gained wider approval. In February 1865 Congress passed the **Thirteenth Amendment,** the law that ended slavery forever in the United States.

With Grant starving and attacking Richmond, and Sherman moving north, Lee realized that the war was over. On April 9, 1865, Lee surrendered to General Grant at Appomattox Court House in Virginia. The Civil War officially ended a few weeks later. Unfortunately, President Lincoln did not live to see it. On April 14, 1865, he was assassinated by John Wilkes Booth, a Southern sympathizer, while watching a play in Washington, D.C. Northerners mourned the loss of the man who had led them through the course of war.

**THE BIG IDEA**

**During 1865 the Union won the Civil War, the United States abolished slavery, and Lincoln was assassinated.**

## GRAPHIC SUMMARY: *Causes and Effects of the Civil War*

| CAUSES |
|---|
| • Regional differences between the North and South grow stronger<br>• Question of slavery in the territories widens the gap between Northern and Southern interests<br>• Congressional compromises are unable to settle the issue of slavery in the territories<br>• Abraham Lincoln, an antislavery Republican, is elected President<br>• Eleven Southern states secede and form the Confederate States of America |

↓

| THE CIVIL WAR |
|---|

↓

| EFFECTS |
|---|
| • The Union is preserved<br>• Slavery is abolished<br>• Over half a million soldiers are dead<br>• Southern farms and cities are left in ruins |

More American soldiers died in the Civil War than in any other war in U.S. history.

## REVIEW QUESTIONS

1. How did the Thirteenth Amendment change the United States?

2. **Diagram Skills** The election of which President helped lead to the Civil War?

Name ______________________ Class ______________ Date ________

# CHAPTER 11 Test

## IDENTIFYING MAIN IDEAS

Write the letter of the correct answer in the blank provided. (10 points each)

____ **1.** As the Civil War began, the South planned
- **A.** a defensive war.
- **B.** a war of attack.
- **C.** a blockade of Northern ports.
- **D.** a war at sea.

____ **2.** During the Civil War, the North had the advantage of
- **A.** fighting for their right of self-government.
- **B.** having a larger population and more factories.
- **C.** having more experienced generals.
- **D.** being able to fight a defensive war.

____ **3.** After the Battles of Shiloh and Antietam
- **A.** Northern generals pushed Lee's army out of Virginia.
- **B.** both sides realized the war would be long and difficult.
- **C.** Lincoln began to consider ending the war.
- **D.** Lee began marching his army toward Washington, D.C.

____ **4.** During the war, the Confederate government
- **A.** offered freedom to slaves if they would join the army.
- **B.** refused to hold a draft.
- **C.** ignored the opinions of England and France.
- **D.** had difficulty gaining cooperation from local governments.

____ **5.** The Emancipation Proclamation freed
- **A.** all slaves everywhere.
- **B.** slaves who fought for the Union.
- **C.** slaves in the Confederate South.
- **D.** slaves in the western territories.

____ **6.** In 1863, Lee marched to Gettysburg with the goal of
- **A.** splitting the Union in two.
- **B.** taking revenge for his defeat at Fredericksburg.
- **C.** fleeing Union troops in Virginia.
- **D.** winning a victory on Northern soil.

____ **7.** The Battles of Gettysburg and Vicksburg were
- **A.** Northern victories which caused the surrender of Lee's army.
- **B.** Southern victories which convinced foreign countries to support the South.
- **C.** Northern victories which were the turning points of the Civil War.
- **D.** Southern victories which secured the South's control of the Mississippi River.

____ **8.** In the Gettysburg Address, Lincoln declared that the purpose of the Civil War was to
- **A.** protest unfair taxes and tariffs.
- **B.** protect and expand freedom in the United States.
- **C.** increase the size of the United States.
- **D.** force the South to leave the Union.

____ **9.** In his campaign to be reelected President in 1864, Lincoln was helped by
- **A.** the death of General Lee.
- **B.** Northern victories on the battlefield.
- **C.** the votes of freed slaves.
- **D.** strong Southern support.

____ **10.** At Appomattox Court House in April 1865,
- **A.** General Lee surrendered to General Grant.
- **B.** Lee's army began to march south to Atlanta.
- **C.** Maryland agreed to join the Confederacy.
- **D.** Lincoln was assassinated.

# Reconstruction (1865–1877)

CHAPTER 12

## SECTION 1 *Presidential Reconstruction*

### TEXT SUMMARY

The Civil War took a terrible toll on people of the South. Railroad lines and factories were destroyed, cities and farmlands lay in ruin, and much of the livestock had been slaughtered. One out of every three Southern men had been killed or wounded.

The period of rebuilding the South and restoring the Southern states to the Union is known as **Reconstruction.** Before the war's end, Lincoln proposed a plan that permitted each Southern state, after 10 percent of the people had sworn allegiance to the Union, to create a new state constitution which needed to ratify the thirteenth amendment. This "ten percent" plan also granted a **pardon,** forgiveness for a crime, to any Confederate, except military and government officials, who swore allegiance to the Union and accepted the end of slavery.

Lincoln's plan was opposed by Congress, who saw the plan as limiting congressional power, and by **Radical Republicans,** who saw the plan as much too lenient. After Lincoln's death, the new President, Andrew Johnson, offered a plan, but it removed the ten percent and allowed pardons to Confederate leaders. Johnson's plan met with much debate.

Meanwhile, African Americans celebrated their new freedom, building churches and schools and looking forward to owning land. Many Northerners, mostly young women, taught in these schools. Congress also established the **Freedman's Bureau,** which set up schools and gave clothing, meals, and medical help to thousands of both black and white war refugees.

**THE BIG IDEA**

**As African Americans celebrated their freedom, Presidents Lincoln and Johnson put forward plans to rebuild the Southern states.**

### GRAPHIC SUMMARY: *African Americans Celebrate Freedom*

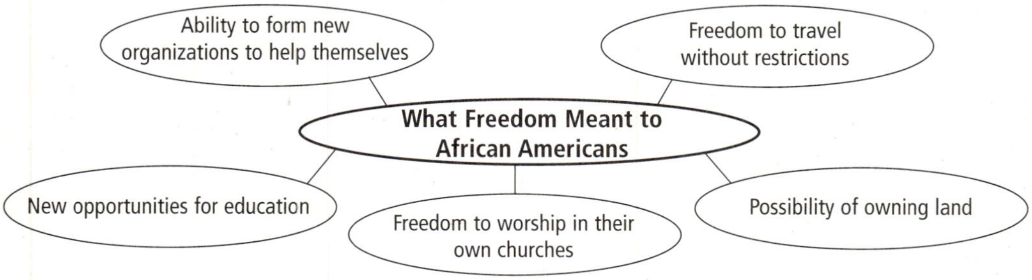


**After the war, African Americans celebrated their new freedom.**

### REVIEW QUESTIONS

1. What was the purpose of Reconstruction?
2. **Diagram Skills** Identify three ways African Americans experienced a new freedom after the Civil War.

# SECTION 2 CONGRESSIONAL RECONSTRUCTION

## TEXT SUMMARY

As Southern states were restored to the Union, their white-run governments began restricting the rights of African Americans through **black codes.** Enraged, Congress in 1866 passed a Civil Rights Act outlawing the black codes. Congress then passed the **Fourteenth Amendment** redefining citizenship to include African Americans and granting equal protection under the law to all citizens.

**THE BIG IDEA**

**Congress took over Reconstruction and passed laws protecting African Americans' freedom.**

Giving **civil rights,** citizens' personal liberties guaranteed by law, to blacks did not please everyone, including President Johnson. He opposed the Fourteenth Amendment, rousing the anger of Radical Republicans, who proposed the Reconstruction Act of 1867. This plan included putting the South under military rule and demanding that the South create new constitutions and give blacks equal rights. President Johnson strongly opposed the plan and fired Edwin Stanton, a friend of the radicals, as Secretary of War.

Because of this, Congress began proceedings to **impeach,** or charge the President with wrongdoing by accusing him of obstructing Reconstruction policies. They did not succeed, but Johnson lost power and the 1868 election. In 1869 Congress passed the **Fifteenth Amendment** stating that "no citizen could be denied the right to vote on account of race, color, or previous condition."

Reconstruction policies led to thousands of African Americans voting throughout the South. Southerners resented the political power of blacks as well as **carpetbaggers,** white Northerners who settled in the South, and **scalawags,** white southern Republicans. Southern Democrats claimed that the newly elected local, state, and federal governments were corrupt and incompetent.

## GRAPHIC SUMMARY: *Major Reconstruction Legislation*

| DATE | LEGISLATION | PURPOSE |
|---|---|---|
| 1865 | Freedman's Bureau | • Provides services for newly freed people |
| 1865 | 13th Amendment | • Abolishes slavery |
| 1866 | Civil Rights Act | • Outlaws the black codes |
| 1867 | Reconstruction Acts | • Establishes Republican Reconstruction program |
| 1868 | 14th Amendment | • Defines citizenship to include African Americans<br>• Guarantees equal protection under law |
| 1870 | 15th Amendment | • Guarantees voting rights to all male citizens |

**The Reconstruction era was marked by important pieces of legislation, including amendments to the Constitution.**

## REVIEW QUESTIONS

1. Describe the black codes, and the reaction of Congress to them.
2. **Chart Skills** What three constitutional amendments were passed during the Civil War and Reconstruction periods? What was the purpose of each?

SECTION 3

# BIRTH OF THE "NEW SOUTH"

## TEXT SUMMARY

In the "New South" of the 1870s, farming changed. Planters no longer had slaves to work their fields. They hired free blacks, as well as whites, in an arrangement called **sharecropping.** The workers farmed for a share of the crop. But many had to pay a planter for housing or food, which usually left them in debt. To escape debt, workers often tried **tenant farming,** renting land and growing and selling their own crops. Tenant farmers had a higher social status than sharecroppers. These new farming methods changed the labor force of the South, put an emphasis on cash crops, and created a cycle of debt for workers and a new class of merchants who often grew rich selling goods on credit to farmers.

Another major change in the South was the growth of cities such as Atlanta, Memphis, and Dallas. Southern leaders encouraged this growth, as well as the expansion of industry, business, and extensive rebuilding of railroads to create trade and commerce. The southern economy continued to thrive off of cotton mills, but the big profits from the cloth went to northern factories because they sold the finished product.

Because much of the South's **infrastructure**—its public property and public services—had to be rebuilt, business opportunities abounded in constructing roads, bridges, canals, telegraph lines, and public buildings. Private investment rebuilt some of the infrastructure, and Congress added funds. The Reconstruction legislatures also poured money into rebuilding by levying heavy taxes on southerners. The people resented paying these taxes, especially since much of the money was lost to corruption.

**THE BIG IDEA**

**During the 1870s southern farming practices changed, while southern cities and industry began to grow.**

## GRAPHIC SUMMARY: *Developments in the "New South"*

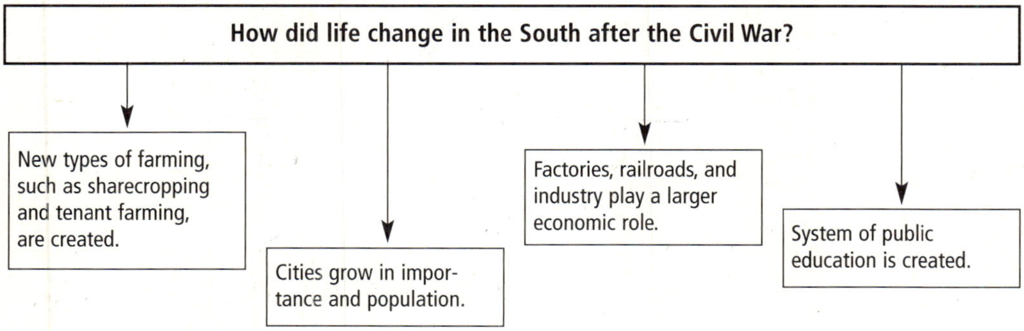


**After the war, the agriculture, industry, and cities of the South all began to change.**

## REVIEW QUESTIONS

1. Describe the difference between sharecroppers and tenant farmers.
2. **Diagram Skills** Identify two ways life changed in the South during Reconstruction.

SECTION 4

# THE END OF RECONSTRUCTION

## TEXT SUMMARY

**THE BIG IDEA**

**Reconstruction came to an end in 1877, leaving a record of both success and failure.**

During the late 1860s and early 1870s, groups of white Southerners launched a series of violent attacks against African Americans and their supporters. The attacks were led by the Ku Klux Klan, or KKK, a secret society of former Confederates, and plantation owners excluded from politics. It also attracted people who were determined to deny blacks equal rights. The goal of the KKK was to keep African Americans from gaining equality with whites.

Congress responded by passing the **Enforcement Act of 1870,** banning the use of terror, force, or bribery to prevent people from voting because of their race. Other laws and the use of the military helped end most Klan activity. But the Klan had prevented many African Americans from exercising their rights.

By the mid-1870s people had grown tired of Republicans' concern over Reconstruction. Scandals in the Grant administration and corruption in Southern Republican legislatures made people weary of Reconstruction. Democrats began to return to power in the South, forming a new bloc of leaders known as the **solid South.** They blocked most federal Reconstruction policies and reversed reforms.

In the presidential election of 1876, both Republicans and Democrats claimed victory. To settle the dispute, the parties reached the **Compromise of 1877.** Democrats agreed to give the presidency to Republican Rutherford B. Hayes if federal troops were removed from the South. The agreement officially ended Reconstruction.

## GRAPHIC SUMMARY: *Reconstruction: Successes and Failures*

RECONSTRUCTION

| SUCCESSES |
|---|
| Union is restored and rebuilding of South begun. |
| Southern economic growth is stimulated. |
| African Americans gain formal rights of citizenship and equal treatment. |
| Many black families helped in obtaining housing, jobs, and schooling. |

| FAILURES |
|---|
| African Americans still lack property and economic opportunity. |
| Southern governments deny African Americans the right to vote. |
| Racist attitudes continue, in both North and South. |
| Lasting bitterness between many Southerners and federal government. |

**Reconstruction was marked by both successes and failures.**

## REVIEW QUESTIONS

1. What was the goal of the Ku Klux Klan?
2. **Chart Skills** In what ways were African Americans helped by Reconstruction?

Name ____________________ Class ____________ Date ________

# CHAPTER 12 Test

## IDENTIFYING MAIN IDEAS

Write the letter of the correct answer in the blank provided. (10 points each)

____ **1.** Reconstruction was the effort to restore
- **A.** Confederate soldiers to the army.
- **B.** the southern states to the Union.
- **C.** voting rights to African Americans.
- **D.** failed southern factories to economic health.

____ **2.** In his plan for Reconstruction, Lincoln insisted that southern states
- **A.** make an official apology to former slaves.
- **B.** ratify the Thirteenth Amendment.
- **C.** remain in the Confederacy.
- **D.** repay the North for war damages.

____ **3.** Unlike Lincoln, President Johnson was willing to
- **A.** support Reconstruction.
- **B.** punish the South for the war.
- **C.** oppose the Thirteenth Amendment.
- **D.** issue pardons to Confederate leaders.

____ **4.** Black codes restricted the
- **A.** rights of African Americans.
- **B.** ability of southern leaders to govern.
- **C.** freedom of tenant farmers.
- **D.** number of northerners allowed to move to the South.

____ **5.** The Fourteenth Amendment gives
- **A.** equal protection of the laws to all citizens.
- **B.** women's right to vote.
- **C.** African Americans the right to vote.
- **D.** freedom of the press.

____ **6.** After the Civil War, one way southern farming changed was that
- **A.** many former slaves became sharecroppers or tenant farmers.
- **B.** plantation owners found it easier to find workers.
- **C.** the South stopped growing cotton.
- **D.** the government gave farmland to all former slaves.

____ **7.** After the war, the growth of southern industry caused
- **A.** the South to stop building railroads.
- **B.** an end to racism.
- **C.** the South to become more industrial than the North.
- **D.** the growth of southern cities.

____ **8.** During Reconstruction, a large amount of public money was spent on
- **A.** lowering taxes.
- **B.** building roads, bridges and public schools.
- **C.** paying off southern debt.
- **D.** building up northern industry.

____ **9.** The Ku Klux Klan used violence to
- **A.** prevent African Americans from exercising their rights.
- **B.** elect Radical Republicans to Congress.
- **C.** keep federal troops in the South.
- **D.** expand economic opportunities for former slaves.

____ **10.** Which was a positive result of the Reconstruction effort?
- **A.** Southern governments vowed to battle racist groups like the Klan.
- **B.** Most African Americans quickly rose out of poverty.
- **C.** New constitutional amendments expanded the rights of African Americans.
- **D.** Bitterness between the North and South came to an end.

CHAPTER 13

# The Expansion of American Industry (1850–1900)

## SECTION 1 A Technological Revolution

### TEXT SUMMARY

During the decades after the Civil War, the United States began to rise as a great industrial nation. Technological advances in new forms of energy, such as oil, and developments such as electricity, the telegraph, telephones, and expanded ways of travel dramatically changed business operations and the daily lives of most Americans. The number of patents at this time soared.

A communications revolution began when Samuel F.B. Morse perfected the telegraph and Alexander Graham Bell invented the telephone. By 1900 millions of messages were sent over wires, and giant communications companies like Western Union were formed.

The development of electricity by Thomas A. Edison stimulated the growth of innumerable businesses. Work in the home was easier with electric lights and appliances like the refrigerators that preserved food and fans that cooled the air.

People and goods traveled faster, easier, and cheaper on an expanding railroad system, including transcontinental railroad from coast to coast. From the **transcontinental railroad,** networks of railroads were created that fostered national markets, lowered production costs, and stimulated new advances in other industries such as steel. The **Bessemer process** made the process of turning iron into steal easier and cheaper. Soon **mass production,** or production in great amounts, of light, flexible steel encouraged a new age in construction of taller buildings and long suspension bridges to help connect cities and improve transportation.

**THE BIG IDEA**

**In the decades following the Civil War, advances in transportation, communications, and electric power changed daily life in the United States.**

### GRAPHIC SUMMARY: *Technology Time Line*

1840 | 1850 | 1860 | 1870 | 1880

- **1844** First Morse code telegram sent
- **1856** Bessemer process makes steel production economical
- **1869** Transcontinental railroad completed
- **1876** Alexander Graham Bell invents the telephone
- **1880** Thomas Edison develops the electric light bulb

The United States experienced a technological revolution during the mid-1800s.

### REVIEW QUESTIONS

1. What was one effect of the transcontinental railroad?
2. **Time Line Skills** What 1880 invention changed the world?

SECTION 2

# THE GROWTH OF BIG BUSINESS

## TEXT SUMMARY

In the late 1800s powerful industrial leaders like Andrew Carnegie and John D. Rockefeller built giant corporations. Carnegie controlled steel; Rockefeller dominated the American oil market. Some historians called them "robber barons," because they raided natural resources and mistreated workers. Other historians called them "captains of industry" who expanded production markets and created jobs.

To explain the need for such industrial giants, the theory of **social Darwinism** argued that government should not interfere in business practices so that those most "fit" would rise to the top and everyone would benefit.

Many factors combined to create a new kind of business in the late 1800s. These industries needed large amounts of capital to start; therefore, only people with large amounts of money could invest in them. Railroads and the telegraph allowed factories owned by the same business to communicate across the nation. Professional managers were hired and new, complex systems of accounting were developed to handle the large volume of money, products, and workers.

Some industrialists gained complete control of one product or service through a **monopoly.** There were two main types of monopolies. The first was **vertical consolidation,** in which one company buys all the phases of a product's development so that it can produce things quicker and cheaper than all other competitors. The other is **horizontal consolidation,** in which a company brings many firms of the same business into one. To avoid state regulations, Rockefeller invented a **trust,** in which a company combined operations with other companies all run by a board of trustees.

The government responded by passing the **Sherman Antitrust Act** in 1890 that outlawed trusts restraining interstate trade.

**THE BIG IDEA**

**Big business helped the nation grow, though people disagreed about whether huge industries were good or bad for the nation.**

## GRAPHIC SUMMARY: *The Impact of Big Business*

| POSITIVE EFFECTS | NEGATIVE EFFECTS |
|---|---|
| • Factories produce a wide variety of goods for consumers to choose from.<br>• Many new jobs are created.<br>• Wealthy industrialists fund charities, libraries, and universities. | • Workers face low wages and poor working conditions.<br>• Monopolies keep prices high, and drive small companies out of business.<br>• Periods of expanding prosperity are often followed by economic hard times. |

**The success of big business brought great wealth and new problems to the United States.**

## REVIEW QUESTIONS

**1.** What is a monopoly?

**2. Chart Skills** Give two positive effects of the success of big business.

# SECTION 3 INDUSTRIALIZATION AND WORKERS

## TEXT SUMMARY

**THE BIG IDEA**

**Working long hours for low wages, millions of industrial workers helped drive the expansion of American industry.**

The demand for workers increased rapidly as American industry expanded and prospered and cities grew. Waves of new immigrants found jobs in factories and shops, while millions of Americans left the countryside for the cities because of poor economic conditions on the nation's farms.

Most workers were not paid by the hour or day but by a system of **piecework,** a fixed amount for each finished piece they produced. Workers also found conditions in many factories unsafe because of fires and accidents, and unhealthy because of poor light and ventilation. This was especially true in the **sweatshops,** where people worked for long hours at low pay.

Anxious to increase productivity and efficiency, employers devised a **division of labor** system in which workers made only one part of a product and never saw the finished item. This took the joy of completion from many workers' jobs.

The relationship between owners and workers deteriorated, as well. Owners of large companies had little contact with workers and often viewed them simply as parts in a large machine. Owners strictly controlled workers for more efficiency, fining or firing them if they broke rules against talking or being late.

Children were especially damaged by poor conditions in factories. Many children left school and took jobs in factories. Girls sometimes took factory jobs so that their brothers could stay in school. In 1880 children made up more than five percent of the labor force.

## GRAPHIC SUMMARY: *The American Labor Force*

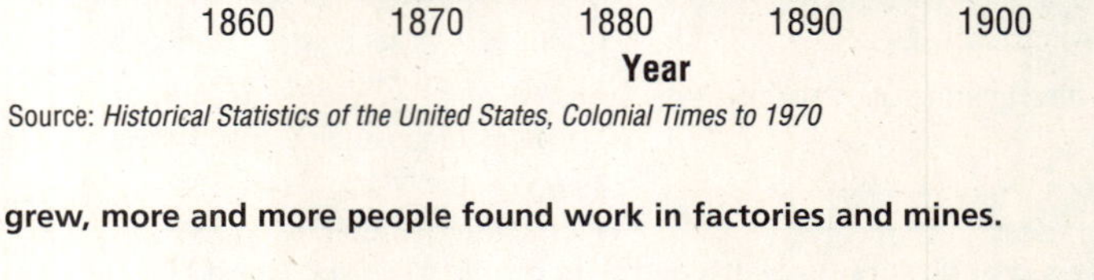


**As industry grew, more and more people found work in factories and mines.**

## REVIEW QUESTIONS

1. Why was factory work unsafe and unhealthy?
2. **Graph Skills** Were there more agricultural workers or industrial workers in 1890?

# SECTION 4 *THE GREAT STRIKES*

## TEXT SUMMARY

Industrialization brought the United States enormous wealth, but a great gap existed between rich and poor. To fight the inequality, many workers turned to **socialism,** the economic and political philosophy that favors public rather than private control of property. Others favored labor unions. By the early 1870s the Knights of Labor was organizing workers from many different trades. The American Federation of Labor (AFL), under the leadership of Samuel Gompers, was a national **craft union,** which organized skilled workers.

Through economic pressures such as strikes and boycotts, the AFL tried to force employers into negotiating with workers through a tactic known as **collective bargaining.** Workers fought for shorter workdays, higher wages, and better working conditions. Employers reacted with measures that included forbidding union meetings, firing union organizers, and refusing to recognize unions.

National labor unrest continued, particularly in the railroad industry. Strikes erupted all over the nation, such as the railroad strike of 1877. In 1893 Eugene V. Debs successfully formed a railway **industrial union,** one that organizes workers from all crafts in a particular industry.

Strikes continued through the late 1800s and often erupted into violence. Employers turned to the federal government and the courts for help. The government responded by sending federal troops, and the courts issued orders against unions. The disorganized and violent nature of the strikes together with court and government actions hampered union progress for many decades.

**THE BIG IDEA**

**In the late 1800s workers formed unions to fight for more pay and better working conditions.**

## GRAPHIC SUMMARY: *An Era of Strikes, Late 1800s*

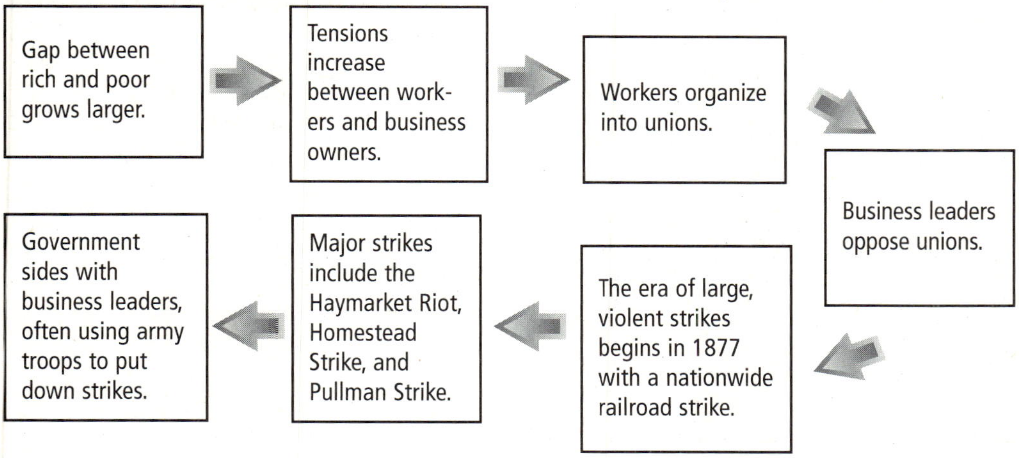


**Increasing tensions between workers and employers led to large, often violent strikes.**

## REVIEW QUESTIONS

**1.** What were two major union goals?

**2. Diagram Skills** When did the era of large, violent strikes begin?

Name ____________________ Class ____________ Date ________

# CHAPTER 13 Test

## IDENTIFYING MAIN IDEAS

Write the letter of the correct answer in the blank provided. (10 points each)

____ **1.** The transcontinental railroad connected
- **A.** northern cities to Mexico.
- **B.** the East Coast to the West Coast.
- **C.** cotton plantations to southern cities.
- **D.** New York to Washington, D.C.

____ **2.** Samuel Morse helped start a communications revolution when he took out a patent on the
- **A.** telephone.
- **B.** telegraph.
- **C.** central power station.
- **D.** phonograph.

____ **3.** The development of the Bessemer process led to
- **A.** refrigeration in every home.
- **B.** the first commercial telephone exchange.
- **C.** a new age of American construction.
- **D.** the development of Morse code.

____ **4.** During the late 1800s, critics of industrial leaders referred to them as
- **A.** captains of industry.
- **B.** philanthropists.
- **C.** robber barons.
- **D.** socialists.

____ **5.** Supporters of social Darwinism believed that if the government did not interfere with business
- **A.** all workers would be able to find jobs.
- **B.** there would be an unfair distribution of wealth.
- **C.** society as a whole would suffer.
- **D.** the smartest and strongest members of society would grow rich.

____ **6.** Which of these best describes working conditions in factories of the late 1800s?
- **A.** brightly lit with a lot of fresh air
- **B.** safe and accident free
- **C.** unhealthy and dangerous
- **D.** inefficient and unprofitable

____ **7.** Many children left school to work in factories because
- **A.** the wages were high.
- **B.** the work was easy and safe.
- **C.** their families needed the money to survive.
- **D.** there were no public schools.

____ **8.** Industrial growth in the United States led to a concentration of wealth in the hands of
- **A.** powerful labor unions.
- **B.** millions of factory workers.
- **C.** a small number of industrial leaders.
- **D.** farmers in the West and South.

____ **9.** Employers fought the power of unions by
- **A.** improving working conditions.
- **B.** paying higher wages.
- **C.** giving union leaders better jobs.
- **D.** firing union organizers.

____ **10.** The federal government responded to large strikes by
- **A.** ignoring them.
- **B.** passing laws against unions.
- **C.** using federal troops to end strikes.
- **D.** forcing employers to raise wages.

# Looking to the West (1860–1900)

CHAPTER 14

## SECTION 1 MOVING WEST

### TEXT SUMMARY

The events and conditions that drove Americans and immigrants west are called **push-pull factors.** Many farmers, former slaves, and other workers were displaced after the Civil War and could not afford eastern farmland. They were pushed west looking for a new start, cheaper farmland, or religious and ethnic freedoms. The West also pushed outlaws on the run. People were pulled by government incentives to settle the great open spaces. Railroads carried people west and also sold settlers portions of land. States sold western land to **land speculators** cheaply, who then resold it to settlers for a large profit. The **Homestead Act** in 1862 sold public land very cheaply and created more than 372,000 farms. The government also protected the rights of farmers, miners, and ranchers by giving them firm private property rights protected under the law.

Settlers came from far and wide. German and Scandinavian immigrants sought farm land in the West. Irish, Italians, European Jews, and Chinese settled in West Coast cities and moved east. Mexicans and Mexican Americans added to the growth of ranching. African Americans also moved west. Benjamin "Pap" Singleton led groups of southern blacks west on a mass "Exodus." These settlers called themselves **Exodusters.** They were fleeing the violence and exploitation that followed Reconstruction for a better life.

**THE BIG IDEA**

**The federal government made western lands available, and settlers moved west to start new lives on their own land.**

### GRAPHIC SUMMARY: *The Homestead Act of 1862*

**The Homestead Act offered 160 acres of land to anyone who met these requirements:**

- Settlers had to be at least 21 years of age, or the head of a family.
- Settlers had to be American citizens or immigrants who had filed for citizenship.
- Settlers had to build a house and live on the land at least six months each year.
- Settlers had to farm the land for five consecutive years.

**President Lincoln signed the Homestead Act to encourage settlement of the West.**

### REVIEW QUESTIONS

1. What were some of the factors that pushed people to the West?
2. **Diagram Skills** For how many consecutive years were settlers required to farm their land?

SECTION 2

# Conflict With Native Americans

## TEXT SUMMARY

THE BIG IDEA

**American expansion onto Native American lands led to many battles and the near destruction of western Native American nations.**

Settling the **Great Plains,** the vast territory between the Mississippi River and the Rocky Mountains, brought settlers into conflict with Native Americans. Most Plains Indians were **nomads,** people who roamed from place to place following their main source of food—herds of buffalo. Competition for land caused a clash between settlers and the Plains Indians.

Settlers believed they had the right to take the land because they would produce more food and wealth. Between 1861 and 1890 battles raged between the United States army and Indian groups. The Indians were outgunned and usually suffered heavy casualties, but they continued to fight. Some key battles were the Sand Creek Massacre that defeated the Cheyenne, and the **Battle of Little Big Horn,** in which the Sioux killed General Custer and all his troops. The last conflict was the **Massacre at Wounded Knee** where American troops killed 200 unarmed Sioux men, women, and children.

The government put the defeated Indian nations on **reservations,** lands set aside for these people. Another government policy of **assimilation** tried to force Indians to adopt the American culture by giving up their religions, traditions, languages, and customs. In 1887 the federal government passed the **Dawes Act** that divided reservation land into plots. Most land was unsuitable for farming, and most Indians had no desire to farm or own land. In 1889 Congress opened up the Indian Territory to thousands of settlers, called **boomers** and **sooners,** pushing Indian groups into smaller areas.

## GRAPHIC SUMMARY: *Key Events in the Native American Conflict*

| | |
|---|---|
| **1864** | Colonel John Chivington and his men slaughter between 150 and 500 Cheyenne of Colorado Territory in the Sand Creek Massacre. |
| **1865** | Federal government decides to build a road through Sioux territory. Sioux launch a two-year war against the United States army. |
| **1874** | Federal government sends Lieutenant Colonel George A. Custer to investigate rumors of gold in the Black Hills of Sioux territory. He reports that there is a lot of gold in the Black Hills. Settlers and miners begin to search the hills for gold. Hostilities resume between the Sioux and the army. |
| **1876** | Nearly 2,000 Sioux warriors attack Custer's troops at the Battle of Little Big Horn. Custer and more than 200 soldiers are killed. |
| **1890** | At the Massacre at Wounded Knee, United States soldiers open fire on unarmed Sioux grieving the death of Sitting Bull, killing 200. |

**Native Americans violently resisted American expansion.**

## REVIEW QUESTIONS

1. How did most Native Americans view white settlers?
2. **Chart Skills** Why did hostilities resume between the United States and the Sioux?

SECTION 3

# MINING, RANCHING, AND FARMING

## TEXT SUMMARY

Once the Indian wars were over, miners, ranchers, and farmers flooded into the West. From California, mining moved inland when gold was discovered in Colorado. Mining became big business when gold was too far underground. Individual miners left, and corporations took over.

Americans learned about ranching from Mexicans in the Southwest, and when the Indians were removed and the buffalo killed, cattle ranching boomed on the Great Plains. Thousands of cattle were herded each year by cowboys and made the **long drive** to railroad towns. As the demand for beef grew, some ranchers became cattle barons, operating spreads of millions of acres of grasslands.

For **homesteaders,** people who farmed claims under the Homestead Act, life was not easy. Most began by living in a **soddie,** a house made of tough prairie soil. Plowing the prairie soil was backbreaking work. Insects were everywhere, and plagues of grasshoppers often wiped out a field of grain. Falling crop prices created debt. Some families headed back east, but most pulled together to make a living.

Plains farmers welcomed technological improvements in the 1870s, including steam-powered corn huskers and wheat threshers. Like ranching, farming soon became big business and **bonanza farms** appeared. These farms, vast estates each devoted to a single cash crop, were owned by corporations and made possible an enormous increase in the nation's food output.

The frontier was full of legend and **stereotypes,** or exaggerated or oversimplified descriptions of reality. Some were true, like Buffalo Bill's Wild West shows. But most were just exaggeration. Historian Jackson Turner claims in the **Turner thesis** that the frontier played a key role in shaping American character.

By 1890 the Census Bureau announced the official end of the frontier. The days of free western land were over.

**THE BIG IDEA**

**The discovery of gold, the cattle ranching business, and new farming techniques brought prosperity to the West.**

## GRAPHIC SUMMARY: *Population Growth of the West, 1860–1900*

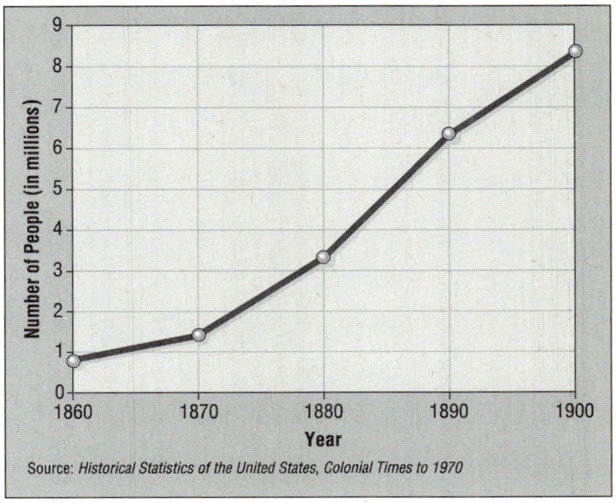


**Millions of people moved west during the late 1800s.**

## REVIEW QUESTIONS

1. Give one reason for the ranching boom of the mid-1800s.
2. **Graph Skills** During which ten-year period did the population of the West grow by about three million people?

# SECTION 4 POPULISM

## TEXT SUMMARY

Great Plains farmers in the late 1800s faced major economic difficulties. When businesses suffered a downturn, crop prices dropped. Tariffs helped protect them from foreign competition but also hurt farmers by raising prices on manufactured goods and farm machinery. Farmers formed alliances and organized protest groups such as the **Grange** to pressure lawmakers to regulate businesses that farmers depended on.

A major political issue for farmers was the **money supply.** In 1873, to prevent inflation, the government changed from a **bimetallic standard,** in which money was backed by gold or silver, to a gold standard. Silver miners and western farmers called for **free silver,** the unlimited coining of silver to increase the money supply. The government responded by passing the **Sherman Silver Purchase Act** that increased the amount of silver purchased by the government every year.

In 1891 alliances of farmers formed the People's Party. The platform of the **Populists** had five main ideas: increased circulation of money, unlimited coining of silver, a progressive tax, government ownership of communications and transportation systems, and an eight-hour work day. Populist William Jennings Bryan ran for the presidency in 1896 with his **Cross of Gold Speech,** but lost.

In the end, populism faded when times improved and crop prices began to rise. But the Populists had begun a movement that would be carried on in the early 1900s.

**THE BIG IDEA**

**During the late 1800s new organizations began fighting to improve conditions for farmers.**

## GRAPHIC SUMMARY: *Election of 1896*

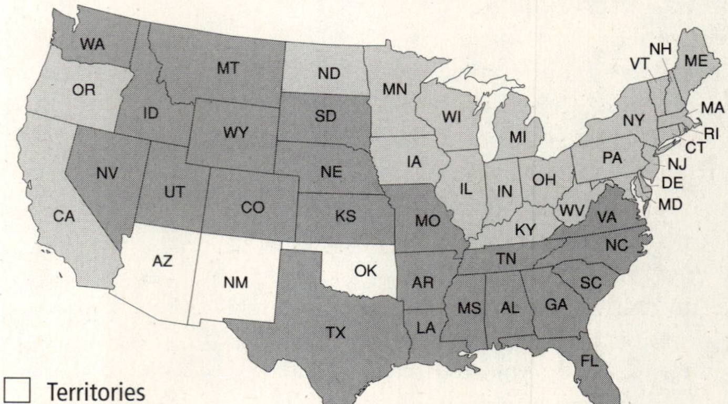


| Candidate/Party | Popular Vote |
|---|---|
| William McKinley (Rep.) | 7,035,638 |
| William J. Bryan (Pop. & Dem.) | 6,497,946 |

The election of 1896 showed that the Populists had strong support in the West and South.

## REVIEW QUESTIONS

1. Give two problems farmers faced in the late 1800s.
2. **Map Skills** Which candidate dominated the North and Midwest?

Name ______________________ Class ______________ Date ________

# CHAPTER 14 Test

## IDENTIFYING MAIN IDEAS

Write the letter of the correct answer in the blank provided. (10 points each)

____ **1.** The Homestead Act of 1862 offered settlers
- **A.** relief from their debts.
- **B.** free public education.
- **C.** loans to expand their farms.
- **D.** western public land at a cheap price.

____ **2.** Which statement best describes life for settlers in the West?
- **A.** Settlers had an easy time farming western lands.
- **B.** Most women worked outside the home.
- **C.** Settlers survived by working together.
- **D.** Farmers enjoyed the mild western climate.

____ **3.** Many settlers felt they had a right to westerns lands because
- **A.** they were welcomed by most Native Americans.
- **B.** Native Americans preferred to move to the East.
- **C.** there were no Native Americans living there.
- **D.** they produced more food and wealth than Native Americans.

____ **4.** The Battle of Little Big Horn marked
- **A.** the last major Indian victory in the West.
- **B.** the end of the Indian wars.
- **C.** an important victory for American troops.
- **D.** the beginning of the Cheyenne wars.

____ **5.** Western farmers were able to survive by
- **A.** relying on manual labor.
- **B.** using new farm machinery and methods.
- **C.** planting only on very fertile soil.
- **D.** not paying their taxes.

____ **6.** One reason western mining was taken over by large corporations was that
- **A.** individual miners could not afford modern mining equipment.
- **B.** the price of gold went down.
- **C.** the government passed laws against searching for precious metals.
- **D.** miners took all the gold from the West during the gold rush.

____ **7.** During the late 1800s many farmers complained about
- **A.** the activities of the Grange.
- **B.** falling crop prices.
- **C.** low tariffs on farm equipment.
- **D.** rising prices for cash crops.

____ **8.** The Populist party fought for
- **A.** the rights of big business.
- **B.** lower taxes for industrialists.
- **C.** better conditions for farmers and workers.
- **D.** a law forbidding workers from striking.

____ **9.** One sign that the frontier no longer existed was that
- **A.** many territories refused to become states.
- **B.** most of the land had been settled.
- **C.** the buffalo continued to dominate the Great Plains.
- **D.** many farms were bought up by corporations.

____ **10.** Which is an accurate statement about the settling of the West?
- **A.** Settlers supported the rights of Native Americans.
- **B.** Settlers included many European and Asian immigrants.
- **C.** Most settlers became rich miners or cattle ranchers.
- **D.** Settlers were all adventurous white males.

CHAPTER 15

# Politics, Immigration, and Urban Life (1870–1915)

## SECTION 1 POLITICS IN THE GILDED AGE

### TEXT SUMMARY

Called the **Gilded Age,** the period following Reconstruction found some Americans very wealthy. But most Americans suffered low wages and poor working conditions. The federal government followed a **laissez-faire** policy of seldom interfering with business practices. Some businesses received a **subsidy,** a payment made by the government to the development of certain key industries, such as railroads.

Many businessmen supported politicians with gifts of money. Scandals often erupted when industries used money to influence leading government officials.

The spoils system was also a problem. Under this system, elected officials appointed friends and supporters to **civil service** posts, government jobs held by nonelected people. In 1877 President Rutherford B. Hayes tried to fight the spoils system, but to no avail. After the assassination of President Garfield, a public outcry went out against the spoils system. President Chester A. Arthur and Congress passed the **Pendleton Civil Service Act** in 1883, which created the Civil Service Commission to test employees.

Tariffs became the top political issue and caused President Grover Cleveland to lose reelection to Benjamin Harrison. The new President increased tariffs, causing an economic collapse in 1893. The economic downturn was blamed on President Cleveland, who returned to office in 1892. Cleveland's second term was marred with economic disaster, leading to the election of Republican President William McKinley. McKinley oversaw a new tariff bill and a stronger gold standard, but he was assassinated in 1901 before he could see the effects of his economic policy.

**THE BIG IDEA**

**During the late 1800s, big business and reform efforts dominated American politics.**

### GRAPHIC SUMMARY: *The Gilded Age*

- Period between 1877–1900 is known as "the Gilded Age"
- *Gilded* means covered in a thin layer of gold
- The term was coined by American writer Mark Twain
- During the Gilded Age, America's big businesses prospered
- Beneath this layer of prosperity were poverty and corruption

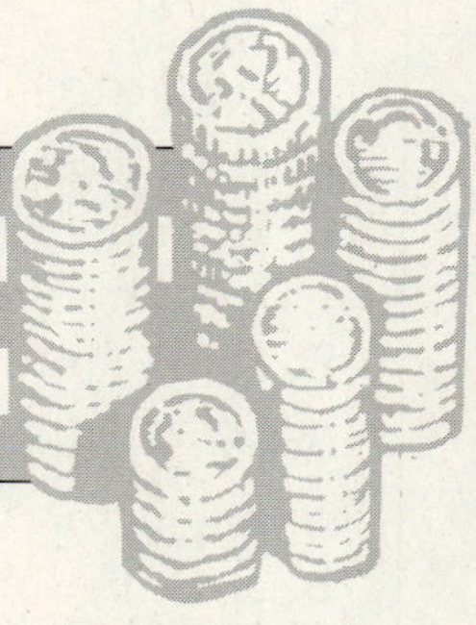

**The term "Gilded Age" paints an unflattering picture of the United States after Reconstruction.**

### REVIEW QUESTIONS

1. Describe the spoils system.
2. **Chart Skills** What writer coined the term "the Gilded Age"?

# SECTION 2 PEOPLE ON THE MOVE

## TEXT SUMMARY

Between 1865 and 1920 close to 30 million immigrants arrived in the United States. Economic opportunities, personal freedom, and the chance to escape religious persecution drew them. Immigrants from Sicily wanted to escape terrible poverty while Jews from Russia were fleeing from **pogroms,** violent massacres of Jews.

Arriving in America, immigrants entered ports like New York, Boston, Philadelphia, and Seattle. In 1892 the federal government established Ellis Island in New York harbor where immigrants came to have physical exams and information was recorded. Most immigrants wanted to settle in communities of their own ethnic backgrounds. In urban areas, these communities became **ghettos,** or places where one racial or ethnic group dominated.

Most immigrants on the West Coast came from China and Japan. Earlier Chinese had arrived in the West to help build the railroads and later settled down into other jobs. The different culture and language of Asians made many Americans suspicious and hostile toward them. In 1882 Congress passed the **Chinese Exclusion Act** prohibiting Chinese laborers from entering the country. California passed the Webb Alien Land Law in 1913, which banned **alien,** or noncitizen, Asians from owning farmland.

The land of the southwest had become fertile farmland, and many Mexicans were "pulled" to America by the lure of jobs. They were "pushed" out of Mexico by the turmoil of the Mexican Revolution. By 1925 Los Angeles had the largest Spanish-speaking population of any North American city outside Mexico.

**THE BIG IDEA**

**During the late 1800s and early 1900s, immigrants from around the world came to the United States in search of a better life.**

## GRAPHIC SUMMARY: *Immigration to the United States by Region, 1871–1920*

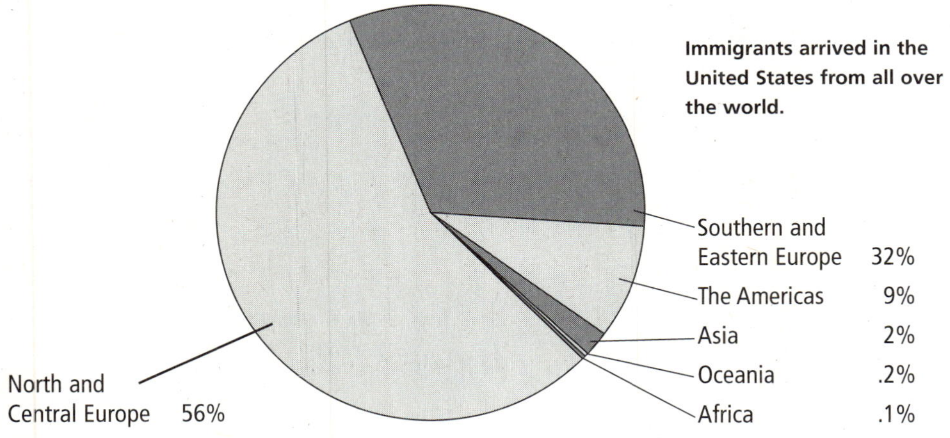


Source: *Historical Statistics of the United States*

## REVIEW QUESTIONS

1. How did the American people act toward Asian immigrants?
2. **Graph Skills** What continent did most immigrants come from between 1871 and 1920?

# SECTION 3 THE CHALLENGE OF THE CITIES

## TEXT SUMMARY

American cities like New York, Boston, Chicago, St. Louis, and New Orleans were jammed with people at the end of the 1800s. Along with the immigrants, Americans were moving in record numbers to cities because factories and machines replaced much of the manual labor of farms. African Americans, facing segregation and violence in the South, also migrated to cities.

**THE BIG IDEA**

**The arrival of millions of new residents brought progress, poverty, and political changes to American cities.**

The face of the nation's cities also changed as features of modern cities began to appear. Public transportation made travel easier, and many people moved from the inner cities to the **suburbs,** residential areas around cities. As space became more limited, tall skyscrapers appeared.

Many people in these cities lived in harsh conditions. They were crowded into **tenements,** low-cost apartment buildings where light, air, and water were often lacking. Fire was a huge hazard, and disease took the lives of thousands. Lack of ventilation and contaminated drinking water led to the spread of disease.

As cities grew, their governments and political figures became more powerful, and **political machines,** run by men called "bosses," often controlled city government. These machines worked to keep one party in power and were often very corrupt. They took bribes and used **graft,** using one's job to gain profit, to support the machine. However, in exchange for votes and support, the machines did provide help to immigrants and the poor when the government did not. One notorious New York City boss, William Marcy Tweed, was brought to justice by the political cartoons of Thomas Nast. His cartoons alerted the people of New York to the illegal activities of "Boss" Tweed. Tweed was arrested and jailed, but the machines continued.

## GRAPHIC SUMMARY: *Political Machines*

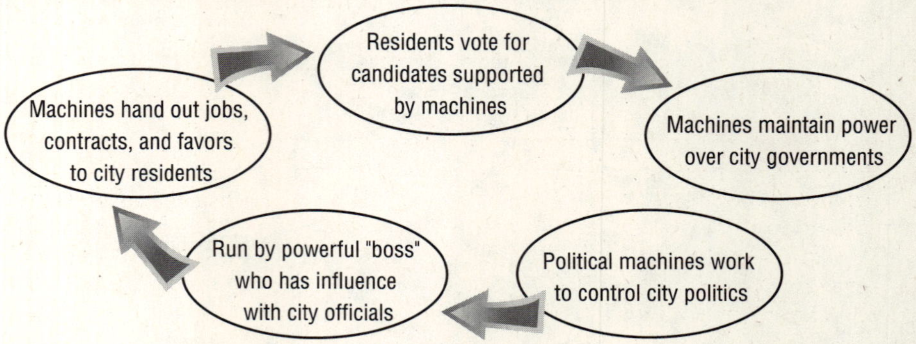


**Political machines gained power through the exchange of favors.**

## REVIEW QUESTIONS

1. What is one reason Americans moved from farms to cities?
2. **Diagram Skills** How did political machines win support from voters?

# SECTION 4 IDEAS FOR REFORM

## TEXT SUMMARY

As cities continued to grow, many Americans were shocked at the conditions of the poor. Out of religious or social impulses, they founded charities to help the needy and improve conditions. Churches provided social services for people, and soon a **social gospel movement** arose among religious institutions seeking to apply the Gospel teachings directly to society.

The social gospel movement was put into practice by young reformers who established **settlement houses,** community centers that offered social services. Soon settlement houses were springing up in large cities around the nation. All of this change led to the development of **sociology,** the study of how people interact with society.

While reformers were helping people and trying to improve conditions, others saw immigrants as the sole cause of problems in the cities. **Nativism,** a policy that favored native-born Americans over immigrants, emerged and demanded policies such as teaching only American culture or language in schools and tighter restrictions on hiring aliens.

Some reformers called "purity crusaders" were determined to stamp out gambling, drugs, alcohol, prostitution, and other forms of **vice.** These people began the **temperance movement,** an organized campaign to eliminate alcohol consumption. To achieve this goal, they supported **prohibition,** a ban on the manufacture and sale of alcohol. However, purity crusaders also attacked corrupt politicians and the political machines.

**THE BIG IDEA**

**The desire to improve conditions in American cities led to the formation of new reform groups.**

## GRAPHIC SUMMARY: *Reactions to Immigration*

**Reactions to Immigration**

- **Nativists**
  - Try to restrict immigration, believe government should support native-born Americans over immigrants.
- **Temperance Movement/ Purity Crusaders**
  - Try to ban alcohol, drugs, gambling, and prostitution.
- **Settlement Movement**
  - Try to help immigrants improve their lives by offering education, child care, and health care.

Increasing immigration inspired a variety of reactions.

## REVIEW QUESTIONS

1. What was the goal of purity crusaders?
2. **Diagram Skills** How did the settlement movement help immigrants?

Name ______________________________ Class ____________________ Date __________

# CHAPTER 15 Test

## IDENTIFYING MAIN IDEAS

Write the letter of the correct answer in the blank provided. (10 points each)

____ **1.** In the Gilded Age, business leaders often influenced American politics by
- **A.** running for political office.
- **B.** offering to pay higher taxes.
- **C.** giving money to government officials.
- **D.** importing more foreign goods.

____ **2.** Under the spoils system, elected officials would
- **A.** campaign for the election of friends and loyal supporters.
- **B.** appoint friends and loyal supporters to civil service posts.
- **C.** work for the defeat of other elected officials from opposing parties.
- **D.** spend money on campaigns for their own reelections.

____ **3.** Which of the following attracted many immigrants to the United States?
- **A.** strong labor unions
- **B.** free colleges
- **C.** cheap, comfortable housing
- **D.** job opportunities

____ **4.** A quarter of a million Chinese immigrants came to the United States to work
- **A.** in midwestern factories.
- **B.** on western farms.
- **C.** for American railroad companies.
- **D.** on cotton plantations.

____ **5.** As more American farms began relying on machines instead of manual labor
- **A.** farmers moved to Europe in search of land.
- **B.** wages in factories rose quickly.
- **C.** farm production dropped steadily.
- **D.** millions of people moved from farms to cities.

____ **6.** What was one way that rapidly growing populations changed American cities?
- **A.** Tall buildings were constructed.
- **B.** Millions of wealthy people moved into urban areas.
- **C.** The government built housing for poor immigrants.
- **D.** Living conditions for the poor improved rapidly.

____ **7.** Many immigrants supported political machines because political machines
- **A.** were free of corruption.
- **B.** helped many immigrants find work.
- **C.** fought against all discrimination.
- **D.** opposed the sale of alcohol.

____ **8.** Nativist groups supported
- **A.** policies favoring Native Americans.
- **B.** favoring the unions over big business.
- **C.** favoring native-born Americans over immigrants.
- **D.** increased immigration from Europe and Asia.

____ **9.** Purity crusaders fought to eliminate
- **A.** vice.
- **B.** pollution.
- **C.** unions.
- **D.** churches.

____ **10.** The main goal of the settlement movement was to
- **A.** end immigration.
- **B.** help settlers in the West.
- **C.** improve conditions for the poor.
- **D.** fight political corruption.

# Life at the Turn of the Twentieth Century (1870–1915)

CHAPTER 16

## SECTION 1 THE EXPANSION OF EDUCATION

### TEXT SUMMARY

In the late 1800s children attended school for only a few years. Pressure from parents to provide their children with more than the basic skills needed to advance in life and from reformers to limit child labor led many states to pass laws requiring children to attend school. By 1910 nearly 72 percent of children went to school.

For immigrants, **literacy,** the ability to read and write, was very important for their children. Reading and writing English would speed the process of **assimilation,** through which immigrant culture could be part of American culture. However, not all education was equal. Minorities attended separate schools that usually received less funding.

Higher education also expanded as more colleges and universities opened. New women's colleges expanded when **philanthropists** gave funds to establish schools of higher learning.

Despite prejudice, many African Americans were also gaining higher education. Black educator Booker T. Washington urged African Americans to study vocational skills to build economic security. But black educator W.E.B. Du Bois encouraged blacks to get a well-rounded education and become leaders in society. Du Bois himself was a leader who helped found the **Niagara Movement,** which called for full civil liberties, an end to racial discrimination, and recognition of human brotherhood.

**THE BIG IDEA**

**By the early 1900s, most American children went to school, and women and African Americans began attending college.**

### GRAPHIC SUMMARY: *College Degrees Earned, 1870–1920*

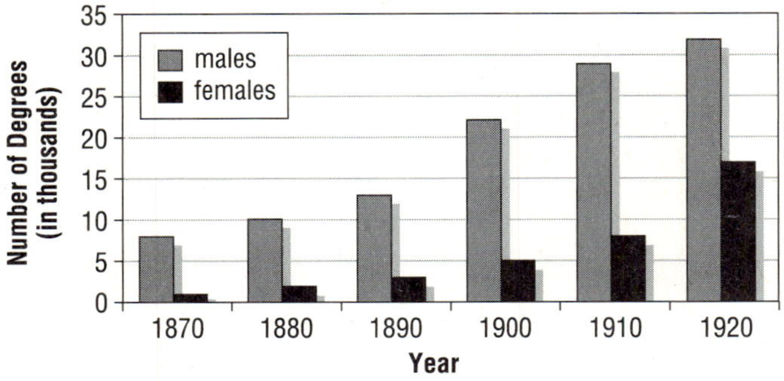


Source: *Historical Statistics of the United States, Colonial Times to 1970*

**The number of women attending college increased quickly in the early 1900s.**

### REVIEW QUESTIONS

1. What did W.E.B. Du Bois encourage African Americans to do?
2. **Graph Skills** In what year did over 15,000 women earn college degrees?

# SECTION 2 NEW FORMS OF ENTERTAINMENT

## TEXT SUMMARY

**THE BIG IDEA**

**Movies, sports, newspapers, and music became popular forms of entertainment in the late 1800s.**

At the turn of the twentieth century, people had more leisure time, and new forms of entertainment became popular. Shows with comic skits, magic acts, songs, and dances called **vaudeville** attracted large audiences. Motion pictures, circuses, and amusement parks also gained popularity.

Sports enjoyed tremendous popularity, and baseball was the most popular. Football emerged, copied from the European game rugby. Basketball, an exclusively American game, was invented.

Newspapers and magazines provided entertainment as well as information. In the competition for readers, some newspapers began covering stories about murders, scandals, and tales of vice. This practice was called **yellow journalism,** and these stories were very popular.

Popular fiction centered on tales of adventure and stories of a rise from "rags to riches." More serious readers turned to the novels of reformers like Edith Wharton, Henry James, and Mark Twain.

New styles of music swept the nation. African American religious folk music, called Negro spirituals, found acceptance by white audiences. Truly new American forms of music emerged, such as **ragtime,** a melody imposed over a marching-band beat, and jazz. Both of these musical forms originated with African American musicians. The player piano and the phonograph allowed people to play this music in their homes. Thanks to these inventions, jazz music was becoming a national passion.

## GRAPHIC SUMMARY: *New Forms of Entertainment*

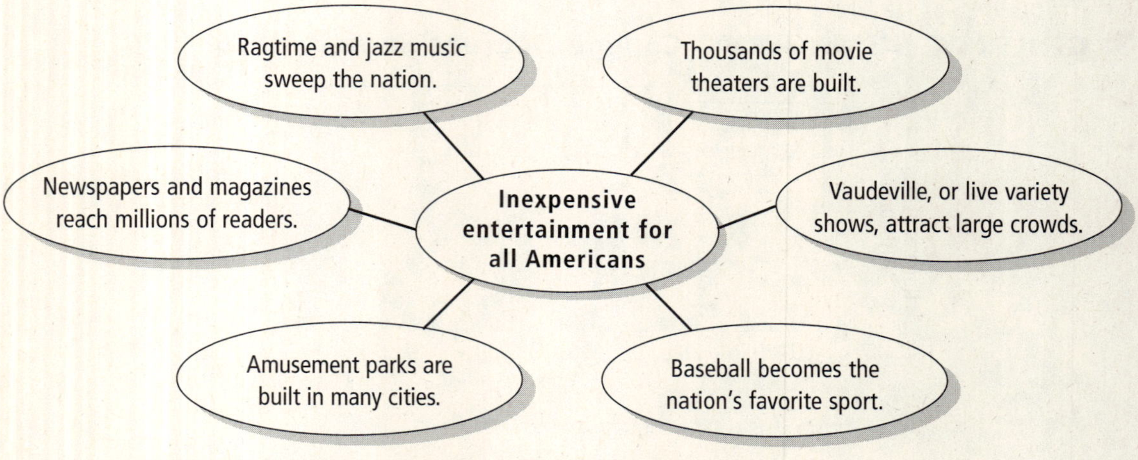


**Americans developed a wide variety of pastimes for people of all ages.**

## REVIEW QUESTIONS

1. Describe yellow journalism.
2. **Diagram Skills** Name three new forms of entertainment.

SECTION 3

# THE WORLD OF JIM CROW

## TEXT SUMMARY

After Reconstruction, African Americans saw their rights begin to disappear. Southern states passed laws requiring blacks to own property and pay a **poll tax,** a special fee, in order to vote. Sometimes they required literacy tests. Most African Americans could not pay these taxes or pass these tests. Many states passed **Jim Crow** laws, or laws designed to prevent African Americans from exercising their equal rights. Jim Crow laws required **segregation,** or separation of people by race, in public places.

The Supreme Court upheld the Jim Crow laws in the landmark case ***Plessy* v. *Ferguson,*** establishing the "separate but equal" doctrine. This doctrine stated that segregation was legal as long as facilities for blacks were equal to those of whites. However, few facilities were equal.

Another effect of racism was violence against African Americans, which included **lynching,** the unlawful killing of a person at the hands of a mob. Between 1882 and 1892 an estimated 1,200 African Americans were lynched.

In response, a group of African Americans and whites founded the **National Association for the Advancement of Colored People (NAACP)** in 1909. While the NAACP fought through the courts, church groups organized settlement houses, and the National Urban League improved job opportunities and housing.

African Americans also began to publish literature, history, and sociological studies. Black-owned businesses began appearing and Booker T. Washington founded the National Negro Business League in 1900.

**THE BIG IDEA**

**New laws limited the rights of African Americans after Reconstruction, but many African Americans achieved success in spite of these obstacles.**

## GRAPHIC SUMMARY: *Jim Crow Laws*

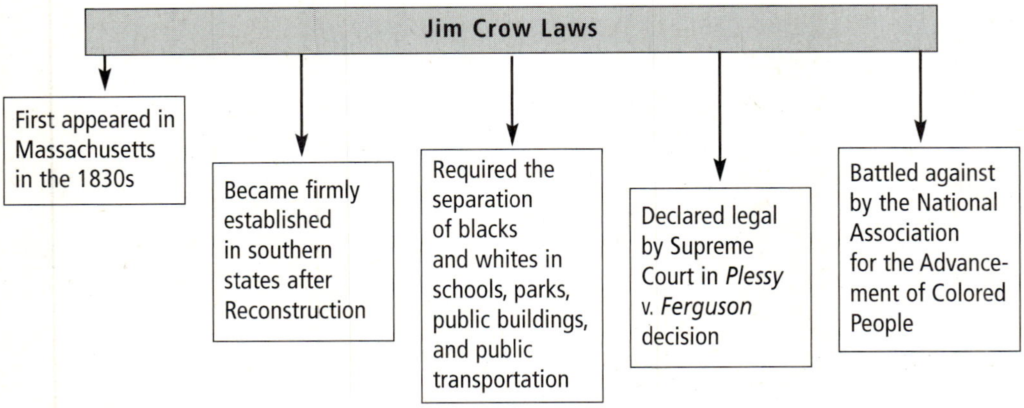


Jim Crow laws were a part of everyday life in the South after Reconstruction.

## REVIEW QUESTIONS

1. What was the goal of Jim Crow laws?
2. **Diagram Skills** Where did the first Jim Crow laws appear?

SECTION 4

# THE CHANGING ROLES OF WOMEN

## TEXT SUMMARY

**THE BIG IDEA**

**As technology changed American life, many women began working outside the home and fighting for equal rights.**

In the late 1800s Americans had different attitudes about what role women should play in society. These attitudes became known as *the woman question.* Many women wanted equality in the forms of the right to vote, the right to control their own property and incomes, and the right to have access to higher education and professional jobs.

People who opposed these ideas argued that society would be permanently damaged if women gained more power. However, new technology was making domestic tasks easier, allowing women more time to pursue outside interests. Women could shop in a **department store,** or order from a **mail-order catalog,** using **rural free delivery (RFD).** Women were now becoming a consumer power.

As a result, many more women worked outside the home, often in domestic service jobs or professional jobs men did not want. They were paid about 30 to 60 percent less than men.

Many women joined volunteer groups, establishing libraries, playgrounds, and education programs. Some groups worked for political and social reform. The National American Women's Suffrage Association fought for voting rights throughout the 1900s.

By the early 1900s *the woman question* included ideas about how women should dress and behave. These "new women" married older and pushed for information on birth control. Women would continue to debate these ideas and the need for women's rights throughout the century.

## GRAPHIC SUMMARY: *The Woman Question*

**For Women's Rights**

- Women should have the right to vote.
- Women should have access to college education.
- Women should have access to all types of professional jobs.
- Women should be paid the same wages as men.

**Against Women's Rights**

- Giving women economic and social power will damage American society.
- Women should continue to focus on traditional roles of mother and homemaker.
- Women lack the mental strength to study difficult subjects such as medicine.

During the early 1900s Americans called the debate over women's rights *the woman question.*

## REVIEW QUESTIONS

1. What technologies allowed women to become a consumer power?
2. **Diagram Skills** What were two rights that many women demanded for themselves?

Name ______________________ Class ______________ Date ________

# CHAPTER 16 Test

## IDENTIFYING MAIN IDEAS

Write the letter of the correct answer in the blank provided. (10 points each)

____ **1.** Parents fought for improved public schools because they felt
**A.** children had too much free time.
**B.** private schools did not provide a good education.
**C.** children needed more than basic skills to advance in life.
**D.** children were taking their factory jobs.

____ **2.** For immigrants' children, literacy would
**A.** help them be part of American society.
**B.** help them avoid deportation.
**C.** grant them citizenship.
**D.** keep them in factory jobs.

____ **3.** W.E.B. Du Bois urged African Americans to
**A.** use violence to fight for civil rights.
**B.** move to Africa.
**C.** accept an inferior role in society.
**D.** become well educated.

____ **4.** Which of these became a popular form of entertainment during the late 1800s?
**A.** television
**B.** baseball
**C.** soccer
**D.** car racing

____ **5.** What form of music was created by black musicians in the 1880s and 1890s?
**A.** rock-and-roll
**B.** jazz
**C.** country and western
**D.** classical

____ **6.** Jim Crow laws were intended to
**A.** end racial discrimination.
**B.** give African Americans the right to vote.
**C.** prevent African Americans from exercising their rights.
**D.** force African Americans to move to the South.

____ **7.** In the case of *Plessy* v. *Ferguson*, the Supreme Court decided that
**A.** black schools were inferior to white schools.
**B.** segregation was illegal.
**C.** blacks had the right to vote.
**D.** segregation was legal.

____ **8.** In 1910 the National Association for the Advancement of Colored People began fighting for
**A.** unions.
**B.** civil rights.
**C.** segregation.
**D.** Jim Crow laws.

____ **9.** Which of these was true of working conditions for women in the late 1800s?
**A.** All men supported their right to work.
**B.** They were paid less than men.
**C.** They were often promoted to high-paying jobs.
**D.** They often received advanced training.

____ **10.** The National American Women's Suffrage Association fought for
**A.** women's right to join unions.
**B.** women's right to vote.
**C.** better jobs for women.
**D.** higher wages for women.

CHAPTER 17

# Becoming a World Power (1890–1915)

SECTION 1

## THE PRESSURE TO EXPAND

### TEXT SUMMARY

In the late 1800s and early 1900s, European **imperialism** reached its peak as stronger nations colonized and dominated weaker nations. Economic, nationalistic, military, and humanitarian factors led to the growth of imperialism. The growth of economic industries created an increased need for natural resources. The European spirit of **nationalism,** the belief that one nation's goals are superior to those of other nations, caused nations to want to protect their interests. Advances in military technology caused Europe to have armies and navies far superior to those in Africa and Asia. Humanitarians believed they had a duty to spread the blessings of Western civilization across the globe.

Recalling its ideas of Manifest Destiny, the United States joined European nations in expanding outward, purchasing Alaska in 1867. Americans convinced Japan to establish trade relations, and signed several treaties with China. Americans also **annexed** the Midway Islands in 1867.

Arguments for expansion included obtaining new markets, protecting investments overseas, rekindling America's pioneer spirit that was lost with the closing of the frontier, and bringing civilization to "heathen" people around the world. Americans eventually warmed up to the idea of imperialism, and a new period of American foreign policy had begun.

**THE BIG IDEA**

**As European imperialism reached new heights in the late 1800s, the United States began to join the search for power and influence abroad.**

### GRAPHIC SUMMARY: *Why Imperialism Developed*

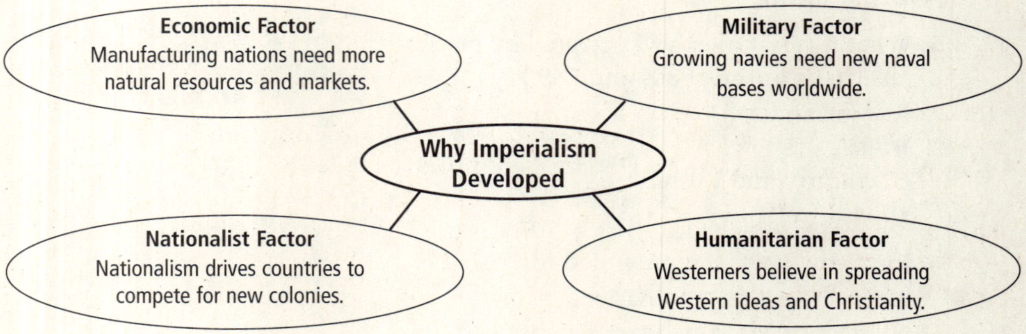


European powers competed for colonies during the late 1800s.

### REVIEW QUESTIONS

1. What were some of the arguments for overseas expansion?
2. **Diagram Skills** What role did nationalism play in the growth of imperialism?

# SECTION 2 THE SPANISH-AMERICAN WAR

## TEXT SUMMARY

The United States displayed its new expansionist policies in Latin America when it intervened in Spain's dispute with its Cuban colony. A rebellion against Spain broke out in Cuba and was harshly put down by Spanish forces. Cuban exiles in the United States urged the government to intervene, and newspapers called for war. Several newspapers indulged in yellow journalism, exaggerating the horrors of the conditions in Cuba. Their stories aroused **jingoism,** or an intense national pride and a desire for action.

Incidents such as the de Lôme letter; the sinking of the battleship *Maine* in Havana harbor, supposedly by the Spanish; and a rebellion in Spain's Philippine colony convinced American officials that war was necessary. On April 11, 1898, President McKinley sent a war message to Congress. The Spanish-American War was short and easy. The United States defeated Spain and took over Cuba, the Philippines, Puerto Rico, and Guam.

These new territories were not happy to be under United States rule. The Philippines revolted and fought a bloody war with the United States. Cuba did not want American intervention in their nation, and the United States finally gave Cuba limited independence with the **Platt Amendment**. Puerto Rico and Guam remained under U.S. control.

American power expanded in the Pacific when Hawaii was annexed in 1898. The United States further established its **sphere of influence,** or areas of economic and political control, in the Pacific with its acquisition of a port on the island of Samoa and its **Open Door Policy** with China, with the goal of access to China's huge markets.

**THE BIG IDEA**

**The United States became a world power with its victory in the Spanish-American War.**

## GRAPHIC SUMMARY: *The Spanish-American War*

**CAUSES**

- United States wants to expand in Latin America and Pacific.
- In Cuba and Philippines, people rebel against Spanish rule.
- Demands for involvement from American expansionists and newspapers.
- Explosion sinks American battleship U.S.S. *Maine* in Cuban harbor. Cause of the explosion is unknown, but angry Americans blame Spain.

**The Spanish-American War**

**EFFECTS**

- United States defeats Spain in three months.
- Spain recognizes Cuba's independence. United States begins to control Cuban politics and economy.
- Puerto Rico, Philippines, and Guam become United States territories.
- United States is recognized as a world power.

With a quick victory in the Spanish-American War, the United States established itself as a new world power.

## REVIEW QUESTIONS

1. What was the goal of the Open Door Policy?
2. **Chart Skills** What territories came under American control as a result of the Spanish-American War?

# SECTION 3 A NEW FOREIGN POLICY

## TEXT SUMMARY

**THE BIG IDEA**

**The United States adopts three distinct types of foreign policy that expand its power but hurt its relations with other nations.**

The Spanish-American War made Americans realize they needed a water route between the Atlantic and Pacific oceans to aid global shipping and allow the U.S. navy to move quickly in a time of war.

The French had bought a **concession,** or a grant for a piece of land in exchange for the promise to use that land for a specific purpose, to build a canal across Panama, a province of Colombia. They had failed, and sold the project to the United States. But, Colombia objected to American involvement. President Theodore Roosevelt then encouraged and supported a revolution in Panama. Panama, grateful, allowed the U.S. to build the canal. Work on the Panama Canal began in 1904 and was completed in 1914.

Roosevelt continued his aggressive foreign policy with the **Roosevelt Corollary,** an extension of the Monroe Doctrine. This addition stated that the United States could intervene in any international affair to prevent intervention from other powers. Roosevelt intervened often in Latin American affairs, causing resentment in other countries. Roosevelt's policies in Asia were similarly aggressive and he won the Nobel Peace Prize for keeping trade with China open to all nations.

President William Howard Taft changed to **dollar diplomacy,** which relied on economic rather than military force to expand American power. Taft's policies were met with little success and created more enemies in Latin America.

President Woodrow Wilson adopted a policy of "moral diplomacy," applying moral and legalistic standards to foreign policy decisions. Skirmishes with Mexico soured relations between the United States and Mexico for years to come.

## GRAPHIC SUMMARY: *United States Expansion*

The United States acquired many new territories around the world.

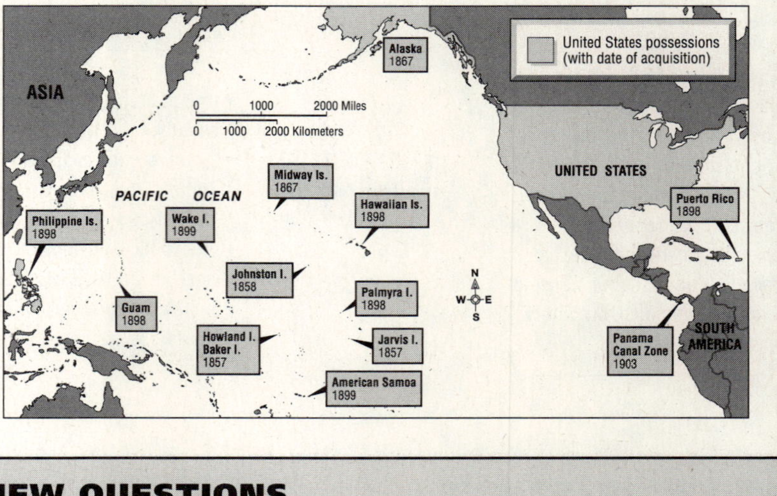


## REVIEW QUESTIONS

1. Why was the United States interested in building the Panama Canal?
2. **Map Skills** In what year did the United States acquire Alaska?

# SECTION 4 DEBATING AMERICA'S NEW ROLE

## TEXT SUMMARY

Following the Spanish-American War, anti-imperialists argued that imperialism was morally and politically wrong. Many also saw that **racism,** the idea that a person's intelligence and character are based on race, was part of imperialism. They argued that imperialism promoted the white, Anglo-Saxon race above all others. Another argument was that heavier taxation and debt would be needed to maintain the necessary armed forces to protect and control overseas territories. They also feared **compulsory,** or required, military service. Samuel Gompers led the argument that imperialism would lead to more laborers coming into the United States and competing for jobs.

The majority of Americans, however, supported imperialism. They argued that it opened up new markets and that it was an expression of American traditions and creative energies. Others argued that military strategy required expansionism. President Roosevelt agreed and sent a new naval force, the **Great White Fleet,** on a world cruise to show the benefits of a strong navy. The gleaming white ships made a huge impression on the world.

The rest of the world had mixed reactions to American imperialism. Imperialism was unpopular in Latin America because the United States often backed governments that were disliked by the local population. However, some countries turned to the United States for economic and military help. The United States was both accepted and rejected on the world stage.

**THE BIG IDEA**

**After the Spanish-American War, Americans debated whether the United States should build an empire.**

## GRAPHIC SUMMARY: *Imperialism*

**Imperialism**

**FOR**

- Americans need a new frontier
- Economy would benefit from more markets
- Military would gain power by having bases around the world
- American ideals of liberty and democracy would be spread

**AGAINST**

- People in territories under American control will be denied their liberties
- Racist beliefs are used to justify controlling other nations
- Overseas involvement is expensive, leading to higher taxes and debts
- United States has enough problems at home, should not take on more responsibilities

**After the Spanish-American War, Americans debated the question of imperialism.**

## REVIEW QUESTIONS

1. Why was American imperialism unpopular in many parts of the world?
2. **Chart Skills** Identify one argument in favor of and one argument against American imperialism.

Name ______________________ Class ______________ Date __________

# CHAPTER 17 Test

## IDENTIFYING MAIN IDEAS

Write the letter of the correct answer in the blank provided. (10 points each)

____ **1.** Under imperialism, strong nations attempted to
- **A.** control weaker nations.
- **B.** prevent immigration.
- **C.** avoid contact with the outside world.
- **D.** decrease the size of their military.

____ **2.** Which of the following was a factor in the growth of imperialism?
- **A.** the shortage of manufactured products
- **B.** the military threat from groups of smaller nations
- **C.** the need for natural resources
- **D.** the desire to learn from the cultures of other nations

____ **3.** An event leading to the Spanish-American War was
- **A.** a rebellion in Puerto Rico.
- **B.** a rebellion in Cuba.
- **C.** Spanish attack on the Philippines.
- **D.** Spain's annexation of the Hawaiian islands.

____ **4.** As a result of its victory in the Spanish-American War, the United States gained
- **A.** important ports in Mexico.
- **B.** Panama.
- **C.** Puerto Rico and the Philippines.
- **D.** a large section of China.

____ **5.** Theodore Roosevelt believed in
- **A.** an aggressive foreign policy.
- **B.** a cautious foreign policy.
- **C.** no American involvement overseas.
- **D.** economic, but not military, intervention.

____ **6.** A main goal of the Panama Canal was to
- **A.** help Latin American economies become independent.
- **B.** improve relations between the United States and Colombia.
- **C.** help European nations trade with Latin America.
- **D.** allow the American Navy to move quickly from ocean to ocean.

____ **7.** In Asia, Roosevelt worked to
- **A.** limit American military power.
- **B.** cause conflicts between other nations.
- **C.** keep markets open for American goods.
- **D.** keep markets closed to American goods.

____ **8.** President Taft believed in
- **A.** promoting American investment in foreign economies.
- **B.** sending troops to support American policies.
- **C.** avoiding all overseas involvement.
- **D.** limiting business investment overseas.

____ **9.** After the Spanish-American War, opposition to imperialism
- **A.** decreased.
- **B.** grew stronger.
- **C.** grew only within the government.
- **D.** was based on the need for new markets.

____ **10.** Anti-imperialists believed imperialism was based on
- **A** racism.
- **B.** ideals of liberty.
- **C.** democracy.
- **D.** humanitarian beliefs.

# The Progressive Reform Era (1890–1920)

CHAPTER 18

## SECTION 1 *THE ORIGINS OF PROGRESSIVISM*

### TEXT SUMMARY

During the **Progressive Era,** the period from about 1890 to 1920, reformers tried to alleviate the effects of industrialization, immigration, and urbanization. Their goals were to make government responsive to its citizens' needs; curb the power of wealthy interests; expand the power of government; and make government more efficient and less corrupt.

Among reformers were leading journalists and writers, whose work influenced public opinion. Sometimes called **muckrakers** because they dug up "muck" about wrongdoing among businesses and politicians, they investigated terrible conditions in slums and sweatshops. Upton Sinclair exposed the filthy conditions in the meatpacking industry. Ida Tarbell revealed the abuses of the Standard Oil Company. Many outraged readers joined reform groups and demanded government action.

Reform organizations included many socialists who favored public control of property and income. They hoped to bring about economic and political reform by ending the capitalist system. Unlike socialists, Progressives did not support ending the capitalist system. Instead they sought to reform it.

Women and women's groups played an active role in the Progressive movement. Florence Kelley's efforts helped limit child labor and regulate sweatshop conditions. Mary Harris "Mother" Jones fought for unions and child labor laws, campaigning nationwide for these things in the mining industry. She helped found the International Workers of the World (IWW) in 1905.

**THE BIG IDEA**

**Beginning in the late 1800s, reformers known as Progressives worked to try to solve the problems of American society.**

### GRAPHIC SUMMARY: *Progressive Goals*

| Progressives urged the government to: |
|---|
| • prevent businesses from treating competing companies unfairly |
| • improve safety and working conditions for workers |
| • outlaw child labor |
| • create programs to help the sick, unemployed, and elderly |
| • reduce government corruption |
| • give women the right to vote |

Progressives argued that the government should take an active role in improving society.

### REVIEW QUESTIONS

1. Who were the muckrakers? How did they help change society?
2. **Chart Skills** What was the Progressive view about child labor?

SECTION 2

# PROGRESSIVE LEGISLATION

## TEXT SUMMARY

**THE BIG IDEA**

**Important progressive reforms were made by city, state, and federal governments during the early 1900s.**

Progressives sought an expanded role for government through **social welfare programs.** These programs would include unemployment benefits, health benefits, and social security. Many of the first reforms occurred at the **municipal,** or city, level. The reformers were successful in getting many cities to take over utilities from monopolies and provide better and more affordable service. Many cities also began to provide welfare services.

On the state level, Progressives helped push through laws giving voters more power. The **direct primary,** in which citizens rather than political leaders choose political candidates, was the result of Progressive efforts. Other Progressive successes at the state level included the **initiative,** the **referendum,** and the **recall.** An initiative allowed voters to put a law they wanted on the ballot by petition; through a referendum, citizens could approve or reject a state law; and recall allowed them to remove public officials from office before an election. Many state governments were also persuaded to make reforms in the workplace. Led by Wisconsin governor Robert M. La Follette, states began to adopt a public-academic alliance to improve government.

On the federal level, President Roosevelt helped the workers by pushing for a "square deal" in a mine strike. This slogan became reflective of the progressive legislation passed during the Roosevelt presidency. His presidency pushed through laws to break up monopolies, to protect the environment and public health, and to improve working conditions. Amendments to the Constitution authorized a federal income tax, direct election of senators, and prohibited production and sale of alcoholic beverages.

## GRAPHIC SUMMARY: *Progressive Era Legislation*

| DATE | LEGISLATION | PURPOSE |
|---|---|---|
| 1890 | Sherman Antitrust Act | Outlawed monopolies and unfair business practices. |
| 1905 | United States Forest Service | Created to manage nation's water and timber resources. |
| 1906 | Meat Inspection Act | Required federal inspection of meat processing to ensure clean conditions. |
| 1906 | Pure Food and Drug Act | Outlawed dishonest labeling of food and drugs. |
| 1913 | Department of Labor | Cabinet department created to promote welfare of working people. |

**Progressive reforms affected many areas of life in the United States.**

## REVIEW QUESTIONS

1. How did the referendum give more political power to citizens?
2. **Chart Skills** What was the purpose of the Meat Inspection Act?

SECTION 3

# PROGRESSIVISM UNDER TAFT AND WILSON

## TEXT SUMMARY

When William Howard Taft was elected President in 1908, he promised to continue progressive policies, but he also sided with big business. Taft favored lowering tariffs and angered **conservationists,** who worked to protect natural resources, by supporting business interests that wanted to develop public lands.

Progressives in the Republican party rebelled against Taft, and former President Theodore Roosevelt turned against him, calling for more reforms in business regulation, welfare laws, workplace protection for women and children, and voting reforms. Roosevelt called his program the **New Nationalism.**

Roosevelt and Progressives formed the Progressive party, nicknamed the **Bull Moose Party,** and in 1912 Roosevelt ran for President. His candidacy split the Republican party, and the election went to Democrat Woodrow Wilson.

Wilson supported many progressive reforms. Tariffs were lowered, and the **Clayton Antitrust Act** strengthened the Sherman Antitrust Act by stating that labor unions were not monopolies, thereby legalizing unions and preventing courts from issuing injunctions. Wilson established the **Federal Trade Commission (FTC)** to enforce regulation on businesses. To regulate the supply of credit, Wilson created the **Federal Reserve System,** a network of federal banks that hold money deposits from national banks and use the money to increase the credit supply when necessary.

But Wilson took little action to pursue social justice reform. Reform was of less interest in America as World War I approached, and Progressivism began to die out. However, the voice for women's suffrage only grew stronger.

**THE BIG IDEA**

**Under Presidents Taft and Wilson, progressive reforms continued until 1916.**

## GRAPHIC SUMMARY: *The Election of 1912*

| CANDIDATE | PARTY | POPULAR VOTE | PERCENT |
|---|---|---|---|
| Woodrow Wilson | Democrat | 6,296,547 | 41.8 |
| Theodore Roosevelt | Progressive | 4,118,571 | 27.4 |
| William H. Taft | Republican | 3,486,720 | 23.2 |
| Eugene V. Debs | Socialist | 900,672 | 6.0 |

**In the election of 1912, each candidate had his own idea of which reforms were most important.**

## REVIEW QUESTIONS

1. Why did Theodore Roosevelt decide to challenge Taft for the presidency in 1912?
2. **Chart Skills** What percentage of the vote did the Socialist candidate receive in 1912?

# SECTION 4 SUFFRAGE AT LAST

## TEXT SUMMARY

**THE BIG IDEA**

**Women finally won the right to vote with the ratification of the Nineteenth Amendment in 1920.**

Women first demanded the right to vote in the mid-nineteenth century. Among the early leaders were Susan B. Anthony and Elizabeth Cady Stanton, who supported **civil disobedience,** the nonviolent refusal to obey a law to change it. Another strategy was to press for a constitutional amendment to give women the vote and pressuring individual states to grant voting rights.

In 1890 Anthony and other veteran leaders of the movement joined with younger leaders to form the **National American Woman Suffrage Association (NAWSA).** Women were gaining more rights, including owning their own property, and many more were demanding the right to vote. However, the two main leaders, Anthony and Stanton, died before their movement was realized.

A new generation of women suffragists, under the leadership of Alice Paul, formed the **Congressional Union (CU),** which called for radical change and staged militant protests for a suffrage amendment. NAWSA also continued its efforts through the leadership of Carrie Chapman Catt.

The CU split from NAWSA and staged a massive protest in front of the White House. They were all arrested and suffered terrible conditions in jail.

When the United States entered World War I in 1917, women committed themselves to the war effort, and arguments that women were not politically equal to men were forgotten. In 1918 Congress proposed the Nineteenth Amendment, giving women the right to vote. Ratified in 1920, the amendment was the last great reform of the Progressive Era.

## GRAPHIC SUMMARY: *Women's Suffrage Before 1920*

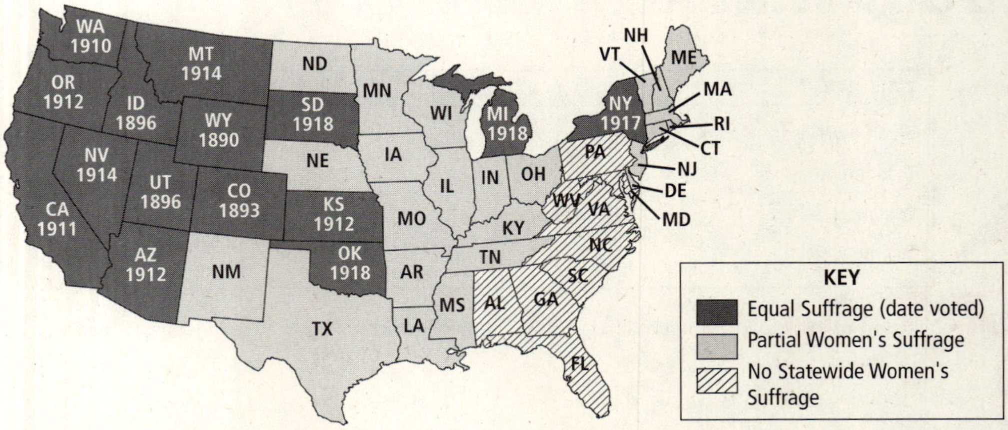


By the time the Nineteenth Amendment became law, many western states had already given women the right to vote.

## REVIEW QUESTIONS

1. Describe the three strategies women used to try to win the right to vote.
2. **Map Skills** What was the only state in the Northeast to grant women voting rights before 1920?

## SECTION 2 THE UNITED STATES DECLARES WAR

### TEXT SUMMARY

As World War I continued in Europe, tensions between the United States and Germany increased. Much of the conflict resulted from a new German weapon, the **U-boat,** a submarine that changed the rules of naval warfare. The U-boat would remain hidden and fire on ships without warning. German U-boats attacked British ships at will as well as neutral American ships suspected of carrying weapons. In 1915 a U-boat torpedoed a British ship, the *Lusitania,* rightly suspected of carrying weapons. Included among the dead were 128 Americans.

As U-boats continued to attack Allied ships, President Wilson demanded that Germany agree to the **Sussex Pledge,** a promise not to attack ships without warning. Then in 1917 Germany withdrew its promise and continued unrestricted submarine warfare. Wilson's hopes of remaining neutral were fading.

Germany did refrain from attacking American ships for a time, but the British intercepted a telegram from the German foreign secretary, Arthur Zimmermann, to the Mexican government promising the American Southwest to Mexico if it declared war on the United States. Most people did not take this **Zimmermann Note** seriously, but it pushed America closer to war.

In 1917 the **Russian Revolution** overthrew the Czar. Americans had always used the non-democratic Russian government as an excuse for not allying themselves with the Allies. With the Czar gone, Americans were now more willing to join the Allies. The final straw came when Germany sank three more American ships. President Wilson officially declared war on the Central Powers on April 6, 1917.

**THE BIG IDEA**

**Attacks by German submarines against American ships pushed the United States to enter World War I on the side of the Allies.**

### GRAPHIC SUMMARY: *The United States Enters World War I*

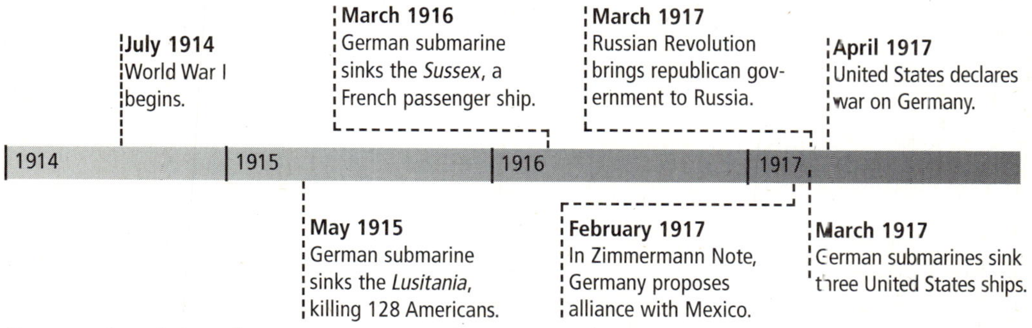


German submarine warfare angered many in the United States, pushing the country toward war.

### REVIEW QUESTIONS

1. Name two events that caused many Americans to turn against Germany.
2. **Time Line Skills** In what year did the United States enter World War I?

SECTION 3

# Americans on the European Front

## TEXT SUMMARY

**THE BIG IDEA**

**American troops joined the war in 1917, helping the Allies to defeat the Central Powers.**

The United States was unprepared for war in 1917. At first, Congress sent a small army with supplies and loans for the Allies. At the same time, Congress passed the **Selective Service Act** authorizing a draft of men into the military. Three million men eventually were selected to serve in the **American Expeditionary Force (AEF).** Thousands of women also contributed to the war effort by volunteering as nurses, drivers, and clerks. African Americans served in segregated units, but few saw combat.

To get the soldiers to Europe without being attacked by German U-boats, Americans used a **convoy** system in which troop and merchant ships sailed to Europe surrounded by armed warships.

The Russians, led by Vladimir Lenin, signed a truce with Germany. This allowed Germany to move all its troops into France and attempt a final offensive before American reinforcements could arrive. Once in Europe, American soldiers fought German forces along the front and deep in Allied territory. Turning the Germans back near Paris, the Allies, with the help of American soldiers, counterattacked in July 1918 and pushed the Germans back.

The war finally ended on November 11, 1918, with an **armistice,** or cease-fire. Around 50,000 American soldiers died in battle, but more died from influenza, a global epidemic that took the lives of some 30 million people around the world. Adding to the casualties was the **genocide,** or deliberate killing of a group of people, of the Armenians by the Turkish government.

## GRAPHIC SUMMARY: *American Soldiers in World War I*

**How did American troops help the Allies win the war?**

- Three million American men serve with United States forces.
- African American 369th Infantry Regiment fights for French Army. Entire regiment awarded France's highest combat medal.
- Thousands of women serve as drivers, nurses, and clerks.
- Americans join Allied counterattack against Germans, forcing Germany's surrender in 1918.
- American troops help save Paris from German attack.

**The turning point of World War I came in 1918, as American troops helped the Allies turn back the German advance.**

## REVIEW QUESTIONS

1. How did American troops travel to Europe without being attacked by U-boats?
2. **Diagram Skills** In what year was Germany forced to surrender?

SECTION 4

# Americans on the Home Front

## TEXT SUMMARY

While soldiers fought in Europe, the U.S. government worked on the home front to finance the war. **Liberty Bonds,** special war bonds sold to Americans, raised a great deal of money. President Wilson also set up new government agencies to help manage the economy. The government managed the production and distribution of food and established **price controls,** through which the government set food prices. The government also instituted a policy of **rationing,** or distributing goods to consumers in a fixed amount. A fuel agency sponsored gasless days and instituted **daylight saving time,** turning the clocks ahead one hour for the summer, to increase the number of daylight hours for work.

To enforce loyalty to the Allied cause, the government also regulated news and information by censoring the press and banning some publications. A public information agency also rallied support through films, pamphlets, and posters.

A fear of foreigners and the possibility of spies approached hysteria as the government repressed civil liberties and passed a **Sedition** Act to quell any disloyal speech or action. Groups of **vigilantes** often took the law into their own hands to hound and even lynch radicals and German immigrants.

World War I made social changes in Americans' lives. The war halted immigration, and the need for workers led many businesses to recruit Mexican, African American, and female workers.

**THE BIG IDEA**

**To strengthen the war effort, the American government expanded its control over the economy and brought changes to American society.**

## GRAPHIC SUMMARY: *Enforcing Loyalty*

**Enforcing Loyalty**

**Committee on Public Education**
Rallies popular support for the war with films, posters, and pamphlets.

**The Sedition Act of 1918**
Makes it illegal to make "disloyal" statements about United States government or military.

**Literacy test for immigrants**
Congress passes law forcing immigrants to prove they can read before entering country. Law leads to nativism and increased anti-German feeling.

**Espionage Act of 1917**
Passed in response to fears that German secret agents might try to weaken American war effort. Act makes it illegal to interfere with the draft.

**President Wilson declared that disloyalty during wartime would be "dealt with with a firm hand of stern repression."**

## REVIEW QUESTIONS

1. What effect did the war have on women and minorities?
2. **Diagram Skills** What did the Sedition Act make illegal?

**SECTION 5**

# GLOBAL PEACEMAKER

## TEXT SUMMARY

**THE BIG IDEA**

**Wilson's plan for world peace met with opposition at home and in Europe.**

To make the world safe from war, President Wilson offered a program called the **Fourteen Points.** It included an end to alliances, removal of trade barriers among nations, reduction of military forces, and the right of ethnic groups to **self-determination,** to make decisions about their own futures.

At the Paris Peace Conference in 1919, Wilson was forced to compromise. Britain, France, and Italy wanted the **spoils,** or rewards of war. Wilson did convince the Allies to accept his plan for a **League of Nations,** an organization of all the nations to work for worldwide security and peace.

But the Allies opposed Wilson's ideas for self-determination and redrew the map of Europe, creating new ethnic minorities and increasing tensions. In addition, Britain, France, and Italy demanded Germany pay **reparations** for economic injuries suffered in the war. The **Versailles Treaty** ended the war officially in June 1919. Germany never forgave or forgot this humiliation.

At home, Wilson was met with resistance to the League of Nations from senators worried that the League would draw the nation into another war. Wilson toured the nation to promote the League, but the treaty was not ratified until 1921, and the United States did not join the League of Nations.

World War I thrust the United States into a position of world leadership, but the aftermath brought problems. Returning soldiers found jobs scarce, and many women and minorities had to give up their jobs. The brutal war with its terrible casualties brought a postwar gloom to the American people.

## GRAPHIC SUMMARY: *After the War*

**United States after the war**

- American economy slows as war-time production ends.
- Returning troops face difficult adjustment to civilian society.
- Many women and minority workers faced with loss of jobs as men return to work force.
- Despite contribution to war effort, returning African American troops continue to face discrimination and segregation.
- Death and destruction of war leads to feelings of gloom among many Americans.

**After World War I, the American people faced a difficult adjustment to peacetime life.**

## REVIEW QUESTIONS

1. Why did the Senate reject American participation in the League of Nations?
2. **Diagram Skills** How did the war's end affect women and minorities?

Name ______________________ Class ____________ Date ________

# CHAPTER 19 Test

## IDENTIFYING MAIN IDEAS

Write the letter of the correct answer in the blank provided. (10 points each)

____ **1.** Germany and Austria-Hungary were opposed at the start of the war by
**A.** Britain, France, and America.
**B.** Britain, France, Russia, and Serbia.
**C.** Britain, France, Italy, and Serbia.
**D.** Britain, Italy, Russia, and Serbia.

____ **2.** The United States responded to the war by
**A.** declaring its neutrality.
**B.** sending troops immediately to Europe.
**C.** stopping its overseas trade.
**D.** forming an alliance with the Central Powers.

____ **3.** Tensions between Germany and the United States grew because of
**A.** German submarine attacks.
**B.** British submarine attacks.
**C.** Germany's refusal to use American U-boats.
**D.** Germany's threats to use U-boats.

____ **4.** After the Russian Revolution in March 1917, Americans were
**A.** frightened of the new Russian government.
**B.** more willing to join the Allies.
**C.** more willing to join Germany.
**D.** more determined to remain neutral.

____ **5.** When the United States joined World War I, it
**A.** refused to loan money to the Allies.
**B.** sent a huge army to Europe right away.
**C.** had already instituted a draft as part of its preparations for war.
**D.** needed to institute a draft to build a large army.

____ **6.** Soon after arriving in Europe, American troops
**A.** helped break through French lines.
**B.** helped save Paris from a German attack.
**C.** were unable to save Paris from capture by the Germans.
**D.** attacked Russia after it had made peace with Germany.

____ **7.** During World War I, the government's role in the American economy
**A.** grew.
**B.** decreased.
**C.** was insignificant.
**D.** was felt only in military production.

____ **8.** During the war, the United States government passed laws to
**A.** prohibit all immigration.
**B.** silence opposition to the American war effort.
**C.** promote freedom of the press.
**D.** protect people's right to criticize the Constitution.

____ **9.** The overall goal of President Wilson's Fourteen Points was to
**A.** create a lasting peace.
**B.** promote imperialism.
**C.** force Germany to pay for war damages.
**D.** preserve Europe's system of alliances.

____ **10.** In the Senate, the main criticism of the League of Nations was that it would
**A.** not be located in the United States.
**B.** be too expensive.
**C.** threaten American independence.
**D.** accept too many nations as members.

CHAPTER 20

# Postwar Social Change (1920–1929)

## SECTION 1 *SOCIETY IN THE 1920s*

### TEXT SUMMARY

**THE BIG IDEA**

**American society changed rapidly during the 1920s, as urban areas grew and women adopted new lifestyles.**

During the 1920s the United States grew rapidly, but many young people disillusioned by the war questioned the ideas and attitudes that had led to war and challenged traditional values.

A symbol of this challenge was the new behavior of many young women. A rebellious, fun-loving, bold young woman who wore short dresses and cut her hair was called a **flapper.** Not every woman was a flapper, and not everyone challenged tradition, but those who did helped create modern American society. Women were working, voting, and attaining political offices. They were laying a foundation for further participation in government.

American **demographics,** statistics that describe a population, were also changing. Millions of people moved from rural to urban areas. Suburbs also grew and cars became more affordable.

The Great Migration of African Americans from the South to northern cities increased in the 1920s as blacks were drawn by urban jobs. Masses of refugees from Asia and southern and eastern Europe also swelled urban areas. Migrants from Mexico settled in cities and created **barrios,** their own Spanish-speaking neighborhoods.

The rapid changes of the 1920s caused many Americans to turn to heroes who seemed to embody values of an earlier and simpler time. Aviation heroes like Charles Lindbergh and Amelia Earhart and sports stars like baseball player Babe Ruth fascinated Americans. With more leisure time and money, many Americans also indulged in recreational activities.

### GRAPHIC SUMMARY: *Women's Changing Roles*

| Style |
|---|
| • Women "bobbed" or cut their hair short<br>• Women wore makeup and shorter dresses<br>• Women smoked and drank in public |

| Work and Politics |
|---|
| • Women moved into office, sales, and professional jobs<br>• Women voted in local and national elections<br>• Women were elected to political office |

**During the 1920s, women adopted new lifestyles and roles in society.**

### REVIEW QUESTIONS

**1.** Who were flappers?

**2. Chart Skills** Name two ways women's styles changed in the 1920s.

SECTION 2

# MASS MEDIA AND THE JAZZ AGE

## TEXT SUMMARY

Before 1920, different regions of the United States held different cultures, attitudes, and interests. This began to change in the 1920s when for the first time, people around the nation saw the same films, heard the same radio broadcasts, and read the same news sources. **Mass media,** the use of print and broadcast methods to communicate to large numbers of people, produced a national culture.

Radio became a popular way to hear music and listen to news, sports, and comedy shows. Radio contributed to the craze for jazz music, a new music that had its roots in the African American music of the South and features improvisation and syncopation. Americans saw this free music as a symbol of the times, and the 1920s adopted the title of the **Jazz Age.**

American artists and writers continued to show American life realistically, recording the culture. Some writers rejected the spirit of the Jazz Age and became known as the **Lost Generation.** These writers and artists rejected materialistic values and scorned popular American culture. Most of them settled in Paris.

For African Americans, New York City's Harlem became their cultural center as African American writers and poets entered the literary scene in the movement known as the **Harlem Renaissance.** Writers like Langston Hughes, Countee Cullen, and Alain Locke wrote about the African American experience. Their writings inspired young blacks and contributed to the overall American culture.

**THE BIG IDEA**

**Radio, movies, jazz music, and great American writers helped make the 1920s a time of creativity and cultural change.**

## GRAPHIC SUMMARY: *Mass Media in the 1920s*

| Radio | Movies | Newspapers |
|---|---|---|
| • By 1930 nearly 14 million American households own radios<br>• Radio networks such as NBC reach nationwide audiences<br>• For the first time, people around the country hear the same music, news programs, and commercials | • Los Angeles suburb of Hollywood becomes center of American film industry<br>• Theaters sell 100 million tickets a week at a time when the United States population is less than 125 million<br>• Film making becomes the 4th largest business in the country | • Newspaper "chains" buy up newspapers around the country<br>• Number of newspapers sold each day increases by 141%<br>• People share the same information, are influenced by the same ideas and fashions |

**The rise of mass media helped create a national American culture.**

## REVIEW QUESTIONS

1. What was the Harlem Renaissance?

2. **Chart Skills** How did radio help create a national culture?

# SECTION 3 CULTURAL CONFLICTS

## TEXT SUMMARY

**THE BIG IDEA**

**Prohibition led to the rise of organized crime, while religious and racial tensions also increased in the 1920s.**

When the Eighteenth Amendment prohibited the manufacture and sale of alcohol, rural areas tended to obey the law. In urban areas, however, the law was largely ignored and demand for alcohol remained strong. This demand created a new kind of criminal, a **bootlegger,** who sold alcohol illegally. Illegal bars called **speakeasies** abounded in the cities.

Producing, transporting, and selling alcohol in the urban areas created organized crime, and gangsters like Al Capone of Chicago built huge profitable crime organizations using violence and power for illegal profit.

Religion was also an issue as **fundamentalism,** which supported traditional Christian views, clashed with scientific theories such as evolution. A major battle between the two forces took place during the **Scopes trial** in Tennessee when a young science teacher challenged a state law prohibiting the teaching of evolution.

Racial tensions rose in the 1920s. Race riots erupted in several northern cities as tensions increased between whites and African Americans. Violence against African Americans returned, as the Ku Klux Klan was revived and intimidated, tortured, and even lynched many blacks. The new KKK not only targeted blacks, but also Catholics, Jews, and immigrants.

The NAACP fought discrimination throughout the 1920s, but not always successfully. Some African Americans supported a movement begun by Marcus Garvey to establish a homeland in Africa. Garvey encouraged black-owned businesses and inspired racial pride, but the movement failed when Garvey was jailed for mail fraud and later deported. However, Garvey's ideas would provide the inspiration for later "black pride" movements.

## GRAPHIC SUMMARY: *The Scopes Trial*

Theory of evolution begins gaining acceptance among many Americans.

↓

Many religious leaders argue evolution contradicts history of creation as stated in Bible and support laws banning teaching of evolution in public schools.

↓

Tennessee passes law against teaching evolution.

↓

Tennessee science teacher John T. Scopes breaks state law by teaching evolution to his students.

↓

Jury finds Scopes guilty, fines him $100. Case causes nationwide debate between Americans holding modern beliefs and those supporting traditional beliefs.

**The Scopes trial highlighted the growing clash between modern and traditional beliefs.**

## REVIEW QUESTIONS

1. How did Prohibition lead to the rise of a new type of criminal?
2. **Diagram Skills** Why did religious leaders oppose the theory of evolution?

Name ______________________________ Class ________________ Date __________

# CHAPTER 20 Test

## IDENTIFYING MAIN IDEAS

Write the letter of the correct answer in the blank provided. (10 points each)

_____ **1.** How did women's roles in society change during the 1920s?
- **A.** Women began earning higher pay than men.
- **B.** Women were elected to state and national governments.
- **C.** Women began to hold more jobs than men.
- **D.** Fewer women went to work.

_____ **2.** The symbol of the 1920s woman was a
- **A.** housewife.
- **B.** maid.
- **C.** flapper.
- **D.** worker.

_____ **3.** A major demographic change in the 1920s was
- **A.** the movement from rural to urban areas.
- **B.** the movement of women into politics.
- **C.** the growth of the suffrage movement.
- **D.** the movement to ban alcohol.

_____ **4.** In the 1920s most African Americans moved to northern cities because they wanted
- **A.** jobs.
- **B.** better schools.
- **C.** less discrimination.
- **D.** higher wages.

_____ **5.** The rise of the mass media led to the
- **A.** development of a national culture.
- **B.** decline of newspaper sales.
- **C.** mass migration to rural areas.
- **D.** decline of the automobile industry.

_____ **6.** The 1920s was called the Jazz Age because
- **A.** people only went to jazz dance halls and dance clubs.
- **B.** poetry and art was filled with jazz.
- **C.** Americans from almost all walks of life embraced jazz music.
- **D.** George Gershwin played jazz music.

_____ **7.** Books by authors of the Lost Generation encouraged many young Americans to
- **A.** want to become rich.
- **B.** seek jobs in government.
- **C.** rebel against popular culture.
- **D.** become more religious.

_____ **8.** Langston Hughes and Countee Cullen were leaders of the
- **A.** labor movement.
- **B.** Lost Generation.
- **C.** Harlem Renaissance.
- **D.** Prohibition movement.

_____ **9.** The main result of Prohibition was that
- **A.** the crime rate fell in most cities.
- **B.** the sale of alcohol rose in rural areas.
- **C.** most Americans in cities stopped drinking.
- **D.** crime organizations grew rich selling alcohol.

_____ **10.** The central issue of the Scopes trial was whether or not
- **A.** Jim Crow laws should be declared illegal.
- **B.** the theory of evolution should be taught in public schools.
- **C.** labor unions should be allowed to strike.
- **D.** Communists should be forced to leave the country.

CHAPTER 21

# Politics and Prosperity (1920–1929)

## SECTION 1 A REPUBLICAN DECADE

### TEXT SUMMARY

**THE BIG IDEA**

**During the 1920s, Republican Presidents worked to limit immigration, while promoting the growth of American business.**

As the 1920s began Americans feared the spread of Russian **communism,** one-party control of people and land. Their fears encouraged a **Red Scare,** an intense fear of communism and other politically radical ideas. In a controversial case, two Italian immigrants, Sacco and Vanzetti, were tried and executed for the robbery and murder of a shoe factory guard. Many believe they were convicted only because they were immigrants with radical beliefs.

The Supreme Court made two important rulings in the 1920s. Justice Oliver Wendell Holmes, Jr., stated that the government had the right to silence free speech when there is a "clear and present danger." In the second ruling the Supreme Court held that the Fourteenth Amendment protected the right of free speech against restriction by state governments as well as the federal government.

Labor unrest added to people's fears, as many Americans thought Communists were behind strikes, riots, and bombings. Distrusting Democrats, people looked to Republicans.

Republican President Warren G. Harding embraced the policy of **isolationism,** avoiding political alliances with foreign countries. Harding proposed **disarmament,** in which nations would voluntarily give up their weapons.

Nativist feelings were strong in the 1920s and the government restricted immigration, placing a **quota,** or numerical limit, on certain ethnic groups.

When Calvin Coolidge became President in 1923, he instituted a laissez-faire policy toward businesses. This helped fuel the 1920s economic boom.

### GRAPHIC SUMMARY: *The Red Scare*

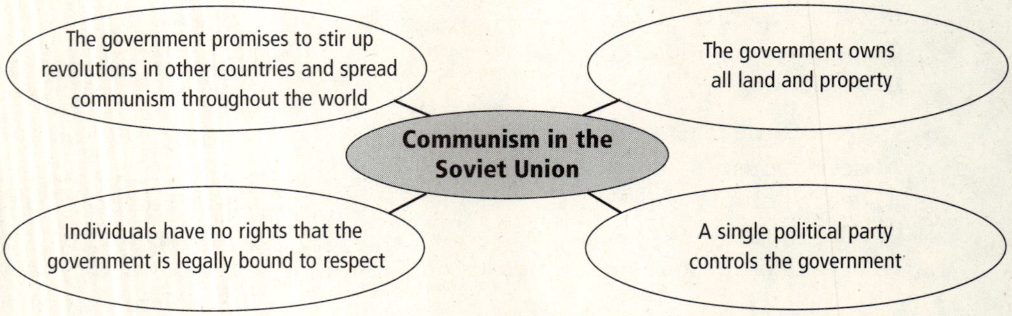


In the 1920s Americans began to fear the spread of communism.

### REVIEW QUESTIONS

1. Define isolationism.
2. **Diagram Skills** Under communism in the Soviet Union, who owned all land and property?

# SECTION 2 A BUSINESS BOOM

## TEXT SUMMARY

Many features of modern American society were born in the 1920s. Fast-food chains and shopping centers appeared. Americans bought new appliances in record numbers, creating a demand for more electrical energy. The 1920s created a **consumer economy** that depended on people spending large amounts. Businesses also introduced paying by **installment plan,** which allowed payment for items over a period of time. This encouraged consumers to spend more money and go into debt.

Mass-media advertising also began in the 1920s, persuading people to buy more and more. Advertisers appealed to people's emotions, promoting products by implying that they would enhance someone's image or make someone socially acceptable.

As consumers bought, productivity rose to meet the demand. The **Gross National Product (GNP),** which is the total value of goods and services a country produces annually, rose at an average of 6 percent per year. One sector of great growth was in the automobile industry, largely due to the efforts of Henry Ford. He wanted ordinary people to have cheap cars, so he adapted the **assembly line,** the process in which each worker does one special task to make it more efficient.

Industrial growth soared for businesses such as oil and steel, and new businesses arose to meet the demands of auto travel.

Some people and industries, however, did not profit from this economic boom. Unskilled laborers and migrant workers remained poor. The farm economy was slumping as Europe recovered from World War I and bought fewer American farm products. The coal and textile industries and the railroads suffered when markets dried up.

**THE BIG IDEA**

**American business boomed during the 1920s as Americans earned more and spent more on exciting new products.**

## GRAPHIC SUMMARY: *Passenger Car Sales, 1920–1929*

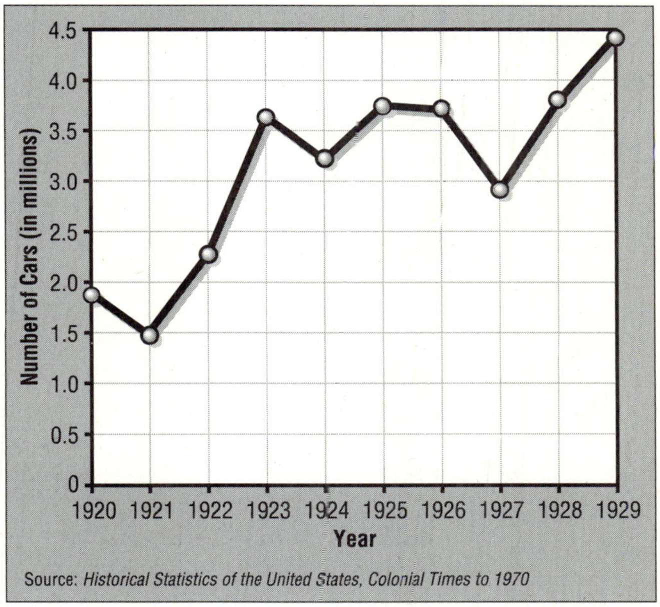


The booming automobile industry helped the American economy prosper during the 1920s.

## REVIEW QUESTIONS

1. What is a consumer economy?
2. **Graph Skills** In what year did car sales first top 3.5 million?

SECTION 3

# THE ECONOMY IN THE LATE 1920s

## TEXT SUMMARY

Entering the late 1920s, the American economy appeared to be in good shape, and people were optimistic about the future. When Herbert Hoover became President in 1928, he sought to keep government out of business and promoted what he called "rugged individualism." People were encouraged to make investments in businesses.

**THE BIG IDEA**

**While the American economy continued growing during the 1920s, there were signs that the good times might not last.**

As the economy stabilized, companies tried to meet labor's demands through **welfare capitalism**. Employers began to pay better wages and provide benefits such as paid vacations and health plans. Welfare capitalism caused a decline in organized labor membership.

However, the economy was not as stable as it seemed. There were warning signs that serious problems existed. There was an uneven distribution of wealth, and large companies dominated the economy. A small number of families held the bulk of the nation's wealth, and tax policies benefited the wealthy. Many Americans bought on credit, increasing their personal debt. Others played the stock market, indulging in **speculation,** the practice of making high-risk investments in the hopes of getting a huge return. Some people invested by **buying on margin,** in which investors bought a stock for a fraction of its price and borrowed the rest.

Overproduction caused problems, too. There were too many goods, more than consumers could buy. Industry began to stagnate and decline. Farmers, factory workers, and coal miners were facing poverty and starvation. Clearly, the economy was in trouble.

## GRAPHIC SUMMARY: *Income Distribution, 1929*

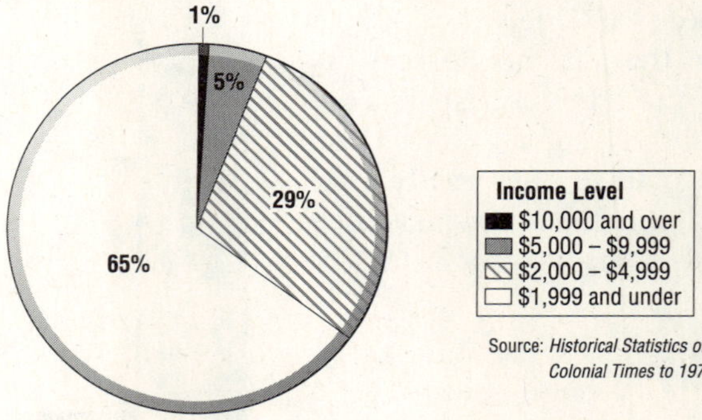


**The prosperity of the 1920s did not bring great wealth to most Americans.**

Source: *Historical Statistics of the United States, Colonial Times to 1970*

## REVIEW QUESTIONS

1. What were some of the signals that the economy was in trouble?
2. **Graph Skills** What percentage of Americans earned over $10,000 in 1929?

Name ______________________ Class ______________ Date __________

# CHAPTER 21 Test

## IDENTIFYING MAIN IDEAS

Write the letter of the correct answer in the blank provided. (10 points each)

_____ **1.** President Warren G. Harding called for
- **A.** a ban on unions.
- **B.** the end of communism.
- **C.** international disarmament.
- **D.** the arrest of all radicals.

_____ **2.** During the Red Scare, many Americans blamed labor strikes on
- **A.** Communists.
- **B.** high rent.
- **C.** the shortage of workers.
- **D.** Republicans.

_____ **3.** President Harding avoided political alliances with other countries in a desire to follow a policy of
- **A.** disarmament.
- **B.** social stability.
- **C.** isolationism.
- **D.** raising tariffs.

_____ **4.** One characteristic of a consumer economy is that
- **A.** people make everything they need.
- **B.** people buy large numbers of products.
- **C.** most people work at home.
- **D.** only the rich can afford modern products.

_____ **5.** The use of the assembly line to manufacture automobiles allowed Henry Ford to
- **A.** sell cars at higher prices.
- **B.** produce cars without factory workers.
- **C.** sell cars at prices ordinary Americans could afford.
- **D.** gain a monopoly in the automobile industry.

_____ **6.** Many farmers struggled to survive in the 1920s because
- **A.** they had no work.
- **B.** farm prices plummeted.
- **C.** most were tenant farmers.
- **D.** they borrowed money.

_____ **7.** Americans elected Herbert Hoover President because he
- **A.** was not corrupt.
- **B.** had served in government before.
- **C.** promised to continue prosperity.
- **D.** built the Hoover dam.

_____ **8.** To meet workers' demands and keep out unions, many companies
- **A.** fired employees.
- **B.** hired women and children.
- **C.** initiated welfare capitalism.
- **D.** closed their businesses.

_____ **9.** One major danger sign that the American economy was in trouble in the 1920s was
- **A.** the increase of personal debt.
- **B.** the demand for more jobs.
- **C.** the growth of industry.
- **D.** a rise in immigration.

_____ **10.** Rising prices on the stock market encouraged people to take risks by
- **A.** selling stocks.
- **B.** increasing savings.
- **C.** putting money in banks.
- **D.** buying on margin.

# CHAPTER 22

# Crash and Depression (1929–1933)

## SECTION 1 THE STOCK MARKET CRASH

### TEXT SUMMARY

**THE BIG IDEA**

**The stock market crashed in October 1929, leading to a long period of serious economic hardship.**

During 1929 stock prices continued to climb. In September the **Dow Jones Industrial Average,** an average of the stock prices of major industries, reached an all-time high. In October, however, stock prices began to fall. President Hoover assured the nation that the problem was not serious, but many investors rushed to get their money out of the market, and stocks dropped even farther. Then on **Black Tuesday,** October 29, the stock market collapsed in what was called the **Great Crash**.

Stock owners were the first to suffer, but the crash soon spread throughout the economy. Banks lost money on loans and people rushed to get their money out of banks, causing bank failures. Businesses cut production, and unemployment rose. Small businesses and factories closed, and farm prices plummeted.

The Great Depression, the worst economic downturn in the nation's history, would last from 1929 until 1941. It caused international trade to crumble, affecting the global economy. The Great Crash and Depression were the result of deep underlying economic problems in the American economy, including speculation, overproduction, borrowing and buying on credit, and uneven distribution of wealth.

### GRAPHIC SUMMARY: *The Stock Market Crash*

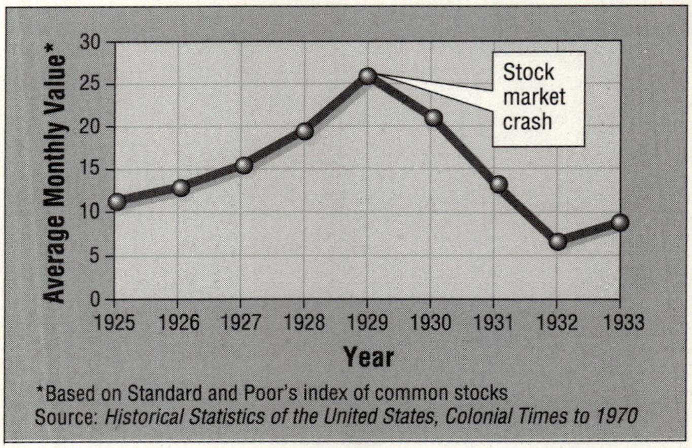


Stock prices continued to fall long after Black Tuesday.

### REVIEW QUESTIONS

1. What happened on Black Tuesday?

2. **Graph Skills** In what year between 1925 and 1933 did stocks reach their lowest point?

# SECTION 2 SOCIAL EFFECTS OF THE DEPRESSION

## TEXT SUMMARY

By 1932 the Great Depression had affected all levels of American society. Although many professionals lost their jobs, those at the bottom of the economic ladder were hardest hit. Unemployment and homelessness increased. Some homeless people built shanty towns called **Hoovervilles**, mocking President Hoover for not resolving the crisis.

Farm prices hit bottom. Many farmers lost their farms when they could not repay bank loans. In the South sharecroppers and tenant farmers were thrown off the land. In the Midwest farmers suffered one of the worst environmental crises of the decade. Prolonged drought and dust storms coupled with faulty farming practices helped create the **Dust Bowl**. Plowing methods had ripped up the grass that held the soil in place, and when it turned to dust, it blew away. Thousands of people left the Dust Bowl, migrating to California in search of work. Relief did not come to the Dust Bowl region until the early 1940s.

The poverty of the Great Depression strained American society as families crowded together in poor living conditions. Morale was low, as men could not provide for their families, and many working women lost their jobs to men. Discrimination increased as African Americans, Hispanics, and Asians were thrown out of work, unemployment soared, and competition for jobs increased racial tension.

**THE BIG IDEA**

**The Great Depression affected almost everyone in the United States, causing widespread poverty, homelessness, and unemployment.**

## GRAPHIC SUMMARY: *Effects of the Depression*

**The Great Depression changed life for most American families.**

## REVIEW QUESTIONS

1. What were some causes of the Dust Bowl?
2. **Diagram Skills** How did the Depression lead to increased racial tensions?

SECTION 3

# Surviving the Great Depression

## TEXT SUMMARY

Americans survived the Great Depression by pulling together and helping one another. Most people were willing to help those they saw as worse off than they were. For example, farmers created what became known as **penny auctions,** where they would bid pennies on land and machines auctioned off by banks, then sell it back to struggling neighbors.

A large number of America's youth left their homes, and many ended up "riding the rails" on freight trains. This was a dangerous life with the possibility of injury or arrest. When the Depression ended, many of these young "railriders" went back to leading a normal life.

To help relieve despair, Americans turned to humor. Humorists like Will Rogers were immensely popular.

As bad as conditions were, most Americans did not call for major political changes. They continued to trust the democratic process. Some, however, such as Socialists and Communists, wanted a fairer distribution of the wealth. At the same time, many people worked together for social justice.

There were some signs of change in the 1930s. The **Twenty-first Amendment** repealed Prohibition in 1933, and most people welcomed it as an end to a failed experiment and a curb on gangsters. Another symbol of hope was the new Empire State Building in New York City in 1931. The tallest building in the world at the time, it represented a triumph over hardship. When gangster Al Capone was finally sent to prison, Babe Ruth retired from baseball, and Calvin Coolidge died, it began to look as if America was entering a new era.

**THE BIG IDEA**

**Americans worked together to survive the Depression, and by the early 1930s they began to see signs of hope.**

## GRAPHIC SUMMARY: *Signs of Change*

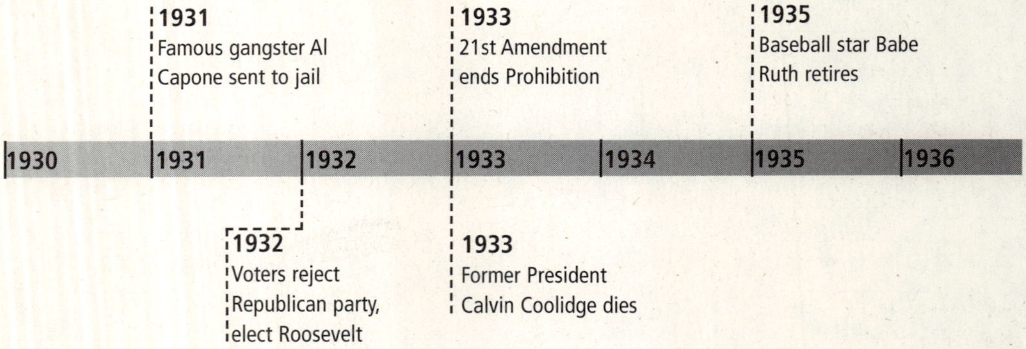


**One by one, symbols of the 1920s faded away.**

## REVIEW QUESTIONS

1. How did farmers support each other during the Depression?
2. **Time Line Skills** In what year was Prohibition ended?

# SECTION 4 *THE ELECTION OF 1932*

## TEXT SUMMARY

Following the Stock Market crash, President Hoover insisted that the key to recovery was confidence. Hoover believed that actions by businesses would resolve the problems and that government did not need to take action.

As conditions worsened, however, Hoover realized he had to do something. He did spend money on public projects. To protect industry, Congress passed the highest import tax in history, the **Hawley-Smoot Tariff,** which backfired when other nations raised their tariffs. Hoover also set up the **Reconstruction Finance Corporation (RFC),** which gave government credits to large industries and lent money to banks.

Hoover's limited actions and his insistence that local governments should provide relief deepened his unpopularity. In 1932 jobless veterans and their families camped in Washington, D.C., demanding payment of a promised bonus. Hoover called in federal troops, who used force to drive the **Bonus Army** out. This image would haunt Hoover in the 1932 election.

In the presidential election of 1932, Franklin Delano Roosevelt (FDR) was the Democratic candidate. FDR believed the government should intervene with direct action and promised "a new deal for the American people." FDR won the election, which was a battle between different views of government's role in society. As President, FDR would make lasting changes in presidential leadership styles and alter the way Americans saw their government and its responsibilities.

**THE BIG IDEA**

**Many Americans blamed Hoover and the Republicans for the Depression, leading to the election of Democrat Franklin D. Roosevelt in 1932.**

## GRAPHIC SUMMARY: *Election of 1932*

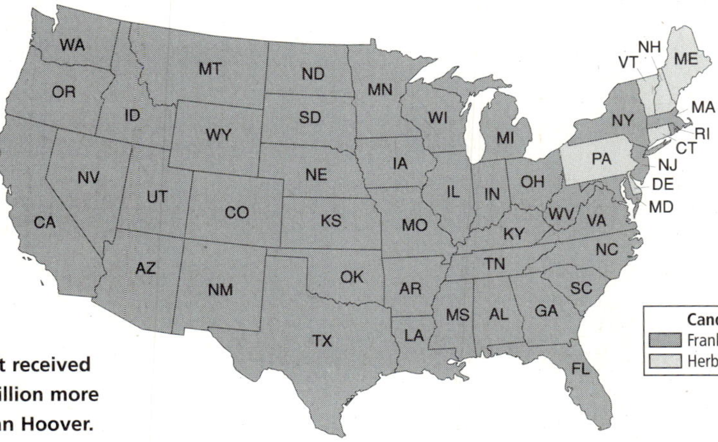


Roosevelt received over 7 million more votes than Hoover.

| Candidate/Party | Popular vote |
|---|---|
| Franklin D. Roosevelt (Dem.) | 22,821,857 |
| Herbert Hoover (Rep.) | 15,761,841 |

## REVIEW QUESTIONS

1. What did Roosevelt mean when he promised the American people a "new deal"?
2. **Map Skills** Was the election of 1932 close? Explain.

Name ______________________________ Class ______________ Date __________

# CHAPTER 22 Test

## IDENTIFYING MAIN IDEAS

Write the letter of the correct answer in the blank provided. (10 points each)

_____ **1.** In the late 1920s most Americans felt the economy would
**A.** soon collapse.
**B.** continue to prosper.
**C.** begin to slow down.
**D.** continue to decline.

_____ **2.** During the 1920s most of the nation's wealth was in the hands of
**A.** small businesses.
**B.** labor unions.
**C.** farmers and workers.
**D.** corporations and rich families.

_____ **3.** The stock market crash of 1929 soon affected
**A.** nearly all Americans.
**B.** only wealthy Americans.
**C.** just those who had invested heavily in stocks.
**D.** everyone except the rich.

_____ **4.** The stock market crash led directly to
**A.** a rapid recovery.
**B.** prosperity in Europe.
**C.** higher farm prices.
**D.** the Great Depression.

_____ **5.** The term "Hooverville" was used to describe
**A.** housing built by the government.
**B.** President Hoover's home.
**C.** shelters built by homeless people.
**D.** the stock market.

_____ **6.** Hard times on the farms in the Dust Bowl caused many farm families to
**A.** move to Canada.
**B.** begin growing cash crops.
**C.** move south to become sharecroppers.
**D.** move to California.

_____ **7.** During the Depression, how did most Americans view the democratic system?
**A.** They thought it was a failure.
**B.** They continued to trust it.
**C.** They preferred Socialism.
**D.** They feared it would make things worse.

_____ **8.** Which of the following became a symbol of hope during the Depression?
**A.** the Empire State Building
**B.** Hoovervilles
**C.** Prohibition
**D.** the Dust Bowl

_____ **9.** Hoover's policy of not taking direct action to try to end the Depression caused
**A.** Hoover's reelection.
**B.** a rapidly improving economy.
**C.** an increase in Republicans' popularity.
**D.** Americans to blame Hoover for their problems.

_____ **10.** Roosevelt won the 1932 presidential election after promising
**A.** a "new deal" for the American people.
**B.** an immediate end to the Depression.
**C.** to close the stock market.
**D.** lower taxes.

# The New Deal (1933–1941)

CHAPTER 23

## SECTION 1 Forging a New Deal

### TEXT SUMMARY

President Franklin Delano Roosevelt (FDR) promised Americans a **New Deal** to ease the effects of the Depression, and in his first **hundred days** in office, he launched programs to provide relief, create jobs, and stimulate the economy. Banks were regulated to prevent failures, and jobs were created through **public works programs** funded by the government. Through the **Civilian Conservation Corps (CCC),** young men were paid to restore parks and forests.

Many of FDR's programs were carried out through a series of new government agencies. FDR surrounded himself with key advisers called the "brain trust," who helped him draft policies. He also relied heavily on his wife, Eleanor, who traveled widely around the nation and reported conditions to her husband. FDR appointed the first woman to a Cabinet post and appointed many African Americans to policy-making positions.

Despite these efforts, the economy faltered. But most Americans supported FDR, and he expanded government programs in what he called the **Second New Deal.** These new programs included more social welfare benefits, support for labor, and stricter controls over business. One program brought electricity to millions of rural Americans, and in 1935 Congress established the **Social Security system** to provide financial security for retirees, the unemployed, and the disabled. In 1936 FDR won the presidency by the largest Electoral College margin in history, 523 to 8.

**THE BIG IDEA**

**As President, Roosevelt began a series of programs designed to help Americans through the Depression.**

### GRAPHIC SUMMARY: *New Deal Agencies*

| AGENCY | PURPOSE |
|---|---|
| • Civilian Conservation Corps | • Provided jobs to young men to work on environmental conservation projects. |
| • Works Progress Administration | • Gave the unemployed work in building construction and arts projects. |
| • Public Works Administration | • Sponsored huge public works projects such as dams. |
| • National Recovery Administration | • Worked with industries to ensure fair business and labor practices. |
| • National Labor Relations Board | • Enforced rights of workers and unions. |
| • Federal Deposit and Insurance Corporation | • Insured people's bank deposits up to $5,000. |

**Roosevelt created many new government agencies to carry out the New Deal.**

### REVIEW QUESTIONS

1. What was the goal of the Social Security system?
2. **Chart Skills** What was the purpose of the Civilian Conservation Corps?

# SECTION 2 THE NEW DEAL'S CRITICS

## TEXT SUMMARY

FDR's victory in the 1936 election showed that most Americans supported his programs, but many became disappointed with the New Deal. Progressive critics claimed that the programs did not go far enough. Women were paid less than men, and African Americans found it hard to get skilled jobs. The New Deal helped promote further segregation in the South and did little to end discrimination in the North.

**THE BIG IDEA**

**Some New Deal critics argued that the government wasn't doing enough to help people, while others claimed that the government was becoming too powerful.**

Other opponents, mostly businesses, argued that many programs were socialistic. A group called the **American Liberty League** charged that the New Deal was un-American. FDR also had to contend with **demagogues,** leaders who manipulate people by scaring them with half-truths and deceptive promises. Among these was Father Charles E. Coughlin, a priest who used the radio to attack the New Deal. Another was Louisiana politician Huey Long, who broke with FDR and advocated a radical program to redistribute wealth.

FDR also got into trouble when he proposed a bill that would allow him to appoint additional Supreme Court justices who favored his programs. Opponents accused him of violating the separation of powers, and he withdrew the bill.

Many modern-day critics have claimed the New Deal hindered economic recovery through high taxes and undermined the free-enterprise system. They also criticized the New Deal's **deficit spending,** paying out more money than the government received in revenues, and government borrowing to finance programs.

## GRAPHIC SUMMARY: *Critics of the New Deal*

| Women and African Americans | Progressives and Socialists | Republicans and other political opponents |
|---|---|---|
| New Deal programs offer more opportunities to white men than to women and minorities. Women and African Americans are paid less for the same work. | New Deal programs are not doing enough to solve the nation's problems. More should be done to distribute the nation's wealth among all Americans. | Government is taking on too much responsibility and becoming too powerful. FDR is like a dictator. New Deal taxes on the wealthy are unfair. New Deal programs are too much like socialism. |

While FDR remained popular, his programs drew criticism from a wide variety of opponents.

## REVIEW QUESTIONS

1. What are demagogues?
2. **Chart Skills** What did Socialists say about the New Deal?

SECTION 3

# LAST DAYS OF THE NEW DEAL

## TEXT SUMMARY

The New Deal led to economic improvement, but in 1937 the economy collapsed into a **recession,** a period of slow business activity, partly because of cuts in New Deal spending. People had less money to spend and some expensive work programs were cut back to slow **national debt,** the amount of money the government borrowed that had to be paid back.

FDR did expand some programs after 1937, and the economy began to improve. During this time, New Deal protections helped labor unions grow. Unskilled workers were organized by a **coalition,** or alliance of groups with the same goals, into the new and powerful Congress of Industrial Organizations. Through **sit-down strikes,** strikes in which laborers stopped work but refused to leave the workplace, workers became more successful in unionizing industries. However, these strikes tended to erupt in violence, and they were outlawed by the Supreme Court in 1939.

The New Deal projects provided many jobs for unemployed artists, musicians, writers, and theater people. Many of these writers, artists, and actors left an enduring cultural legacy on American society.

The New Deal's lasting achievements include public works as well as federal agencies that regulate businesses. The New Deal also profoundly changed ideas about the roles of government and the President.

**THE BIG IDEA**

**The New Deal lessened suffering during the Depression and helped change the way Americans thought about government.**

## GRAPHIC SUMMARY: *Cultural Life During the Depression*

**Literature**

John Steinbeck's *The Grapes of Wrath* tells the story of victims of the Dust Bowl.

Zora Neale Hurston's *Their Eyes Were Watching God* describes the life of an African American woman in Florida.

**Radio**

Radio becomes a major source of entertainment for American families.

Comedy shows and soap operas are especially popular.

**Movies**

At 25 cents for a double feature, movies offer affordable entertainment.

Films such as *The Wizard of Oz*, Marx Brothers movies, and Disney cartoons help Americans escape hard times.

**Books, radio, and movies helped Americans get through the Great Depression.**

## REVIEW QUESTIONS

1. Why did FDR cut back on government spending in 1937?
2. **Chart Skills** Who wrote *The Grapes of Wrath*?

Name ______________________ Class ______________ Date ________

# CHAPTER 23 Test

## IDENTIFYING MAIN IDEAS

Write the letter of the correct answer in the blank provided. (10 points each)

____ **1.** A main goal of the New Deal was to
- **A.** oppose labor unions.
- **B.** decrease the size of government.
- **C.** create jobs.
- **D.** lower taxes.

____ **2.** Public works programs were government-funded programs to
- **A.** encourage immigration.
- **B.** reform the banking system.
- **C.** eliminate segregation.
- **D.** build or improve roads, parks, and airports.

____ **3.** Eleanor Roosevelt helped FDR by
- **A.** reporting to him on conditions around the country.
- **B.** leading the National Recovery Administration.
- **C.** traveling to Europe to gain support for the New Deal.
- **D.** becoming a powerful member of Congress.

____ **4.** Which New Deal program was created to offer payments to people who could not support themselves?
- **A.** Federal Reserve Board
- **B.** Tennessee Valley Authority
- **C.** Social Security
- **D.** Civilian Conservation Corps

____ **5.** New Deal programs were most helpful to
- **A.** white men.
- **B.** women.
- **C.** African Americans.
- **D.** immigrants.

____ **6.** Progressives attacked the New Deal for
- **A.** limiting people's freedom.
- **B.** not doing enough to help poor people.
- **C.** raising taxes on the rich.
- **D.** increasing the national debt.

____ **7.** The American Liberty League thought the New Deal was
- **A.** too weak.
- **B.** un-American and limited individual freedom.
- **C.** promoting racism.
- **D.** abandoning the poor.

____ **8.** In order to influence the Supreme Court, FDR tried to
- **A.** amend the Constitution.
- **B.** remove opposing judges from the Court.
- **C.** appoint judges favoring the New Deal.
- **D.** ignore Supreme Court rulings.

____ **9.** The economic collapse of 1937 was caused in part by
- **A.** war in Europe.
- **B.** reduced government spending on New Deal programs.
- **C.** crop failures in the South.
- **D.** lower Social Security taxes.

____ **10.** During the New Deal, labor unions
- **A.** opposed FDR.
- **B.** lost many members.
- **C.** were declared illegal.
- **D.** grew in size and power.

# World War II: The Road to War (1931–1941)

CHAPTER 24

## SECTION 1 The Rise of Dictators

### TEXT SUMMARY

In the 1920s and 1930s, **totalitarian** governments appeared in Germany, Italy, and the Soviet Union. These governments used terror and force to suppress opposition. **Fascism,** a philosophy adopted by Adolf Hitler in Germany and Benito Mussolini in Italy, stressed nationalism and the supreme authority of the leader.

To stem the economic failures of communism, the Soviet dictator Josef Stalin tried to modernize agriculture and industry by placing all farms under state control. His methods caused famine and starvation. To keep control, Stalin conducted a series of **purges,** killing or imprisoning political enemies and possible opposition.

Mussolini improved Italy's failing economy, but suppressed individual rights and established a fascist dictatorship. In Germany Adolf Hitler, a discontented World War I veteran, rose to power through the Nazi party, whose philosophy, **Nazism,** included fanatical ideas of nationalism and German racial superiority.

As depression hit Germany, Hitler vowed to rebuild the economy and restore lands lost after World War I. In defiance of the Treaty of Versailles, Hitler and the Nazis began rearming Germany. Neither Britain nor France tried to stop Hitler when Germany invaded Austria and Czechoslovakia. Britain and France adopted a policy of **appeasement,** giving in to Hitler's demands to keep peace.

In Spain the military was waging a brutal war against a new republican government. General Francisco Franco overthrew the government and established a fascist state in Spain that lasted until 1975.

**THE BIG IDEA**

**Dictators in the Soviet Union, Italy, Germany, and Spain formed brutal, repressive governments in the 1930s.**

### GRAPHIC SUMMARY: *The Rise of Dictators*

| Dictator | Country | Philosophy | Characteristics |
|---|---|---|---|
| Josef Stalin | Soviet Union | Communism | rapid industrialization; state control of farms and industry; violent political purges |
| Benito Mussolini | Italy | Fascism | loss of individual freedoms; need for expansion; violent gang raids |
| Adolf Hitler | Germany | Nazism | extreme German nationalism and racial superiority; expansion through military conquest |
| Francisco Franco | Spain | Fascism | military dictatorship; tight government control |

**Each dictator implemented a different philosophy in his totalitarian government.**

### REVIEW QUESTIONS

1. How did Stalin try to stem the economic problems in the Soviet Union?
2. **Chart Skills** What are some of the characteristics of Nazism in Germany?

SECTION 2

# EUROPE GOES TO WAR

## TEXT SUMMARY

**THE BIG IDEA**

**Germany's invasion of Poland in 1939 marked the start of World War II. War quickly spread across Europe.**

Peace in Europe was destroyed in 1939 when Hitler aggressively began to push westward across Europe. Hitler was willing to go to war with France and Britain, but he feared an eastern attack from the Soviet Union. To prevent such an attack, Hitler signed a pact with Stalin in which the Soviet Union promised not to invade from the east in exchange for land in the newly conquered Eastern Europe. At the same time, Britain and France signed a treaty with Poland pledging support if Hitler invaded.

## GRAPHIC SUMMARY: *Axis and Allies, 1941*

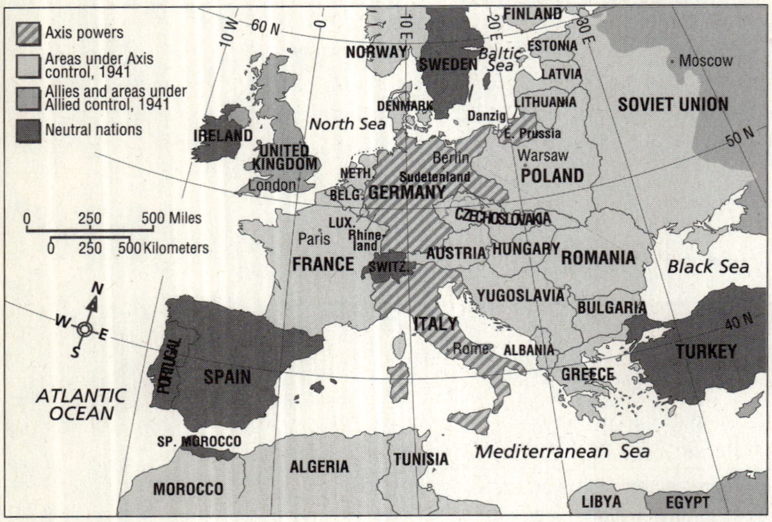


By 1941, the Axis powers controlled most of Europe.

In September 1939 Germany invaded Poland in a ***blitzkrieg*** attack, a lightning-quick land and air assault that conquered Poland in less than a month. Britain and France declared war on Germany, and France prepared defenses on the Maginot Line, a massive string of fortifications along France's border with Germany. However, France was open to attack through Belgium.

In April 1940 Hitler launched another massive *blitzkrieg,* conquering Norway, Denmark, the Netherlands, and Belgium. He attacked France from behind the Maginot Line, invading through northern France to the English Channel. British and French troops retreated to the coastal French city of Dunkirk where thousands were rescued by a flotilla of makeshift boats that carried them to Britain.

Germany conquered nearly all of France, leaving only an area in the south under French supervision. Called Vichy France, this French government entered into **collaboration,** or close cooperation, with Germany.

All that remained for Hitler to conquer was Great Britain. At the end of 1940 Germany began a series of massive bombings called the Battle of Britain. But the British people remained steadfast, and Britain's Royal Air Force (RAF) fought back as its outnumbered fighter planes shot down German bombers, inflicting heavy damage. The raids eventually ended in late 1941, leaving thousands of British civilians killed or injured.

## REVIEW QUESTIONS

1. What were two problems with the Maginot Line?
2. **Map Skills** Who controlled France in 1941?

# SECTION 3 JAPAN BUILDS AN EMPIRE

## TEXT SUMMARY

In Asia, Japan emerged from a series of economic recessions in the 1920s. As conditions worsened, nationalism increased, and the military became more powerful. At the same time, the government was looking for more land and resources for a rapidly growing population. Japan began to expand into China and Southeast Asia.

In 1931, in the **Manchurian Incident,** the Japanese army seized Manchuria from Chinese troops and set up a **puppet state** supposedly independent but under the control of Japan. Although Europe and the United States protested, nothing was done, and Japan's military continued to gain power.

Manchuria became a base for Japanese expansion, and in 1937 Japan resumed its war against China. The Japanese army occupied major cities and overwhelmed the Chinese Nationalist army in the north with superior weapons and ruthless air raids. The United States condemned Japan's actions but maintained its neutrality.

With European countries caught up in the war, Japan announced it would free Asia from European colonizers. In 1940 Japan named itself leader of a **Greater East Asia Co-Prosperity Sphere,** and set its sights on colonies such as the Dutch East Indies and French Indochina.

Later in that year, Japan allied itself with Germany and Italy in the Tripartite Pact, moving troops into French Indochina. In 1941 Japan signed a neutrality pact with the Soviet Union.

**THE BIG IDEA**

**The Japanese military expands into China and Southeast Asia.**

## GRAPHIC SUMMARY: *Japan's Military Rise to Power*

**Japan aggressively increased its military power and world influence in the 1930s and 1940s.**

1930 | 1935 | 1940 | 1945

**1930** Population of Japan nears 65 million people.

**1932** Japan takes control of Manchuria in the Manchurian Incident. Japan sets up a puppet state in Manchuria.

**1937** Japan resumes its war with China.

**1939** Japan's war with China reaches a stalemate.

**1940** Japan establishes the Greater East Asia Co-Prosperity Sphere to liberate Asia from European colonizers. Japan signs the Tripartite Pact, allying with Germany and Italy, and moves troops into French Indochina.

**1941** Japan signs a neutrality pact with the Soviet Union.

**1949** Communists take over China.

## REVIEW QUESTIONS

**1.** Why did Japan establish the Greater East Asia Co-Prosperity Sphere?

**2. Time Line Skills** In what year did Japan resume its war with China?

SECTION 4

# *From Isolationism to War*

## TEXT SUMMARY

During the 1930s the United States was focused on solving domestic problems. The government did not want to get involved in foreign affairs, even when Germany, Italy, and Japan threatened world peace.

Under President Franklin Roosevelt, the United States maintained its neutrality through a series of **Neutrality Acts,** one of which prohibited the United States from giving military goods and loans to warring nations. Another policy, called **cash and carry,** required warring nations to pay cash for all nonmilitary goods and their transport from the United States.

**THE BIG IDEA**

**America moves from neutrality to Allies' supporter to participant in the war.**

However, American opinion changed as German aggression increased, and after the fall of France, public opinion favored increasing aid to Europe. Congress responded by giving Britain 50 old destroyers in exchange for permission to build military bases on British territory in the Western Hemisphere.

This move prompted a group of isolationists to form the **America First Committee.** This group lobbied to block any aid to Britain. Despite this opposition, Roosevelt proposed "lending" war supplies to Britain, and he persuaded Congress to pass the **Lend-Lease Act** in 1941. This act gave the President the authority to aid any nation whose defense he believed was vital to the security of the United States.

Roosevelt's growing concern over Japanese aggression in Asia prompted him to restrict trade between Japan and the United States. However, as Japanese and American diplomats met to try to avoid war, Japan's military struck. On December 7, 1941, a massive Japanese air attack on the U.S. Navy base at Pearl Harbor in Hawaii caused the United States to enter World War II.

## GRAPHIC SUMMARY: *America Moves Toward War*

| REASONS TO SUPPORT THE WAR | REASONS TO OPPOSE THE WAR |
|---|---|
| • The Allies were defending American principles of democracy and freedom. | • The memories of World War I and the lives and people lost |
| • The United States would eventually be attacked by the Axis powers. | • Domestic problems from the Great Depression needed all of the government's attention. |
| • America was already helping militarily and financially; they should send troops to help as well. | • Public opinion, while sympathetic, favored the United States' continued neutrality. |

**There were many reasons for and against the United States entering the war.**

## REVIEW QUESTIONS

1. How did the Lend-Lease Act help the Allies?
2. **Chart Skills** What was one reason for the United States not to enter the war?

Name ______________________ Class ______________ Date __________

# CHAPTER 24 Test

## IDENTIFYING MAIN IDEAS

Write the letter of the correct answer in the blank provided. (10 points each)

____ **1.** In which country did Adolf Hitler rise to power?
**A.** Italy
**B.** Germany
**C.** Japan
**D.** Soviet Union

____ **2.** How did Josef Stalin try to modernize the Soviet Union?
**A.** He allowed some private enterprise.
**B.** He executed his enemies.
**C.** He placed all farms under state control.
**D.** He purified the Communist party.

____ **3.** One of the goals of Italy's fascist dictatorship was
**A.** to expand Italy's territory.
**B.** to imitate the success of the Soviet Union.
**C.** to do away with the Versailles Treaty.
**D.** to invade Germany.

____ **4.** How did Hitler defy the Versailles Treaty?
**A.** He improved the nation's economy.
**B.** He silenced opposition.
**C.** He criticized the Jewish population.
**D.** He rearmed and expanded the military.

____ **5.** War began in Europe when Germany invaded which nation?
**A.** Poland
**B.** Soviet Union
**C.** Great Britain
**D.** France

____ **6.** How did Hitler attempt to destroy England in the Battle of Britain?
**A.** He invaded Britain.
**B.** He launching a *blitzkrieg*.
**C.** He launched a massive air assault.
**D.** He signed a pact with the Soviet Union.

____ **7.** A major reason for Japan's military expansion was
**A.** a threat from the United States.
**B.** the rise of nationalism.
**C.** a growing population.
**D.** the Kellogg-Briand Pact.

____ **8.** Japan announced its influence in Asia through
**A.** a treaty with Germany.
**B.** the Burma Road.
**C.** the Manchurian Incident.
**D.** the Greater East Asia Co-Prosperity Sphere.

____ **9.** Which of the following reflected the isolationism of the United States?
**A.** Neutrality Acts
**B.** Lend-Lease Act
**C.** Hawley-Smoot Tariff
**D.** cash and carry policy

____ **10.** The United States entered World War II after
**A.** Japan invaded Manchuria.
**B.** Japan attacked Pearl Harbor.
**C.** Germany invaded Poland.
**D.** Germany attacked Britain.

# CHAPTER 25 World War II: Americans at War (1941–1945)

## SECTION 1 MOBILIZATION

### TEXT SUMMARY

**THE BIG IDEA**

**The United States mobilized quickly both militarily and on the home front to fight in World War II.**

In order for the United States to enter World War II, the nation's armed forces had to be strengthened. The government also needed to increase defense spending. Congress responded by authorizing the **Selective Training and Services Act,** a draft that required all men from ages 21 to 36 to register for military service. More than 16 million men and women from all ethnic and racial backgrounds served in the armed forces. They were called **GIs,** an abbreviation for "Government Issue."

The United States also needed to prepare the economy for war and gather a labor force. President Roosevelt created the War Production Board to set priorities and allocate raw materials, and he established the **Office of War Mobilization** to centralize the nation's resources and maximize production.

The unemployment brought about by the Depression dropped drastically when thousands of men and women found work in defense industries or joined the military. To pay for the war, the government raised taxes and borrowed from banks, private investors, and the public. A high level of deficit spending enabled the armed forces to be equipped and helped make workers prosperous as defense-related industries hummed at full capacity.

On the home front, food and products that were needed for the war effort were rationed, and the price of consumer goods was monitored by the Office of Price Administration to keep inflation under control. Morale was high. As war became part of everyday life, Americans at home increased their war efforts by recycling products, planting **victory gardens,** and participating in blackouts. Americans worked hard to support the war effort.

### GRAPHIC SUMMARY: *The Wartime Workers*

Wartime production finally lifted the American economy out of the Great Depression.

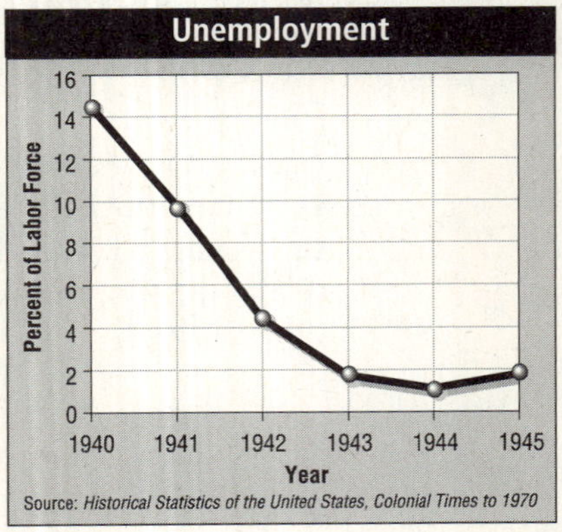


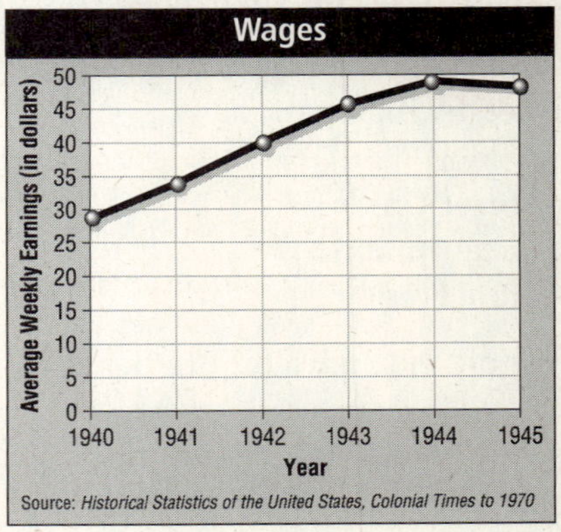


There were many reasons for and against the United States entering the war.

### REVIEW QUESTIONS

1. How did the federal government pay for the war?
2. **Graph Skills** In what wartime year did employment reach its lowest point?

# SECTION 2 RETAKING EUROPE

## TEXT SUMMARY

When the United States entered the war in 1941, Germany had conquered most of Europe and North Africa, and German submarines were sinking Allied ships in the Atlantic. So U.S. warships began escorting convoys of merchant ships. In 1942 American troops joined the British in North Africa, and by 1943 the Allies had defeated German forces.

Roosevelt and Churchill then turned their efforts to Europe, beginning by invading Italy. From 1943 until 1945, Allied troops battled through Italy until German forces finally surrendered.

At the same time, Hitler invaded the Soviet Union, despite his pact with Stalin. By 1942 Germany had captured huge areas of the Soviet Union, and was closing in on Moscow. With no aid from the Allied forces, the Red Army launched its comeback at Stalingrad, and by 1943 was pushing Germany back into Eastern Europe.

In 1944, after increased Allied **carpet bombing** of German targets, the Allies launched a full invasion of Western Europe. On June 6, a day known as **D-Day,** in the world's largest invasion by sea, the Allies landed on the coast of France and fought their way into Europe. At the same time, Soviet forces from the east drove deep into Germany. Germany counterattacked in the **Battle of the Bulge,** the largest battle ever fought by U.S. forces. With Germany's defeat, most of its leaders realized the war is lost. Germany surrendered on May 8, 1945.

Roosevelt, Churchill, and Stalin met in Yalta and decided to divide Germany and its capital into four zones, each controlled by a different Allied power. But Stalin's desire for land in Eastern Europe would fuel a future European conflict.

**THE BIG IDEA**

**The Allies finally defeated Germany after six years of bitter fighting in North Africa, Western Europe, and the Soviet Union.**

## GRAPHIC SUMMARY: *Victory in Europe and Africa*

| | |
|---|---|
| November 1942 | British troops win victory at El Alamein, Egypt. German forces begin to retreat west. |
| Winter 1942–1943 | Soviet and German armies clash at Stalingrad. Soviet army begins pushing Germans back toward Germany. |
| May 1943 | British and American armies trap Axis armies in Tunisia. Nearly 240,000 German and Italian soldiers surrender. |
| July 1943 | American troops begin invasion of Italy. |
| June 1944 | In operation known as D-Day, Allies invade Europe at French beaches of Normandy. |
| December 1944 | Germans counterattack in the Battle of the Bulge, the largest battle ever fought by the United States Army. After battle, most German leaders realize the war is lost. |
| May 1945 | Germany surrenders. |

Germans counterattacked in the Battle of the Bulge, the largest battle ever fought by U.S. forces. With Germany's defeat, most of its leaders realize the war is lost.

Suffering heavy casualties, Allied forces slowly recaptured Europe from Germany.

## REVIEW QUESTIONS

1. How did the United States deal with the German threat at sea?

2. **Chart Skills** What was the largest battle ever fought by American troops?

SECTION 3

# THE HOLOCAUST

## TEXT SUMMARY

THE BIG IDEA

**Under Adolf Hitler, the Nazis murdered six million Jews and millions of other people.**

For centuries Jews in most of Europe had faced **anti-Semitism,** the term used to describe discrimination or violent hostility directed at Jews. When Hitler took power in Germany in 1933, he made anti-Semitism an official German policy. Determined to rid Germany, and Europe, of Jews, Hitler eventually launched the **Holocaust,** the systematic murder of European Jews.

In Germany, Nazi policies included stripping Jews of citizenship, forcing them out of business, attacking their homes and synagogues, and encouraging them to leave Germany. Many Jews did escape, but not all nations were ready to welcome thousands of refugees.

Worse was the outcome for Jews living not only in Germany, but also in German-occupied nations. In Poland Nazis sealed off the **Warsaw Ghetto,** dooming thousands of Jews to starvation and death. Determined to eliminate all of Europe's Jews, Hitler launched his policy of genocide, the deliberate destruction of an entire group, which was carried out through mass murders in **death camps** across Eastern Europe.

Many Jews fought back through resistance groups or rebellion in the camps. The United States government knew about the murders, but it was not until 1944, when Roosevelt created the **War Refugee Board (WRB),** that a movement to rescue Jews in Eastern Europe took hold in the United States.

Despite these efforts, millions of Jews had perished by the time the Allies liberated Europe. Horrified by this Holocaust, the Allies conducted the **Nuremberg Trials** in Germany, prosecuting top Nazi leaders for crimes against humanity. Of the 24 leaders tried, 12 were sentenced to death for their crimes.

## GRAPHIC SUMMARY: *Estimated Jewish Losses in the Holocaust*

**Estimated Jewish Losses in the Holocaust**

| Country | Estimated Minimum Loss | Percentage of Initial Jewish Population Lost |
|---|---|---|
| Poland | 2,900,000 | 88–91% |
| Soviet Union | 1,000,000 | 33–36% |
| Hungary | 550,000 | 67–69% |
| Romania | 271,000 | 44–47% |
| Czechoslovakia | 146,150 | 71% |
| Lithuania | 140,000 | 83–85% |
| Germany | 134,500 | 24–25% |
| Netherlands | 100,000 | 71% |
| France | 77,320 | 22% |
| Latvia | 70,000 | 77–78% |
| Greece | 60,000 | 78–87% |
| Yugoslavia | 56,200 | 72–81% |
| Austria | 50,000 | 27% |
| Belgium | 28,900 | 44% |
| Italy | 7,680 | 17% |

The Holocaust affected Jews in many nations throughout Europe.

## REVIEW QUESTIONS

**1.** What were the Nuremberg Trials?

**2. Chart Skills** Which country lost the most Jews during the Holocaust?

SECTION 4

# The War in the Pacific

## TEXT SUMMARY

Following the attack on Pearl Harbor, Japanese forces advanced throughout the Pacific, seizing American, Dutch, and British colonies and capturing the Philippine Islands. The brutal treatment of Filipino prisoners of war by the Japanese during the **Bataan Death March** went against the standards of conduct set out in the third **Geneva Convention.**

Japanese battleships also advanced across the Pacific Ocean but met resistance from the remains of the U.S. Pacific fleet. In the **Battle of the Coral Sea,** U.S. naval forces prevented Japan from establishing bases from which to attack Australia. The war in the Pacific reached a turning point in 1942 with the American victory at the **Battle of Midway.** The United States gained control of the first piece of Japanese-held territory at the **Battle of Guadalcanal,** then took the offensive with a campaign of **island hopping,** attacking and capturing strategic Pacific islands.

Under American General Douglas MacArthur, U.S. forces fought to regain the Philippines, and in the greatest naval battle in history, the **Battle of Leyte Gulf,** the United States emerged victorious, despite Japan's use of ***kamikazes,*** or suicide planes. As U.S. forces drew closer to Japan, fighting became deadlier. In the **Battle of Iwo Jima** and the **Battle of Okinawa,** Japanese troops fiercely resisted American forces, and both sides suffered severe casualties.

At the same time, in the top-secret **Manhattan Project,** scientists were developing an atomic bomb. President Harry Truman believed an invasion would cost millions of American lives. Therefore, in early August 1945 two atomic bombs decimated the Japanese cities of Hiroshima and Nagasaki. On September 2, 1945, Japan signed a formal surrender agreement.

**THE BIG IDEA**

**After years of bitter fighting in the Pacific, Japan surrendered in 1945.**

## GRAPHIC SUMMARY: *Victory in the Pacific*

| | |
|---|---|
| June 1942 | Japanese Navy suffers devastating blow at the Battle of Midway. United States goes on the offensive in the Pacific. |
| August 1942– February 1943 | United States Marines engage in bitter jungle warfare in the Battle of Guadalcanal. Japanese forces leave the island in February 1943. |
| October 1944 | American troops regain the Philippines from the Japanese. |
| November 1944– June 1945 | In some of the bloodiest battles in American history, American forces capture key islands of Iwo Jima and Okinawa. |
| August 1945 | Americans drop atomic bombs on Japanese cities of Hiroshima and Nagasaki. Japan surrenders. |

**In some of the fiercest fighting Americans had ever seen, the United States defeated Japan in the Pacific.**

## REVIEW QUESTIONS

**1.** What was the Manhattan Project?

**2. Chart Skills** When did Japanese forces leave the island of Guadalcanal?

SECTION 5

# The Social Impact of the War

## TEXT SUMMARY

Ethnic and racial minorities did not always benefit from the opportunities offered by the war. African Americans still suffered prejudice in the workplace. To end such discrimination and provide employment, in 1941 President Roosevelt signed an Executive Order stating that jobs and training be given to African Americans in defense plants. As a result of this order, more than 2 million African Americans migrated from the South to cities in the North.

However, the armed forces remained segregated, and groups like the **Congress of Racial Equality (CORE)** protested and demonstrated against this discrimination, using nonviolent techniques. This group was leading the way for the civil rights movement of the next decade.

Mexican Americans and Native Americans also faced discrimination as they tried to join the armed forces and began moving into cities to work. A program to bring ***braceros,*** farm laborers from Mexico, to help relieve the shortage of farm workers swelled the Latino population of many cities like Los Angeles, where the workers lived in crowded ***barrios*** and often suffered prejudice. Native Americans moving to cities adapted to a new life in urban centers and often felt a loss of their traditions.

Japanese Americans suffered official discrimination as the government ordered all people of Japanese descent to be **interned,** or confined, in desolate camps in remote areas. Families were uprooted and their businesses and homes were taken from them. Over the years, Americans came to realize that the internment, which ended in 1945, was unjustified. In 1988 the government awarded money to survivors and formally apologized.

Women found new work outside the home as men went off to war. Women, too, often faced hostile reactions for taking these jobs, and they received less pay than men. Once the war ended, women were expected to return to their homes, and those who did not lost their jobs to men.

**THE BIG IDEA**

**World War II brought job opportunities to many minorities, although discrimination against Japanese Americans increased.**

**More than two million African Americans migrated to the North during World War II.**

## GRAPHIC SUMMARY: *African American Migration, 1940–1945*

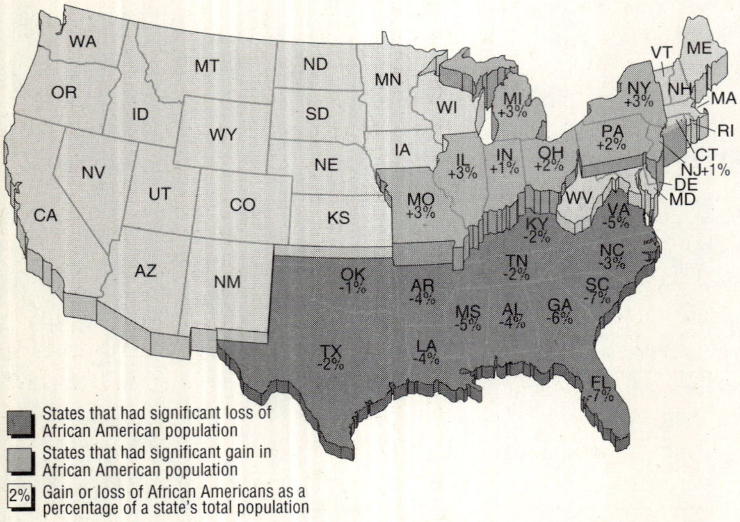


## REVIEW QUESTIONS

1. Who was forced into internment camps during the war? How did the government try to make up for this injustice?
2. **Map Skills** Which southern states lost 7 percent of their African American population during the 1940s?

Name ______________________ Class ______________ Date __________

# CHAPTER 25 Test

## IDENTIFYING MAIN IDEAS

Write the letter of the correct answer in the blank provided. (10 points each)

____ **1.** In order to mobilize the armed forces, Roosevelt authorized
- **A.** the Four Freedoms.
- **B.** the Selective Service and Training Act.
- **C.** the integration of the armed forces.
- **D.** building Liberty ships.

____ **2.** Which was an important part of Americans' war efforts on the home front?
- **A.** the rise of union membership
- **B.** consuming more food
- **C.** conserving and recycling materials
- **D.** spending more money

____ **3.** How did Allied forces prepare for the invasion of Europe?
- **A.** by executing an intensified air war
- **B.** by beginning the invasion of Italy
- **C.** by waging the Battle of Stalingrad
- **D.** by strengthening the German forces

____ **4.** A major event that marked the end of German resistance in Europe was
- **A.** the Allied landing in France.
- **B.** the Allied victory at the Battle of the Bulge.
- **C.** the liberation of Paris.
- **D.** the German retreat in Belgium.

____ **5.** In the 1930s Nazi persecution of Jews in Germany included
- **A.** forcing Jews to live in ghettos.
- **B.** stripping Jews of German citizenship.
- **C.** sending millions of Jews to death camps.
- **D.** all of the above.

____ **6.** Nazi policy to eliminate all of Europe's Jews resulted in
- **A.** deporting Jews to other nations.
- **B.** destroying death camps in Germany.
- **C.** a Holocaust of the Jewish people.
- **D.** liberation of concentration camps.

____ **7.** Which of the following was a major Allied strategy to regain Pacific islands held by Japan?
- **A.** island hopping
- **B.** controlling the Burma Road
- **C.** bombing Japan's cities
- **D.** retaking the Philippines

____ **8.** Which of the following made an Allied invasion of Japan unnecessary?
- **A.** Allied victory at Okinawa
- **B.** Allied demands for Japan's unconditional surrender
- **C.** the development and use of the atomic bomb
- **D.** a naval blockade of Japan

____ **9.** During the war, a major problem for ethnic and racial minorities at home was
- **A.** the lack of voting rights.
- **B.** the movement to large urban centers.
- **C.** segregation in the armed forces.
- **D.** economic discrimination.

____ **10.** What was the result of prejudice against Japanese American citizens during the war?
- **A.** They were denied employment.
- **B.** They were deported to Japan.
- **C.** They were confined in internment camps.
- **D.** They were imprisoned for spying.

CHAPTER 26

# The Cold War (1945–1960)

## SECTION 1 ORIGINS OF THE COLD WAR

**THE BIG IDEA**

**At the end of World War II, tensions between the United States and the Soviet Union grew into a conflict known as the Cold War.**

### TEXT SUMMARY

Different goals for a postwar world caused conflict between the United States and the Soviet Union. The United States envisioned a Europe of free, democratic nations. However, the Soviet Union was determined to create satellite nations in Eastern Europe. **Satellite nations** are countries dominated by a more powerful neighbor. Both nations did agree, however, on the formation of the United Nations (UN) as an international peacekeeping organization.

The Soviet Union tightened its hold on nations in Middle and Eastern Europe. Stalin installed a repressive government in the eastern part of Germany and declared that communism would triumph over capitalism.

In response, Britain's former prime minister Winston Churchill declared that an **iron curtain** of Communist domination had fallen over Europe and called upon the United States to prevent any more Soviet takeovers.

These speeches set the tone for the **Cold War,** the competition for world power and influence between the United States and the Soviet Union. The United States adopted a policy of **containment.** It called for the United States to resist Soviet attempts to form new Communist governments. President Harry Truman applied this policy when he gave aid to Greece and Turkey to keep them from becoming Soviet satellite nations.

In the **Truman Doctrine,** the President called on the United States to take a leading role in supporting free people around the world. The Truman Doctrine and the policy of containment would become the basis of U.S. foreign policy for the next 40 years.

### GRAPHIC SUMMARY: *The Cold War in Europe*

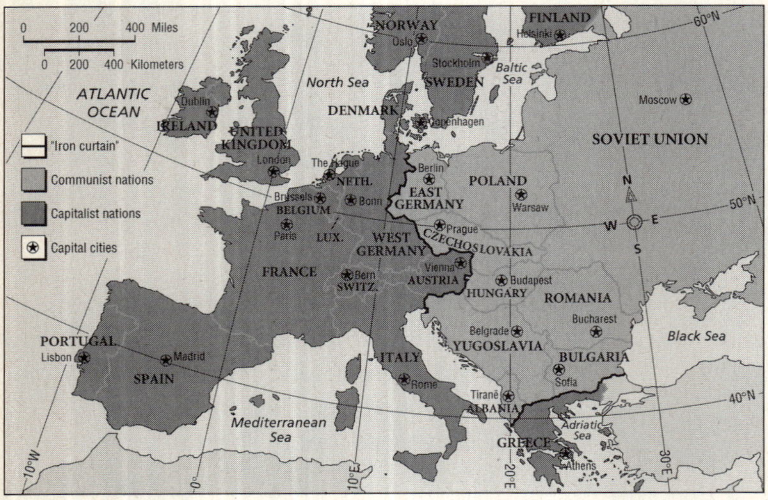


In a 1946 speech, former British prime minister Winston Churchill stated that "an iron curtain has descended across the Continent."

### REVIEW QUESTIONS

1. What was containment?
2. **Map Skills** Which country was divided into two parts by the iron curtain?

SECTION 2

# The Cold War Heats Up

## TEXT SUMMARY

As the Cold War intensified, the United States focused on strengthening Western European democracies and economies. Through the **Marshall Plan,** named for Secretary of State George C. Marshall, the United States gave financial aid to Europe, gaining allies and trading partners.

Many European nations looked to the UN for protection. But the Soviet Union vetoed all UN attempts to solve postwar problems. Therefore, in order to strengthen European alliances and deal with postwar problems, the United States, Canada, and some Western European nations formed the **North Atlantic Treaty Organization (NATO)** of mutual military assistance. The Soviet Union responded with the **Warsaw Pact,** a military alliance with its satellite nations.

In 1949 the Soviet Union successfully tested an atomic bomb, and Communists finally took control of China under their leader Mao Zedong. These two events convinced many Americans that communism was a serious domestic threat, and a new Red Scare threatened civil rights.

Congress hunted for Communists in government agencies and in the film industry through the **House Un-American Activities Committee (HUAC),** which relentlessly pursued anyone it suspected of supporting Communist ideas. Hollywood studios circulated a **blacklist** of industry people who were denied work in films because they opposed HUAC and spoke out.

Adding to the anti-Communist campaigns were the trials of Alger Hiss, a former high-ranking State Department employee, and Julius and Ethel Rosenberg, all accused of spying. Following a controversial trial that is still debated, the Rosenbergs were executed for treason.

**THE BIG IDEA**

**As the United States worked to rebuild Western Europe, Cold War tensions increased and the fear of communism grew.**

## GRAPHIC SUMMARY: *Early Days of the Cold War*

**1944** Soviet Union begins domination of Eastern Europe.

**1947** President Truman promises to oppose Communist expansion.

**1948** Marshall Plan begins rebuilding Europe.

**1948–1949** Berlin airlift supplies West Berlin during Soviet blockade.

**1949** NATO formed.

**1949** Soviet Union explodes its first atomic bomb.

**1949** Communists take over China.

1944 | 1945 | 1946 | 1947 | 1948 | 1949

**After fighting as allies in World War II, the United States and the Soviet Union faced each other as enemies in the Cold War.**

## REVIEW QUESTIONS

1. How did the Cold War affect the American movie industry?

2. **Time Line Skills** What two events frightened many Americans in 1949?

# SECTION 3 THE KOREAN WAR

## TEXT SUMMARY

The United States fought communism in a "hot" war in Korea from 1950 to 1953. Following World War II, the United States and the Soviet Union temporarily agreed that the Soviet army would occupy Korean territory north of the 38th parallel, the line running across the midsection of the Korean peninsula, while the Americans would occupy South Korea.

**THE BIG IDEA**

**American and UN troops fought against Communist forces in North Korea, resulting in a return to prewar Korean borders.**

Communist North Korea invaded the south, and United States and UN troops fought to push the North Koreans back. Heading the combined forces was U.S. General Douglas MacArthur, a World War II hero and strong anti-Communist.

When UN forces pushed the North Koreans close to the Chinese border, General MacArthur ignored a Chinese warning not to advance and Chinese troops poured into Korea, forcing a UN retreat. Determined to rid Asia of communism, MacArthur opposed the President's policy of a limited war. Truman eventually removed MacArthur from command.

Americans were frustrated by the **Korean War.** However, the Communists were contained behind the **38th parallel,** and a nuclear war had been avoided. In addition, for the first time, African American and white troops fought side by side in the same units.

The Korean War increased defense spending tremendously. By 1960 a strong **military-industrial complex** had evolved in the United States, employing millions. The Korean War also impelled the United States to sign a peace treaty with Japan to help maintain a balance of power in Asia. But relations with China were poisoned for years to come.

## GRAPHIC SUMMARY: *Events of the Korean War*

**1945**
Korea is divided at the 38th parallel.

**1949**
Communists come to power in China.

**1950**
Korean War begins when North Korean troops cross the 38th parallel into South Korea. MacArthur announces his "Home by Christmas" offensive, and is pushed back into South Korea by Chinese troops.

**1953**
After the threat of atomic weapons, President Eisenhower signs a truce with Korea. Korea remains divided at the 38th parallel.

1945 — 1950 — 1955

The Korean War lasted three years with high losses and few gains.

## REVIEW QUESTIONS

1. Why was MacArthur removed from his position?
2. **Time Line Skills** When did the Korean War begin?

SECTION 4

# The Continuing Cold War

## TEXT SUMMARY

During the 1950s the Cold War spread to several other nations around the world, while an anti-Communist crusade at home spread fear and suspicion.

Continued fear of Communist expansion led many Americans to believe the charges of Senator Joseph McCarthy that Communists had infiltrated the government. Using smear tactics and baseless accusations that came to be called **McCarthyism,** the senator targeted high-ranking government officials and even proclaimed that the army was full of Communists. At hearings viewed by millions of Americans, people saw through McCarthy's tactics, and he soon lost public support.

In foreign affairs, President Eisenhower continued Truman's policies of containment, while the United States and the Soviet Union increasingly vied for world leadership. They competed in an **arms race** to gain weapons superiority. The United States wanted to establish a policy of **deterrence,** making the United States so powerful that no enemy would dare attack.

Using a policy of **brinkmanship,** going to the edge of war to protect interests, the United States tested the Soviet Union. Meanwhile, the Soviets were building powerful intercontinental ballistic missiles, or **ICBMs.** When the Soviet Union launched ***Sputnik,*** the first artificial satellite to orbit the Earth, the United States realized the extent of Soviet technology. While trying to gain access to these technologies, a U.S. spy plane was shot down over Soviet territory. What became known as the **U-2 incident** shattered the confidence of the United States and made the country willing to spend considerable resources to catch up to, and surpass, the Soviet Union.

**THE BIG IDEA**

**During the 1950s the Cold War spread around the globe, while the fears of communism at home reached new levels.**

## GRAPHIC SUMMARY: *The Cold War Worldwide*

| Asia | Middle East | Latin America |
|---|---|---|
| **1950–1953**<br>American and UN forces battle Communist expansion in Korean War. | **1948**<br>Nation of Israel is created. United States backs Israel, Soviet Union supports surrounding Arab nations. | **1954**<br>United States helps overthrow government of Guatemala, claiming it supports radical causes. |
| **1954**<br>Vietnam is divided into Communist North Vietnam and anti-Communist South Vietnam. United States provides support for South Vietnam. | **1957**<br>President Eisenhower states that United States will use force to oppose communism in Middle East. | **1959**<br>Fidel Castro takes over Cuba, eventually forming alliance with Soviet Union. |

**The Cold War quickly developed into a global struggle between the United States and the Soviet Union.**

## REVIEW QUESTIONS

**1.** What was McCarthyism?

**2. Chart Skills** What year did Fidel Castro take over Cuba?

Name ______________________________ Class ____________________ Date __________

# CHAPTER 26 Test

## IDENTIFYING MAIN IDEAS

Write the letter of the correct answer in the blank provided. (10 points each)

____ **1.** Which of the following was a major postwar goal of the United States?
**A.** testing the atom bomb
**B.** bringing democracy to conquered European nations
**C.** dividing Germany into four occupied zones
**D.** signing a treaty with the Soviet Union

____ **2.** How did the Soviet Union gain political control in postwar Europe?
**A.** They signed a peace treaty with Germany.
**B.** They allowed free elections in Eastern Europe.
**C.** They established satellite nations.
**D.** They invaded Eastern Europe.

____ **3.** A major goal of the Truman Doctrine was
**A.** to support free peoples in Europe.
**B.** to give aid to Great Britain.
**C.** to drive Communists from Eastern Europe.
**D.** to raise the iron curtain.

____ **4.** The United States promoted economic aid to Europe through
**A.** the Berlin airlift.
**B.** the Marshall Plan.
**C.** the containment policy
**D.** the United Nations.

____ **5.** What was one U.S. response to the Communist takeover of China?
**A.** the development of a hydrogen bomb
**B.** the formation of NATO
**C.** greater efforts to protect the rest of Asia
**D.** massive aid to Nationalist China

____ **6.** Congress sought to root out suspected Communists in the government through
**A.** the McCarran-Walter Act.
**B.** the House Un-American Activities Committee.
**C.** the Hollywood Ten.
**D.** the blacklist.

____ **7.** The North Korean invasion of South Korea was an attempt to
**A.** drive out American forces.
**B.** fight Chinese forces.
**C.** remove the 38th parallel line.
**D.** unify all of Korea.

____ **8.** What was one of the effects of the Korean War?
**A.** Improved relations with China.
**B.** The military was integrated.
**C.** Defense spending declined.
**D.** General Douglas MacArthur was promoted.

____ **9.** Senator Joseph McCarthy spread suspicion and fear of communism when he
**A.** denounced the Cold War.
**B.** accused other senators of treason.
**C.** used smear tactics and untrue accusations.
**D.** found Communists in the State Department.

____ **10.** The United States and the Soviet Union struggled for world leadership by
**A.** confronting each other in Europe.
**B.** settling conflicts in the Middle East.
**C.** engaging in an arms race.
**D.** avoiding war at all costs.

# The Postwar Years at Home (1945–1960)

CHAPTER 27

## SECTION 1 THE POSTWAR ECONOMY

### TEXT SUMMARY

In the postwar years, the American economy prospered. The gross national product and the **per capita income,** the average annual income per person, nearly doubled from 1945 to 1960. A few large firms dominated many industries, forming **conglomerates,** corporations of smaller unrelated businesses, to protect themselves from economic downturns. At the same time, a new business, the **franchise,** began as entrepreneurs opened businesses under the name of a parent company. Fast-food restaurants, clothing stores, and other franchises began popping up all over the country.

Advances in technology, such as television, computers, **transistors,** and nuclear power also spurred industrial growth as businesses met demands for new technologies. Medicine also took huge leaps. Dr. Jonas Salk and Dr. Thomas Francis discovered a vaccine for poliomyelitis, a disease claiming more than 20,000 lives a year. The workforce changed as more workers entered white-collar jobs, especially in service industries.

A growing economy and more affluence helped increase the birthrate, causing a **baby boom** in the 1950s. With growing incomes and families, many Americans left the cities for the suburbs, buying homes and depending on cars to carry them to jobs in cities and new suburban shopping centers. The **GI Bill of Rights** gave veterans low-interest loans so that they could purchase homes and provided educational stipends to attend college or graduate school.

The government encouraged these changes by building new and better highways across the nation, which in turn inspired new businesses and resorts. Consumer credit, and debt, started to grow as lending agencies offered credit cards.

**THE BIG IDEA**

**Economic prosperity in the years after World War II brought many changes to American life.**

### GRAPHIC SUMMARY: *Postwar Changes*

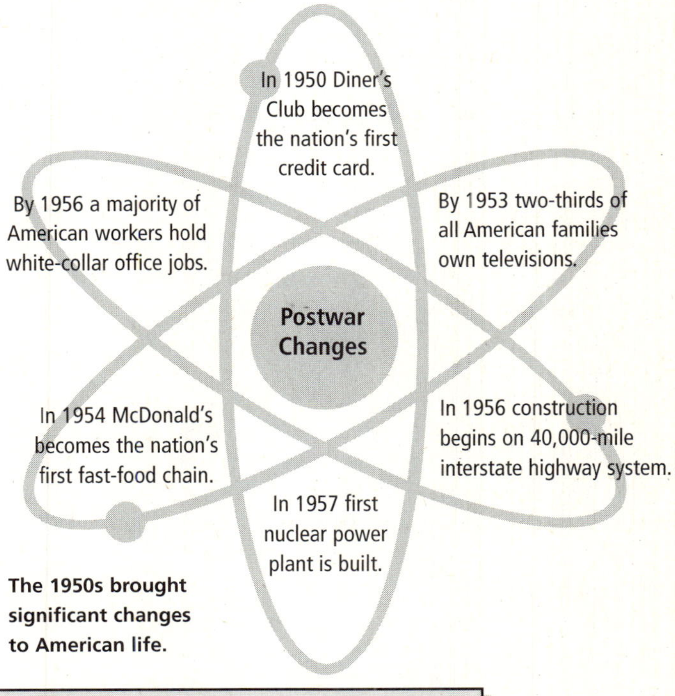


**The 1950s brought significant changes to American life.**

### REVIEW QUESTIONS

1. What was the GI Bill of Rights and how did it help the economy?
2. **Diagram Skills** In what year was the nation's first nuclear power plant built?

# SECTION 2 THE MOOD OF THE 1950S

## TEXT SUMMARY

**THE BIG IDEA**

**Many Americans enjoyed the stability and prosperity of the 1950s, while some young people began to rebel against their parents' society.**

During the 1950s many Americans lived comfortable lives. After a depression and a war, people valued security and comfort over individuality. Most young people, sometimes called the "silent generation," were content to enjoy their parents' affluence rather than become involved in the outside world. Businesses seized this opportunity to sell products to this new youth culture. Americans also showed a renewed interest in religion. Religious affiliations increased dramatically during the 1950s in response to the struggle against "godless communism." Conformity to traditional roles was the norm. Men worked in the public arena, while women worked at home or as secretaries, teachers, nurses, and sales clerks, and not in professions such as medicine or law, which were reserved for men.

Some young people felt confined by the conformity of the 1950s and looked for a style of their own. Many turned to music, becoming fans of the new **rock-and-roll** music, especially the songs of Elvis Presley. Most adults disliked this music, seeing it as a potential cause of immorality.

Other people, not just teenagers, challenged society's attitudes. These people were referred to as the "Beat Generation," or **beatniks.** This group consisted of artists and writers who challenged the traditional patterns of respectability and shocked most Americans with their open sexuality and use of illegal drugs.

## GRAPHIC SUMMARY: *The 1950s Mood*

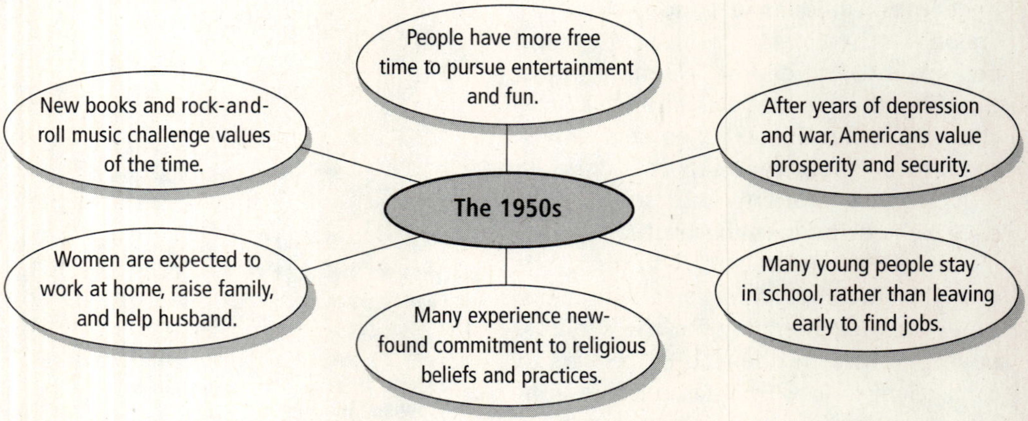


**The mood of the 1950s reflected a nation recovering from years of depression and war.**

## REVIEW QUESTIONS

1. Why were most young people of the 1950s called the "silent generation"?
2. **Diagram Skills** What did most Americans seem to value during the 1950s?

SECTION 3

# Domestic Politics and Policy

## TEXT SUMMARY

Becoming President just as World War II was ending, Harry Truman faced the challenges of America's **reconversion,** the transition from a wartime to a peacetime economy.

Truman proposed the "Fair Deal" program that included more benefits for workers, national health insurance, and control over atomic energy. He also moved to increase civil rights for African Americans by ordering the armed forces to end segregation.

Truman's Fair Deal ran into trouble with a conservative Congress. His popularity fell, and he was expected to lose the 1948 presidential election. Campaigning vigorously, Truman won an upset victory, and Democrats won control of Congress. Truman continued to push for his programs but with limited success.

Concerns over FDR's third term led Congress to pass the Twenty-second Amendment in 1951. It set term limits on the President, and even though it made an exception for Truman, he declined to seek a third term.

Republicans supported Dwight D. Eisenhower for President, and his background and charm won him the election in 1952. Eisenhower promoted **Modern Republicanism,** the major goal of which was to slow federal government growth and limit presidential power.

Eisenhower favored business, reduced spending, and cut taxes. Eisenhower also helped establish the **National Aeronautics and Space Administration (NASA),** an independent agency for space exploration. He also signed the **National Defense Education Act,** giving money to improve science and mathematics education.

**THE BIG IDEA**

**Presidents Truman and Eisenhower pursued different policies and used different styles to meet the challenges of the postwar period.**

## GRAPHIC SUMMARY: *The Truman and Eisenhower Years*

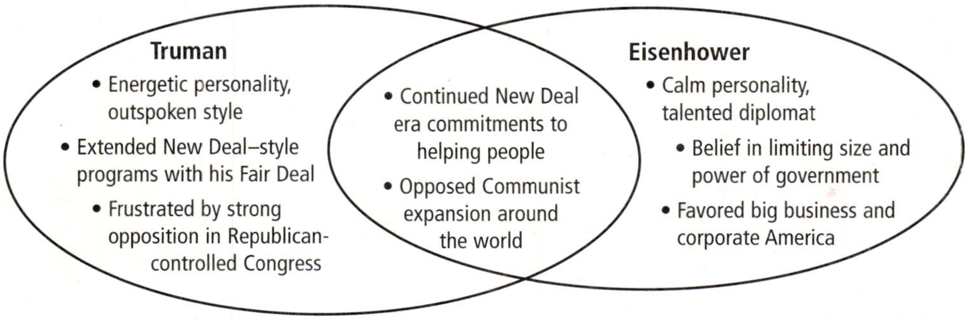


Truman and Eisenhower brought different styles and different programs to the presidency.

## REVIEW QUESTIONS

1. How did Truman work to continue pursuing the goals of the New Deal?
2. **Chart Skills** Identify one common aspect of the presidencies of Truman and Eisenhower.

Name ______________________ Class ______________ Date __________

# CHAPTER 27 Test

## IDENTIFYING MAIN IDEAS

Write the letter of the correct answer in the blank provided. (10 points each)

____ **1.** Between 1945 and 1960 the American economy
**A.** enjoyed great prosperity.
**B.** went into a steep decline.
**C.** stayed at the same level of production.
**D.** had periods of rapid growth and steep decline.

____ **2.** Which was an important part of American business during the 1950s?
**A.** the rise of national restaurant and store chains
**B.** the decline of most large corporations
**C.** the lack of technological development
**D.** the drop in the national per capita income

____ **3.** One result of the growth of the suburbs was the
**A.** drop in the per capita income.
**B.** growth in the automobile industry.
**C.** decline in the computer industry.
**D.** slowing of road construction projects.

____ **4.** In the 1950s most Americans wanted to
**A.** fight another world war.
**B.** imitate European ways of life.
**C.** rebel against American society.
**D.** enjoy the prosperity of the times.

____ **5.** During the 1950s women were expected to
**A.** earn money to support their family.
**B.** make important political decisions.
**C.** work at home and raise children.
**D.** go to college.

____ **6.** Which of the following was seen as a challenge to the values of the 1950s?
**A.** television
**B.** religion
**C.** nuclear power
**D.** rock-and-roll music

____ **7.** Truman's Fair Deal was designed to
**A.** continue policies of the New Deal.
**B.** reduce the size of government.
**C.** lower taxes for the wealthiest Americans.
**D.** end the government's active role in society.

____ **8.** Which action did Truman take to improve civil rights for African Americans?
**A.** He hired Martin Luther King as an adviser.
**B.** He ordered the armed forces to end segregation.
**C.** He declared segregation in public schools unconstitutional.
**D.** He banned discrimination in professional sports.

____ **9.** One of Eisenhower's main goals was to
**A.** continue the Fair Deal.
**B.** reduce the size of government.
**C.** continue the Korean War.
**D.** raise taxes and government spending.

____ **10.** How did the United States attempt to meet the Soviet technology challenge?
**A.** It raised federal taxes.
**B.** It formed a new agency to explore space.
**C.** It gave loans to businesses.
**D.** It reversed the Fair Deal.

# The Civil Rights Movement (1950–1968)

CHAPTER 28

## SECTION 1 DEMANDS FOR CIVIL RIGHTS

### TEXT SUMMARY

The racial climate in the United States began changing after World War II. Working through the courts, the NAACP challenged segregation laws throughout the nation. It won a historic Supreme Court decision in 1954 in the case ***Brown* v. *Board of Education of Topeka, Kansas.*** The Court ruled that segregation in public education was unconstitutional.

In the South, civil rights leaders began a new battle in Montgomery, Alabama. They launched the **Montgomery bus boycott,** during which African Americans refused to ride the segregated public buses. Thousands walked, bicycled, or organized car pools. Montgomery refused to change its policy, but in 1956 the Supreme Court ruled that bus segregation was illegal. The boycott began the career of a 26-year-old Baptist minister, Martin Luther King, Jr., who became the spokesperson for this protest movement.

White resistance continued, however. In Arkansas, Governor Orval Faubus defied the ruling to bring the races together through **integration.** He used the National Guard to prevent nine black students from entering a high school in Little Rock. Eisenhower had to send federal troops to protect the students.

Mexican Americans and Native Americans also struggled in the 1950s for equal rights, but their protests were not as successful as those of African Americans.

**THE BIG IDEA**

**After World War II, African Americans began winning important victories in the battle for civil rights.**

### GRAPHIC SUMMARY: *Civil Rights Milestones*

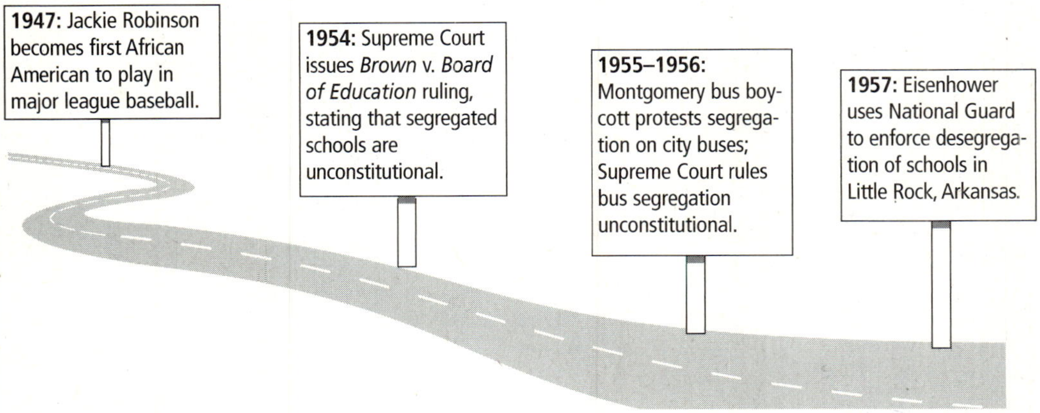


### REVIEW QUESTIONS

1. Who became the spokesperson for the Montgomery bus boycott?

2. **Diagram Skills** How were the events of 1954 and 1957 related?

SECTION 2

# LEADERS AND STRATEGIES

## TEXT SUMMARY

Several important civil rights groups laid the foundation for the civil rights movement of the 1960s. Since 1909 the NAACP, an **interracial** group with both African American and white members, had been working through the courts to challenge laws that prevented African Americans from achieving full equality. The National Urban League helped African Americans moving into northern cities find homes and jobs.

Another interracial group, the **Congress of Racial Equality (CORE),** was founded by pacifists during World War II and was dedicated to peaceful protests. In 1957 Martin Luther King, Jr., and others founded a new group, the **Southern Christian Leadership Conference (SCLC).** Headed by southern church leaders like King, SCLC focused the civil rights movement on the South. King and the SCLC advocated **nonviolent protest,** peaceful resistance against racism, as the most effective tool for change. To fight for justice, King advocated civil disobedience to unjust laws through nonviolence. He taught that protesters should not use violence, even when attacked.

Another group was created by the movement's youth. The **Student Nonviolent Coordinating Committee (SNCC)** was formed to give young African Americans a stronger voice in the civil rights movement. Under the leadership of activists like Robert Moses, SNCC called for more immediate change and was less patient with the gradual change advocated by groups like the NAACP and SCLC.

**THE BIG IDEA**

**The civil rights movement of the 1960s was made up of a variety of groups, united by their desire to achieve equal rights for all Americans.**

## GRAPHIC SUMMARY: *Civil Rights Organizations*

**CORE**
- Used peaceful confrontations, such as sit-ins, to bring about change.

**SNCC**
- Gave young activists an important role in civil rights movement.

**NAACP**
- Worked through the courts to secure legal equality for all Americans.

**National Urban League**
- Assisted people moving to major American cities.

**SCLC**
- Organized nonviolent protests against racism and segregation.

The struggle for civil rights was led by activists of all ages and backgrounds.

## REVIEW QUESTIONS

1. Describe Martin Luther King's strategy for promoting change.
2. **Diagram Skills** What role did SNCC play in the civil rights movement?

SECTION 3

# THE STRUGGLE INTENSIFIES

## TEXT SUMMARY

The continuing civil rights movement brought intensified strife in the South. Young African Americans protested through **sit-ins,** in which a group simply sat down in segregated public places and refused to move. They faced arrest and sometimes violence. The tactic drew thousands of young African Americans, who staged sit-ins throughout the South.

When the Supreme Court banned segregation on interstate buses in 1960, young activists organized **Freedom Rides.** They rode buses south, stopping at stations along the way to test the Court's ruling. A clash occurred in Anniston, Alabama, when an armed mob met one bus, attacked the riders, and burned the bus. The violence prompted the federal government to act to protect the Freedom Riders.

In 1962, when James Meredith tried to enroll at the all-white University of Mississippi, the governor, Ross Barnett, defied a Supreme Court ruling and barred Meredith's way. Violence erupted, several hundred people were hurt, and federal marshals had to escort Meredith to classes.

In Birmingham, Alabama, Martin Luther King, Jr., planned a series of nonviolent marches and boycotts and was arrested. From jail, King wrote a letter defending his tactics. He also decided to let children join the marches, and an entire nation watched on television as Birmingham police turned fire hoses and attack dogs on the marchers, including children. The police brutality horrified people, and the nonviolent protest gained wider support, causing Birmingham to finally begin desegregating its facilities.

**THE BIG IDEA**

**Civil rights protests succeeded in battling segregation, though protesters often faced violent opposition.**

## GRAPHIC SUMMARY: *The Birmingham Protests, 1963*

Martin Luther King, Jr., calls Birmingham, Alabama, "the most segregated city in the country."

↓

King invited to Birmingham to lead protests against segregation.

↓

Birmingham police commissioner Eugene "Bull" Conner vows to arrest King and other demonstrators.

↓

King is arrested during protest march and spends a week in jail.

↓

After being released, King leads another protest march. Birmingham police respond with violence and more arrests.

↓

Nation watches police violence on television, sympathy for civil rights activists grows.

↓

Birmingham ends policies of segregation.

Civil rights activists won a major victory in Birmingham in 1963.

## REVIEW QUESTIONS

1. Describe a sit-in.
2. **Diagram Skills** Who was the police commissioner of Birmingham in 1963?

SECTION 4

# The Political Response

**THE BIG IDEA**

**The civil rights movement gained the support of Presidents Kennedy and Johnson, leading to the passage of important civil rights legislation.**

## TEXT SUMMARY

Early in his term, President John F. Kennedy moved slowly on civil rights issues, but as violence escalated against protesters, he was disturbed at what he saw and urged Congress to pass a strong civil rights bill. However, powerful southern congressmen blocked its passage.

To focus national attention on the President's bill, civil rights leaders organized a **March on Washington** in August 1963. More than 200,000 people marched and gathered in the nation's capital to call for jobs and freedom. They listened to songs and speeches, including Martin Luther's King, Jr.'s famous "I Have a Dream" address, which was heard around the nation.

Following Kennedy's assassination in 1963, President Lyndon Johnson used his political skill to push through Congress the **Civil Rights Act of 1964,** which expanded civil rights by prohibiting discrimination in jobs, schools, and voting. Despite the act, voting rights continued to be denied in the South, and protests continued.

To push for stronger voting rights, King and others led a march of about 25,000 people from Selma, Alabama, to Montgomery, Alabama. Although police attacked the marchers, the march was highly effective. Johnson responded by forcing the **Voting Rights Act of 1965** through Congress. This act gave federal officials the right to register voters if state officials blocked registration. Another legal landmark was the **Twenty-fourth Amendment,** which outlawed the poll tax. Because of these two laws, thousands of new black voters elected many African Americans to political offices.

## GRAPHIC SUMMARY: *Major Protests, 1955–1965*

**1955** Montgomery Bus Boycott

**1962** James Meredith wins the right to attend University of Mississippi

**1963** Protest marches in Birmingham, Alabama

1955 | 1957 | 1959 | 1961 | 1963 | 1965

**1961** Freedom Rides

**1963** March on Washington

**1965** Selma March

Years of protests convinced politicians to pass new civil rights laws.

## REVIEW QUESTIONS

1. What was the goal of the Voting Rights Act of 1965?

2. **Time Line Skills** In what year did the March on Washington occur?

SECTION 5

# THE MOVEMENT TAKES A NEW TURN

## TEXT SUMMARY

For many African Americans, change was too slow, and protests continued over persistent discrimination. More militant, radical leaders emerged in the civil rights movement, and division occurred.

Author James Baldwin expressed his anger in his writings. Malcolm X, a leader in the **Nation of Islam,** often called the Black Muslims, opposed integration and preached self-help and **black nationalism,** the separate identity and racial unity of African Americans. He was assassinated in 1965, but his legacy lived on in the **black power** movement.

Under the radical leader Stokely Carmichael, SNCC urged taking up arms in self-defense and challenged moderate civil rights leaders. Black power was also reflected in the Black Panther political party, which often directly confronted authorities, leading to violent encounters.

Early civil rights leaders fought ***de jure* segregation,** racial separation created by law. However, ***de facto* segregation,** the separation caused by social and economic conditions, persisted in most American cities. Discrimination in jobs, housing, and schools fueled several riots in northern cities in 1964 and 1965, and the deadly riots in Watts, California.

Adding to the continuing discontent of the 1960s were two major tragedies of 1968. The assassination of Martin Luther King, Jr., caused African Americans to lose faith in the idea of nonviolent change. The assassination of Robert Kennedy, who had taken up the cause of civil rights, caused many to wonder if equal civil rights could ever be achieved. Nevertheless, the struggle of the 1960s had brought tremendous changes. Segregation was illegal, African Americans could vote, and thousands of African Americans gained political offices and power.

**THE BIG IDEA**

**The slow pace of progress encouraged some civil rights leaders to call for more radical action.**

## GRAPHIC SUMMARY: *Black Power*

| | |
|---|---|
| **Elijah Muhammad** | Founds the Nation of Islam in 1925. Often called the Black Muslims, the group teaches black separation and self-help. |
| **Malcolm X** | Uses fiery speeches to spread the idea of black nationalism, the belief that African Americans should build their own communities and culture. |
| **James Baldwin** | Becomes a strong voice for civil rights through his powerful novels and essays on the African American experience. |
| **Stokely Carmichael** | Coins the phrase "black power" as he calls on African Americans to unite and build strong communities. |

**Malcolm X became one of several spokesmen for African Americans who were frustrated by the slow pace of change.**

## REVIEW QUESTIONS

1. Describe the philosophy of Malcolm X.
2. **Chart Skills** How did James Baldwin contribute to the civil rights movement?

Name ______________________ Class ______________ Date ________

# CHAPTER 28 Test

## IDENTIFYING MAIN IDEAS

Write the letter of the correct answer in the blank provided. (10 points each)

____ **1.** In the struggle for civil rights, the NAACP focused on working through
**A.** the court system.
**B.** peaceful protest marches.
**C.** violent riots.
**D.** boycotts.

____ **2.** One of the founders of the Southern Christian Leadership Conference was
**A.** James Baldwin.
**B.** Malcolm X.
**C.** Martin Luther King, Jr.
**D.** Robert Moses.

____ **3.** Martin Luther King, Jr., believed that the most effective tool for change was
**A.** armed confrontation.
**B.** lawsuits.
**C.** inaction.
**D.** nonviolent protest.

____ **4.** Freedom Rides were organized to protest segregation in
**A.** northern housing.
**B.** southern bus stations.
**C.** the military.
**D.** government offices.

____ **5.** James Meredith advanced the cause of civil rights when he
**A.** refused to join the Air Force.
**B.** enrolled at the University of Mississippi.
**C.** organized the Freedom Rides.
**D.** was elected to Congress.

____ **6.** Violent treatment of civil rights marchers by the police in Birmingham, Alabama,
**A.** ended the civil rights movement in Alabama.
**B.** angered most Americans.
**C.** was supported by Kennedy.
**D.** was ignored across the country.

____ **7.** After seeing the violence committed against civil rights protesters, President Kennedy
**A.** refused to introduce a new civil rights bill.
**B.** became a strong supporter of civil rights.
**C.** lost interest in the civil rights movement.
**D.** decided to support segregation.

____ **8.** What happened after Congress passed the Voting Rights Act of 1965?
**A.** African Americans began playing a larger role in politics.
**B.** Many African Americans were elected to the United States Senate.
**C.** The civil rights movement came to an end.
**D.** President Johnson vetoed the Act.

____ **9.** Malcolm X believed that African Americans should
**A.** wait patiently for change.
**B.** reject white society and build a separate culture.
**C.** imitate white culture.
**D.** fight to end segregation.

____ **10.** Which of these was a political party that called on African Americans to confront authorities?
**A.** CORE
**B.** SCLC
**C.** the Black Panthers
**D.** the National Urban League

# The Kennedy and Johnson Years (1961–1969)

CHAPTER 29

## SECTION 1 *The New Frontier*

### TEXT SUMMARY

In the 1960 presidential campaign, Democrat John F. Kennedy ran against Republican Richard M. Nixon. The two candidates faced each other in the nation's first televised debate. Kennedy appeared to most viewers as relaxed and confident while Nixon seemed tired and strained. The debate had a significant impact on American politics. Politicians could now use television as a more effective means of communicating with the public.

Kennedy was the youngest person to run for President and the first Roman Catholic to win the presidency. He won by a narrow margin, which denied him a strong **mandate,** or public endorsement of his ideas. However, he actively pursued his programs to improve the economy, fight poverty and inequality, and develop the space program. These policies, which he called the **"New Frontier,"** were frequently blocked by Congress. Therefore, Kennedy sought to achieve his goals through executive orders. During his short presidency he succeeded in enacting measures to improve the economy, the standard of living for the poor, and the environment. Kennedy also pushed the space program to put a man on the moon. NASA reached this goal in 1969, but Kennedy never got to see it.

On a campaign visit to Dallas, Texas, in November 1963, Kennedy was assassinated by Lee Harvey Oswald, who was then murdered by Jack Ruby before he could be tried. Vice President Lyndon B. Johnson took over as President and immediately appointed a commission to investigate the assassination.

The **Warren Commission,** headed by Supreme Court Chief Justice Earl Warren, concluded that Oswald acted alone. However, many people still believe that Oswald was part of a larger conspiracy.

**THE BIG IDEA**

**As President, John F. Kennedy worked to improve the economy and battle poverty. Kennedy was assassinated in 1963.**

### GRAPHIC SUMMARY: *The Space Program*

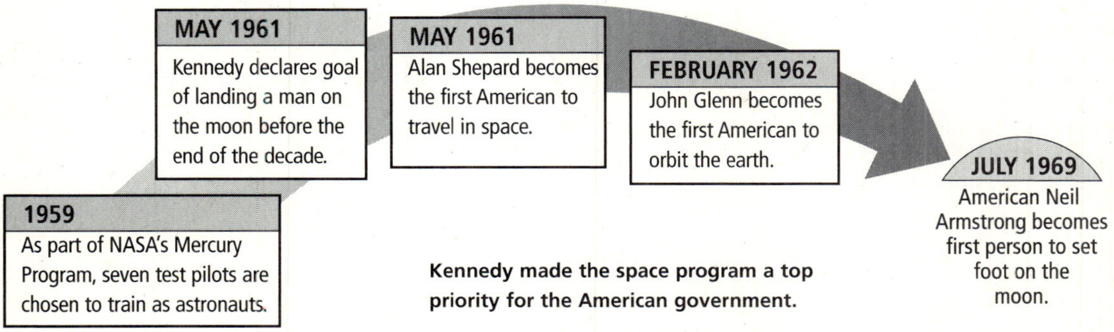


### REVIEW QUESTIONS

1. What were the goals of Kennedy's New Frontier?
2. **Diagram Skills** Who was the first American to travel in space?

# SECTION 2 *THE GREAT SOCIETY*

## TEXT SUMMARY

Before becoming President in 1963, Lyndon Johnson had served more than 20 years in Congress, gaining fame for his legislative and persuasive skills.

**THE BIG IDEA**

**With his Great Society program, President Johnson created new government programs to battle poverty and improve education and health care.**

To carry on Kennedy's policies, Johnson proposed a sweeping program of domestic reform he called the **Great Society.** It included poverty relief, education aid, health care reform, voting rights reform, conservation efforts, and urban renewal.

Elected President in his own right in 1964, Johnson pushed through Kennedy's tax cut with an addendum to cut government spending, causing the GNP to grow, the deficit to shrink, unemployment to fall, and inflation to remain in check. He instituted **Head Start,** a preschool program for children from low-income families, and **Volunteers in Service to America (VISTA),** which sent people to help poor communities. Johnson's medical assistance plan included **Medicare,** medical insurance for Americans age 65 and older, and **Medicaid,** medical coverage for low-income Americans.

At the same time, the Supreme Court, under Chief Justice Earl Warren, outlawed prayer in public schools, redefined obscenity laws, and struck down laws prohibiting birth control. To safeguard the constitutional rights of individuals, the Court mandated the **Miranda rule,** which states that police must inform criminal suspects of their rights before questioning. The Court also moved to reform state legislatures through **apportionment,** the redrawing of state electoral districts.

By 1968, however, the war in Vietnam was draining the federal budget and undermining Johnson's Great Society. Nevertheless, Johnson cut poverty in half because of his programs.

## GRAPHIC SUMMARY: *The Warren Court*

| *Mapp* v. *Ohio* (1961) | *Gideon* v. *Wainright* (1963) |
|---|---|
| Ruling: Evidence seized illegally cannot be used in a trial. | Ruling: Suspects who cannot afford a lawyer have the right to free legal aid. |
| *Escobedo* v. *Illinois* (1964) | *Miranda* v. *Arizona* (1966) |
| Ruling: Individuals accused of a crime must be given access to an attorney while being questioned. | Ruling: Police must inform accused persons of their rights before questioning them. |

Earl Warren and other members of the Supreme Court were concerned with protecting the rights of individuals accused of crimes.

## REVIEW QUESTIONS

**1.** Describe Medicare and Medicaid.

**2. Chart Skills** What did the Supreme Court decide in the case of *Miranda* v. *Arizona*?

# SECTION 3 FOREIGN POLICY IN THE EARLY 1960S

## TEXT SUMMARY

When President Kennedy took office in 1961, he immediately faced his first foreign crisis. With U.S. backing, Cuban opponents of leader Fidel Castro launched the **Bay of Pigs invasion** of Cuba in 1961. Castro easily defeated the invasion forces, and Kennedy was criticized for the disaster.

Cold War tensions also increased in Germany when the Soviet Union built the **Berlin Wall.** The wall cut Communist East Berlin off from West Berlin. Kennedy responded by promising to protect West Germany's freedom.

The most dangerous event of the Cold War erupted in October 1962, with the **Cuban Missile Crisis.** The Soviet Union was building missile bases in Cuba, and Kennedy responded with a naval "quarantine" around Cuba and called on the Soviets to withdraw the missiles. Tensions and stakes were high, but war was averted. An agreement was made that the United States would stay out of Cuba and the Soviets would withdraw the missiles.

Afterward, a step toward peace was taken when the United States and the Soviet Union signed the **Limited Test Ban Treaty,** prohibiting nuclear testing above ground.

Kennedy also initiated the **Alliance for Progress,** calling on all Western Hemisphere nations to work together to satisfy the basic needs of people in North, Central, and South America, and the **Peace Corps,** a program to send volunteers worldwide as health workers, educators, and technicians.

When Johnson became President in 1963, he continued Kennedy's policy in Vietnam, sending advisers and economic aid to South Vietnam. By 1965 American involvement in Vietnam was deepening.

**THE BIG IDEA**

**Kennedy's presidency was filled with ambitious international programs and dangerous Cold War crises.**

## GRAPHIC SUMMARY: *Kennedy's Foreign Policy Goals*

**GOALS:**
- Reduce risk of nuclear war
- Encourage countries to ally themselves with United States

**1961 Peace Corps established**
Sends volunteers around the world to help developing nations

**1961 Alliance for Progress**
Provides money for economic development and social reform throughout Latin America

**1963 Limited Test Ban Treaty**
United States and Soviet Union agree to ban above-ground nuclear testing

**Kennedy developed programs aimed at spreading peace and American influence around the world.**

## REVIEW QUESTIONS

1. How was the Cuban Missile Crisis solved?
2. **Diagram Skills** What did the Limited Test Ban Treaty of 1963 accomplish?

Name ______________________ Class ______________ Date ________

# CHAPTER 29 Test

## IDENTIFYING MAIN IDEAS

Write the letter of the correct answer in the blank provided. (10 points each)

____ **1.** Television was a major factor in the election of 1960 because during the campaign
**A.** television became popular across the country.
**B.** the candidates faced each other in the nation's first televised debates.
**C.** the candidates refused to debate on television.
**D.** only Kennedy appeared on television.

____ **2.** Kennedy's New Frontier included efforts to
**A.** raise taxes.
**B.** decrease the size of government.
**C.** improve the space program.
**D.** protect the environment.

____ **3.** The Warren Commission decided that the Kennedy assassination was
**A.** the act of a single man.
**B.** part of a large conspiracy.
**C.** due to poor security.
**D.** an act of Soviet agents.

____ **4.** As a member of Congress, Lyndon Johnson was known for his
**A.** lack of experience in politics.
**B.** support for Richard Nixon.
**C.** opposition to the New Deal.
**D.** great skills as a legislator.

____ **5.** Johnson called his plan for improving the nation the
**A.** Fair Deal.
**B.** New Frontier.
**C.** Great Society.
**D.** New Deal.

____ **6.** Medicare and Medicaid were programs designed to help people afford
**A.** housing.
**B.** education.
**C.** health care.
**D.** legal aid.

____ **7.** During the 1960s the Supreme Court made several decisions which
**A.** declared Great Society legislation unconstitutional.
**B.** opposed civil rights.
**C.** supported school segregation.
**D.** protected the rights of people accused of crimes.

____ **8.** The goal of the Bay of Pigs invasion was to
**A.** capture Soviet missiles.
**B.** force Fidel Castro from power.
**C.** prevent a revolutionary war in Cuba.
**D.** support Fidel Castro's army.

____ **9.** Why did the Soviets build the Berlin Wall?
**A.** to protect against an American invasion
**B.** to stop Americans from entering the Soviet Union
**C.** to protect the people of Cuba
**D.** to stop people from escaping from East Germany

____ **10.** The Cuban Missile Crisis ended when
**A.** Castro was removed from power.
**B.** the Soviets removed their missiles from Cuba.
**C.** Kennedy was assassinated.
**D.** American planes destroyed the Soviet missiles in Cuba.

# An Era of Activism (1960–1975)

CHAPTER 30

## SECTION 1 *The Women's Movement*

### TEXT SUMMARY

During women's early struggles for equal rights, the word **feminism** was first used to describe the idea of political, economic, and social equality of men and women. In the 1960s women, inspired by the civil rights movement, realized that organized protests and legal action could bring about change.

In 1966 a group of professional women founded the **National Organization for Women (NOW).** Its goal was to bring women into full participation in American society. It called for equal pay and opportunity. It challenged the idea that women should be expected to stay home, and called for men to share parenting and household responsibilities.

By the early 1970s thousands of women were supporting equality for women. Many people's attitudes began to change as more women entered professional fields. A controversial issue was abortion and a woman's right to legally end an unwanted pregnancy. Women won the right to choose through the 1973 ***Roe* v. *Wade*** decision of the Supreme Court that struck down state regulation of abortion.

Many women also campaigned to add the **Equal Rights Amendment (ERA)** to the Constitution to prohibit discrimination based on gender. Congress passed the ERA, but it was not ratified by the states because of growing opposition.

**THE BIG IDEA**

**Inspired by the success of the civil rights movement, women began to organize and work for equal rights.**

### GRAPHIC SUMMARY: *Median Incomes of Men and Women*

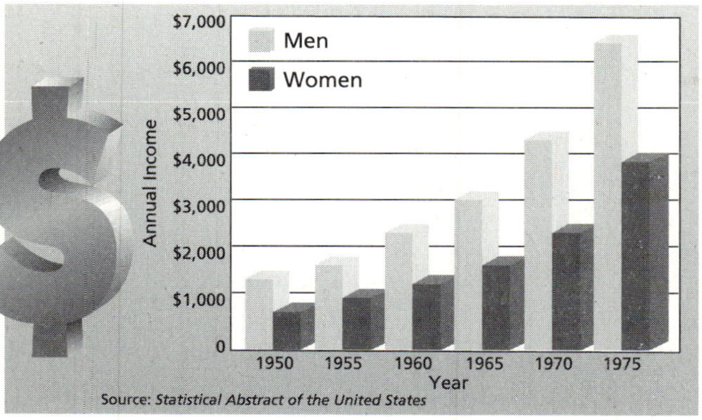


Equal pay was a main goal of the women's movement.

### REVIEW QUESTIONS

1. Describe the goals of the National Organization for Women.
2. **Graph Skills** What was the average woman's income in 1975?

SECTION 2

# ETHNIC MINORITIES SEEK EQUALITY

## TEXT SUMMARY

During the 1960s and 1970s racial and ethnic minorities in America also fought for equality. **Latinos,** people whose origins are in Spanish-speaking Latin America, organized against discrimination in housing, education, and jobs.

Led by César Chávez, Latino farm workers struggled for equality. A farm worker himself, Chávez founded the **United Farm Workers (UFW)** union to improve conditions for **migrant farm workers,** people who moved around the country to plant and harvest crops under backbreaking conditions. Chávez believed in nonviolence, and he used boycotts against California grape growers to demand change. Supported by many people, the boycotts brought improvements for farm workers.

Asians also protested racial discrimination. Through the **Japanese American Citizens League (JACL),** Japanese Americans sought compensation for their losses because of World War II internment. The government eventually made small payments to Japanese Americans. Asian Americans made economic advances faster than most ethnic groups, but still faced discrimination.

Native Americans had many grievances with the federal government over equal rights, broken treaties, and land rights. Poor living conditions, high unemployment, and poverty on the reservations led to the formation of the **American Indian Movement (AIM).** They sought **autonomy,** or self-government, and other legal rights. After many confrontations with the government, new laws were passed to improve educational facilities for Native Americans and grant self-determination.

**THE BIG IDEA**

**During the 1960s Latinos, Asian Americans, and Native Americans began effective equal rights movements of their own.**

## GRAPHIC SUMMARY: *Latino Victories in the 1960s*

**Latino Victories**

**Labor**
- Under leadership of César Chávez, United Farm Workers union makes important financial, health, and safety gains for farm workers.

**Politics**
- Voters elect Texans Henry González and Elizo de la Garza to the House of Representatives. José Angel Gutiérrez creates La Raza Unida, a political party to support Latino interests.

**Civil Rights**
- Mexican American Legal Defense and Education Fund helps Mexican Americans gain civil rights and encourages Mexican American students to become lawyers.

**Latinos began to organize against discrimination in the 1960s.**

## REVIEW QUESTIONS

1. How did César Chávez help win better working conditions for workers on grape farms?
2. **Diagram Skills** What state did Henry Gonzáles represent in Congress?

# SECTION 3 THE COUNTERCULTURE

## TEXT SUMMARY

During the 1960s and 1970s the values of many young Americans ran counter to those of traditional American culture. Those in this **counterculture** promoted freedom and individuality and challenged the authority of mainstream America. Their freer fashions and styles, like working-class clothing and long hair and beards, rejected the stiffness of the corporate world. Often they identified with the poor and downtrodden.

The new generation also demanded freedom in personal relationships, leading to a "sexual revolution." Young men and women experimented with different living arrangements, including living together outside of marriage. Part of this new freedom involved using psychedelic drugs. Drug use, especially marijuana, became more widespread.

Music also contributed to the cultural changes of the 1960s, with popular youth rock groups such as the Beatles and the Rolling Stones. Symbolic of the new wave of music was the 1969 gathering of counterculture youth at the **Woodstock festival** in upstate New York. Some 400,000 people listened to major rock bands and enjoyed fellowship with each other. Some looked at it as a model for the new, more peaceful world. Many others, both young and old, deplored Woodstock, disturbed by what they saw as a rejection of traditional morals and important mainstream values. By the 1980s the young people of the counterculture had grown older, and most, who came from middle-class America, drifted back into the mainstream culture.

**THE BIG IDEA**

**During the 1960s many young Americans experimented with new ideas about clothes, drugs, and personal relationships.**

## GRAPHIC SUMMARY: *The Counterculture*

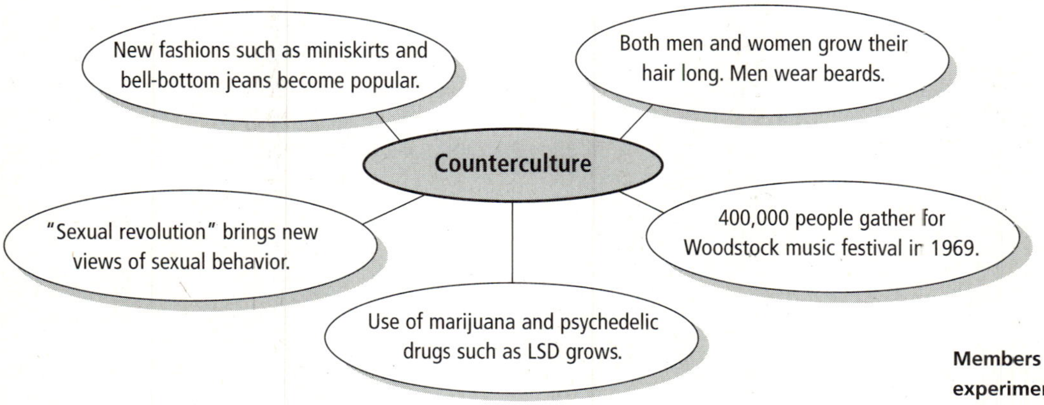


Members of the counterculture experimented with a variety of new ideas and attitudes.

## REVIEW QUESTIONS

1. Describe the contrasting views of the Woodstock festival.
2. **Diagram Skills** What impact did the counterculture have on drug use in the United States?

SECTION 4

# THE ENVIRONMENTAL AND CONSUMER MOVEMENTS

## TEXT SUMMARY

The 1960s and 1970s also saw the birth of the environmental and consumer protection movements. Environmental movements demanded preservation and restoration of Earth's environment. Inspired by Rachel Carson's book *Silent Spring,* condemning the chemicals that were poisoning the environment, groups organized around the country. Activists protested pollution and toxic wastes. The government responded to environmentalists' fears over possible nuclear accidents by establishing the **Nuclear Regulatory Commission (NRC)** in 1974 to oversee the safety of nuclear power plants.

As concerns about environmental damage grew among the public, the government also established the **Environmental Protection Agency (EPA)** to set national antipollution standards. The EPA enforced these standards through the **Clean Air Act** and the **Clean Water Act,** which controlled air and water pollution by industries. Because of concerns of business that new regulations would cost them too much and cause loss of jobs, the government tried to balance the demands of economic development and environmental protection.

The consumer movement demanded safety for consumers and workers. It had roots in early-20th-century efforts, such as those of the muckrakers, to protect the public. But in the 1960s and 1970s the movement grew larger and stronger. Led by consumer activist Ralph Nader, who has devoted his life and work to consumer protection, scores of volunteers investigated the automobile and food industries. They reported on the safety of products from baby food to insecticides and inspired consumers to demand protection from harmful products.

**THE BIG IDEA**

**During the 1960s activists began movements to protect the environment and improve the safety of consumer products.**

## GRAPHIC SUMMARY: *Major Environmental and Consumer Protection Laws*

| Year | Law | Purpose |
|---|---|---|
| 1964 | Wilderness Act | Set aside lands to be preserved for future generations. |
| 1966 | National Traffic and Motor Vehicle Safety Act | Forced the automobile industry to confront safety problems. |
| 1967 | Wholesome Meat Act | Set regulations for the meat-packing industry. |
| 1970 | Clean Air Act | Developed program to prevent air pollution. |
| 1972 | Clean Water Act | Created to protect the nation's water resources. |
| 1973 | Endangered Species Act | Established protection for plants and animals in danger of extinction. |

**The environmental movement of the 1960s led to strong new environmental laws.**

## REVIEW QUESTIONS

1. What was the impact of Rachel Carson's *Silent Spring*?
2. **Chart Skills** What was the purpose of the Endangered Species Act?

Name ________________________ Class ____________ Date ________

# CHAPTER 30 Test

## IDENTIFYING MAIN IDEAS

Write the letter of the correct answer in the blank provided. (10 points each)

____ **1.** The word *feminism* describes the theory that
**A.** women are superior to men.
**B.** women should have equal rights with men.
**C.** women should focus on traditional roles.
**D.** women should not work outside the home.

____ **2.** Which of these was a result of the women's movement of the 1960s?
**A.** The Equal Rights Amendment became law.
**B.** Women began earning more than men in most jobs.
**C.** Women won the right to end an unwanted pregnancy.
**D.** Women were no longer allowed to join the military.

____ **3.** Many women rejected the women's movement because they
**A.** preferred traditional roles.
**B.** thought it was too weak to be effective.
**C.** did not support women's right to vote.
**D.** opposed equal pay for women.

____ **4.** The Latino population in the United States is made up of people whose family origins are in
**A.** Africa. **B.** Latin America.
**C.** Spain. **D.** Asia.

____ **5.** César Chávez fought to improve the lives of
**A.** farm workers. **B.** Latino students.
**C.** Native Americans. **D.** miners.

____ **6.** Which of these was a goal of Japanese American activists?
**A.** To gain compensation for losses suffered during their World War II internment.
**B.** To convince Congress to pass anti-Asian immigration laws.
**C.** To prevent Hawaii from becoming a state.
**D.** To allow Japanese American students to attend American colleges.

____ **7.** The American Indian Movement worked to
**A.** secure citizenship rights for Native Americans.
**B.** gain Native American self-government and to regain traditional Native American lands.
**C.** convince Native American children to accept white culture.
**D.** sell Native American lands to large industries.

____ **8.** The counterculture of the 1960s valued and promoted
**A.** corporate and business influence.
**B.** personal freedom and individuality.
**C.** beautifying America.
**D.** classical music.

____ **9.** In *Silent Spring,* Rachel Carson warned Americans of the dangers of
**A.** chemical pesticides.
**B.** nuclear power.
**C.** unsafe automobiles.
**D.** strong environmental laws.

____ **10.** The consumer movement of the 1960s was spearheaded by
**A.** passage of the Clean Water Act.
**B.** Ralph Nader's campaign to improve auto safety.
**C.** the government's effort to enforce environmental laws.
**D.** the falling price of food and other products.

CHAPTER 31

# The Vietnam War (1954–1975)

## SECTION 1 THE WAR UNFOLDS

### TEXT SUMMARY

American involvement in Vietnam grew out of the Cold War and fears that Southeast Asia would become dominated by Communist governments. United States' foreign policy subscribed to the **domino theory** that if one nation fell to communism, its neighbors would follow.

THE BIG IDEA

**The United States entered the war in Vietnam with the goal of stopping the spread of communism.**

Following World War II, nationalists in Vietnam, then a French colony, began a war of independence. When their forces, the **Vietminh,** drove the French from northern Vietnam, an international conference met in 1954 and through the **Geneva Accords** divided the nation at the 17th parallel into Communist North Vietnam, led by Ho Chi Minh, and anti-Communist South Vietnam, led by Ngo Dinh Diem.

The legacy of the Vietnam War began when President Eisenhower sent about 675 military advisers to aid South Vietnam in their struggle against North Vietnam. President Kennedy pledged support and sent more advisers. However, he became disillusioned with the Diem government, and in 1963 U.S. military leaders helped organize a coup in South Vietnam. Despite the establishment of a new military government in South Vietnam, North Vietnamese forces, aided by the **Viet Cong,** Communist guerrillas in the South, gained more territory and won over many South Vietnamese who had no confidence in their new government.

Communist advances alarmed President Lyndon Johnson. In 1964 he announced that North Vietnamese forces had attacked U.S. ships off the coast of North Vietnam. Although reports of an attack were sketchy, he persuaded Congress to pass the **Gulf of Tonkin Resolution,** giving him power to take whatever action he deemed necessary to prevent aggression against U.S. forces in Vietnam without an official declaration of war. Johnson had expanded presidential power and gained total control over U.S. involvement in Vietnam.

### GRAPHIC SUMMARY: *The United States in Vietnam, 1960–1964*

During the early 1960s the American military slowly expanded its involvement in the Vietnam War.

| | |
|---|---|
| 1960 | President Eisenhower sends 675 United States military advisers to assist South Vietnam. |
| 1963 | President Kennedy increases number of military advisers to over 16,000. |
| 1964 | Congress passes Gulf of Tonkin Resolution, giving President Johnson power to expand American involvement in the war. |

### REVIEW QUESTIONS

**1.** What was the domino theory?

**2. Chart Skills** What power did the Gulf of Tonkin resolution give President Johnson?

## SECTION 2 *FIGHTING THE WAR*

### TEXT SUMMARY

Thousands of American soldiers in Vietnam faced hard battlefield conditions. The Viet Cong conducted guerrilla warfare, attacking from jungle hideouts. They had the advantage of knowing the land, and they often had the support of the local population. American soldiers could never be sure who was an enemy or a friend as they struggled with heavy weapons through swamps and rice paddies. Viet Cong booby traps were a constant danger. A soldier could be killed or mangled by stepping on a **land mine,** an explosive device planted in the ground.

Vietnamese civilians, both North and South, also suffered terribly from the war. An air war over the North included **saturation bombing,** as U.S. planes dropped thousands of tons of explosives over wide areas. Many of these bombs threw pieces of thick metal casings in all directions when they exploded. These **fragmentation bombs** were not only used in North Vietnam, but also killed countless civilians in South Vietnam. The United States also used chemical warfare, dropping **Agent Orange,** a herbicide, and **napalm,** a jellylike substance that burned uncontrollably, from planes.

As the war intensified, the Viet Cong expanded within South Vietnam, using the **Ho Chi Minh Trail,** a supply route through Laos and Cambodia. In response, American soldiers and supplies were poured into South Vietnam, causing divisions to appear in the United States. Those called **hawks** supported the war, while **doves** criticized the **escalation,** or expansion, of the conflict.

In 1968 the North Vietnamese army and the Viet Cong launched a massive attack on cities and military bases across the South. Called the **Tet Offensive,** the campaign was a major turning point in the war. North Vietnamese forces were turned back, but they had won a psychological victory. They had shown unprecedented brutality toward civilians, causing similar reactions in the actions of the U.S. troops, culminating in events like the massacre at My Lai village. This caused dissent at home, and President Johnson's popularity plunged.

**THE BIG IDEA**

**Both soldiers and civilians suffered from the brutal fighting in Vietnam.**

### GRAPHIC SUMMARY: *Vietnam, 1968*

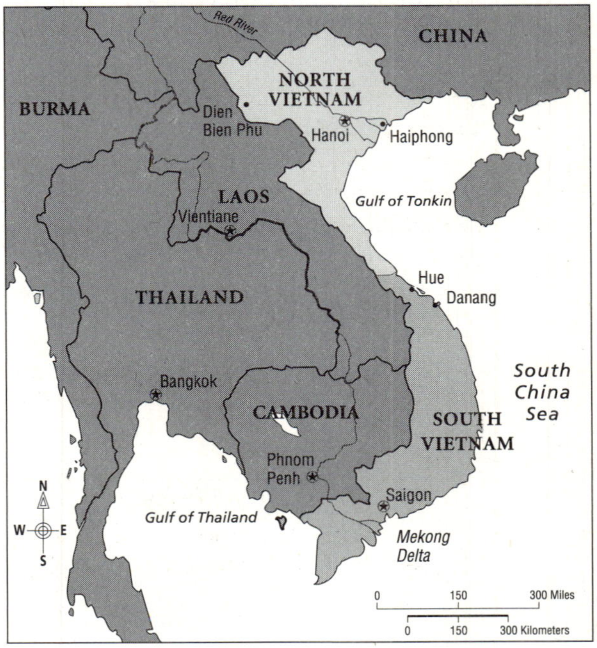


### REVIEW QUESTIONS

1. What advantages did the Viet Cong soldiers have?
2. **Map Skills** What country bordered North Vietnam to the north?

SECTION 3

# POLITICAL DIVISIONS

## TEXT SUMMARY

In the 1960s opposing political viewpoints created divisions in American society, mostly over the Vietnam War. Many young people rebelled against their elders' values, widening the **generation gap.**

Student activists called for radical changes, and their efforts were a major influence on a new political movement known as the **New Left.** The New Left was antiwar and demanded radical change to poverty and racism. Some university teachers protested the Vietnam War through methods such as **teach-ins,** holding separate classes to discuss the war. Other protests came from those who resisted the military draft. Protests and demonstrations erupted as American casualties mounted in Vietnam.

**THE BIG IDEA**

**The Vietnam War created deep divisions in the Democratic Party and in the nation as a whole.**

The war had political effects as well. It split the Democratic party. As the 1968 presidential elections approached, antiwar candidates like Robert Kennedy and Senator Eugene McCarthy opposed President Johnson's policies. Johnson's popularity plummeted, and he chose not to run for reelection. At the Democratic National Convention in 1968, conflict broke out among delegates, and violence erupted in the streets as antiwar protesters faced police clubs.

Vice President Hubert Humphrey became the Democratic candidate, facing Republican candidate Richard Nixon. Although many disillusioned Democrats stayed away from the polls, the 1968 election was close. Nixon's win signaled a political shift toward republicanism and reflected the desire of mainstream Americans, sometimes called **Middle America,** for stability.

## GRAPHIC SUMMARY: *Public Opinion of the Vietnam War*

Americans were asked, "Do you approve of the way President Johnson is handling the situation in Vietnam?"

| | Approve | Disapprove | No opinion |
|---|---|---|---|
| December 1965 | 56% | 26% | 18% |
| May 1966 | 41% | 37% | 22% |
| April 1967 | 43% | 42% | 15% |
| July 1967 | 33% | 54% | 15% |
| February 1968 | 35% | 50% | 15% |

The student protest movement reflected growing opposition to the war in Vietnam.

## REVIEW QUESTIONS

1. What were the goals of the New Left?
2. **Chart Skills** On what date did over 50 percent of the public say they disapproved of President Johnson's handling of the Vietnam War?

# SECTION 4 THE END OF THE WAR

## TEXT SUMMARY

President Johnson had proposed a peace plan for Vietnam, but the **Paris peace talks** of 1968 failed to reach a settlement. Once in office, President Nixon initiated a new policy, **Vietnamization,** to withdraw American forces from Vietnam and replace them with South Vietnamese soldiers. Nixon also intensified bombing and expanded the war into Cambodia, causing new waves of protest.

Nixon called for law and order, appealing to those he called the **silent majority,** those who opposed antiwar protesters and radical change. In 1970 tensions came to a head between antiwar activists and law-and-order supporters with violent clashes on college campuses. Americans were horrified when four students were killed and nine wounded at Kent State, and when two were killed and eleven wounded at Jackson State, by National Guardsmen.

The Vietnam War dragged on until 1973, when the United States agreed to withdraw its troops and leave Vietnam still divided. The Vietnamese continued to fight, however, until South Vietnam fell to North Vietnamese forces in 1975.

The Vietnam War was the longest and least successful of any American war, with 58,000 Americans killed and 300,000 wounded. **POWs,** prisoners of war, and **MIAs,** missing in action, accounted for more than 2,500 Americans lost. The cost to the Vietnamese and Cambodians was even worse. Millions of Vietnamese were killed and vast stretches of territory scarred for years to come. In Cambodia the Khmer Rouge, a force of Communists led by fanatical leader Pol Pot, declared war on their own people, killing up to a fourth of the population.

In 1979 Vietnam veterans decided to create a memorial in Washington, D.C. They held a design contest, and college student Maya Ying Lin won with her simple, long wall of black granite set into a hillside and inscribed with the names of all the people who had died.

**THE BIG IDEA**

**American forces withdrew from Vietnam in 1973. In 1975 North Vietnam defeated South Vietnam.**

## GRAPHIC SUMMARY: *The United States in Vietnam, 1968–1975*

| | |
|---|---|
| **1968** | United States and North Vietnam begin peace talks in Paris, France. |
| **1969** | President Nixon begins withdrawing American troops from Vietnam. |
| **1970** | United States troops invade Cambodia to clear out Communist camps there. |
| **1972** | North Vietnam launches major attack on the South. Nixon orders massive bombing campaign of North Vietnam. |
| **1973** | United States agrees to withdraw its troops from Vietnam. |
| **1975** | Last American officials rush to leave Vietnam as North Vietnam completes its conquest of South Vietnam. |

**The United States failed in its goal of stopping the Communists from taking over South Vietnam.**

## REVIEW QUESTIONS

**1.** What was Vietnamization?

**2. Chart Skills** In what year did United States troops invade Cambodia?

Name ______________________ Class ______________ Date ________

# CHAPTER 31 Test

## IDENTIFYING MAIN IDEAS

Write the letter of the correct answer in the blank provided. (10 points each)

____ **1.** In 1954 Ho Chi Minh became the
**A.** pro-American leader of South Vietnam.
**B.** emperor of Vietnam.
**C.** military leader of the Viet Cong.
**D.** Communist leader of North Vietnam.

____ **2.** President Kennedy's goal in Vietnam was to
**A.** help North Vietnam win the war.
**B.** prevent the Communists from defeating South Vietnam.
**C.** stop France from colonizing Vietnam.
**D.** keep the American military out of the war.

____ **3.** When Lyndon Johnson became President he quickly began to
**A.** increase the number of American troops in Vietnam.
**B.** negotiate for peace with North Vietnam.
**C.** withdraw American forces from Vietnam.
**D.** end American bombing of North Vietnam.

____ **4.** American soldiers in Vietnam had to deal with
**A.** a lack of training.
**B.** surprise attacks and guerrilla warfare.
**C.** poor military equipment.
**D.** working side by side with Communists.

____ **5.** In fighting the North Vietnamese, the American military used
**A.** nuclear weapons.
**B.** traps and land mines.
**C.** bombs and chemical weapons.
**D.** germ warfare.

____ **6.** In what became known as the My Lai massacre,
**A.** American troops killed Vietnamese villagers.
**B.** Ho Chi Minh was assassinated.
**C.** The North Vietnamese capital of Hanoi was bombed.
**D.** Viet Cong soldiers killed American prisoners.

____ **7.** What role did student activists play in the antiwar effort?
**A.** They refused to participate.
**B.** They helped lead the protest movement.
**C.** They marched in favor of the draft.
**D.** They focused on other civil rights issues.

____ **8.** Many mainstream Americans opposed youth activism because they thought it
**A.** was old-fashioned.
**B.** promoted violence.
**C.** threatened traditional values.
**D.** would support drug use.

____ **9.** As Nixon withdrew American troops from Vietnam, he also
**A.** sent troops into China.
**B.** declared a cease-fire.
**C.** expanded the war into Cambodia.
**D.** stopped bombing North Vietnam.

____ **10.** The Vietnam War ended when
**A.** South Vietnam defeated North Vietnam.
**B.** the United States captured most of North Vietnam.
**C.** North Vietnam defeated South Vietnam.
**D.** American troops began withdrawing.

# Nixon, Ford, Carter (1969–1981)

CHAPTER 32

## SECTION 1 Nixon's Domestic Policy

### TEXT SUMMARY

Richard Nixon entered the presidency in 1969 determined to confront the antiwar movement, the government bureaucracy, the press, and his political opponents.

On domestic issues, Nixon attempted to halt inflation and control federal spending. It was difficult, and he turned to **deficit spending,** spending more money in a year than the government takes in through revenues, to help the economy. In another attempt to control inflation, Nixon froze wages and prices, but this caused inflation to soar when an energy crisis and a war in the Middle East resulted in the **Organization of Petroleum Exporting Countries (OPEC)** placing an **embargo,** or ban, on oil to the United States. This raised foreign oil prices, resulting in a recession.

Nixon called for a new partnership between the federal government and the state governments, known as **New Federalism.** Under this policy, states would take more responsibility, using revenues from the federal government as they wished.

To win votes of southern white Democrats, Nixon embarked on a "southern strategy," slowing down advances in African American voting rights and opposing busing. Nixon also appointed four new justices to the Supreme Court, each reflecting his conservative views.

**THE BIG IDEA**

**President Nixon worked to lead the country in a new direction and develop a conservative approach to domestic issues.**

### GRAPHIC SUMMARY: *Nixon's Domestic Policies*

Nixon's Policies

- Try to slow inflation
- Decrease support for Great Society social programs
- Strengthen law and order, discourage protests
- Move slowly on civil rights, appoint conservative justices to Supreme Court

Nixon sought to lead the United States in a more conservative direction.

### REVIEW QUESTIONS

1. What was New Federalism?
2. **Diagram Skills** Identify two of Nixon's domestic policies.

# SECTION 2 *NIXON'S FOREIGN POLICY*

## TEXT SUMMARY

President Nixon's greatest achievements took place in the area of foreign policy. Together with National Security Adviser and later Secretary of State Henry Kissinger, Nixon changed the direction of American foreign policy. Kissinger was Nixon's most trusted and influential adviser, and the President followed Kissinger's policy of ***realpolitik,*** in which a nation makes decisions based on maintaining its own strength rather than following moral principles.

**THE BIG IDEA**

**President Nixon's foreign policy led to improved relations with the Soviet Union and China.**

Nixon embarked on a policy of **détente** with both China and the Soviet Union, relaxing tensions between the United States and these two nations. Nixon took a realistic approach, understanding that China's Communist government was not going to disappear. He also believed that friendlier U.S. relations with China could be a bargaining chip in negotiating with the Soviet Union. In February 1972 Nixon took a trip to China to meet with leaders and discussed ways of solving international problems. He was the first United States President to ever travel to China, and his trip would lead to future diplomatic relations with China.

Nixon's next foreign visit was to the Soviet Union, where he and Soviet premier Leonid Brezhnev agreed to work together to explore space, ease trade limitations between the two nations, and conclude a weapons pact. Viewing arms control as vital, the United States and the Soviet Union began negotiating the Strategic Arms Limitation Treaty, **SALT I,** which froze intercontinental ballistic missiles at the 1972 level. The treaty was a triumph for Nixon, showing that arms control treaties were possible and paving the way for future progress.

## GRAPHIC SUMMARY: *Opening Relations with China*

In a 1970 report to Congress, Nixon states that "The Chinese are a great and vital people who should not remain isolated..."

↓

In January and February 1970 American and Chinese ambassadors meet in Poland.

↓

In March 1971 the United States government ends its ban on travel to China.

↓

In June 1971 the United States ends its 21-year embargo on trade with China.

↓

In February 1972 Nixon travels to China and receives a warm welcome from Chinese leaders.

**Nixon eased Cold War tensions by improving relations with China.**

## REVIEW QUESTIONS

1. What important agreement did the Soviet Union and the United States make in 1972?
2. **Diagram Skills** What American policies did Nixon end as part of his process of improving relations with China?

SECTION 3

# The Watergate Scandal

## TEXT SUMMARY

During his presidency, Nixon was determined to battle his political enemies, a stance that led to a number of unethical and illegal acts. In addition to compiling an "enemies list," Nixon instituted **wiretaps,** listening devices, on the phones of some of his staff as well as reporters suspected of leaking information. Although legal at the time, the wiretaps led to illegal wiretaps for political purposes.

During Nixon's reelection campaign of 1972, further illegal acts erupted into the **Watergate scandal,** when five men were caught trying to wiretap phones in the headquarters of the Democratic National Committee at the Watergate apartment complex in Washington, D.C. Nixon did not plan the break-in, but he tried to cover it up. As more details began emerging, Nixon denied any involvement, but the Senate began televised public hearings. As millions watched, Nixon aides testified that the President knew about the Watergate break-in and tried to cover it up. Aides also testified that Nixon kept audiotapes of all of his conversations and phone calls in the Oval Office that could provide critical evidence.

Nixon agreed to appoint a **special prosecutor,** one who works for the Justice Department but leads an independent investigation, to investigate the charges. When the prosecutor asked for the tapes, Nixon refused and fired him. The President's action led to congressional hearings to **impeach** him, charging him with misconduct in office.

Nixon finally delivered the tapes, which clearly showed his involvement, and Congress proceeded with the impeachment process to remove him from office. The outcome seemed clear, and on August 9, 1974, Richard Nixon resigned, the first President to ever do so.

**THE BIG IDEA**

**As a result of the Watergate scandal, President Nixon resigned from office in August 1974.**

## GRAPHIC SUMMARY: *Watergate Time Line*

1972 | 1973 | 1974

- **June 1972** Five men arrested breaking into Democratic National Committee headquarters.
- **April 1973** Nixon denies knowledge of break-in.
- **May 1973** Senate committee begins hearings.
- **June 1973** Former Nixon aide John Dean tells committee Nixon approved the cover-up.
- **August 1974** Nixon forced to release tapes of White House conversations which prove his role in cover-up.
- **August 1974** Nixon resigns.

**More than two years after the Watergate break-in, Nixon became the first American President to resign from office.**

## REVIEW QUESTIONS

1. What action marked the beginning of the Watergate scandal?
2. **Time Line Skills** What former Nixon aide testified that Nixon had approved the cover-up?

# SECTION 4 *THE FORD ADMINISTRATION*

## TEXT SUMMARY

**THE BIG IDEA**

**As President, Gerald Ford faced economic difficulties and the lasting effects of the Watergate scandal.**

Taking over as President when Nixon resigned, Gerald Ford faced the effects of the Watergate scandal and an economy in trouble. One of his first acts was to pardon Nixon for any crimes, an action that brought instant criticism from many sides, and Ford lost a great deal of his popularity. Many felt it was unfair for Nixon to escape punishment when many of his advisers and aides went to prison.

Economically, Ford had to deal with a recession. Both inflation and unemployment had soared in the early 1970s, causing **stagflation,** a stalled economy. Favoring limited government, Ford hesitated to take direct action, but he was finally forced to support tax cuts and more federal spending to try to improve the economy. Ford was also often at odds with a Democratic Congress, which consistently overrode his vetoes of programs for housing, education, and health care.

In foreign affairs, Ford followed Nixon's policy of détente. He continued improved relations with China and developed relationships with several newly independent African nations. However, his power in Southeast Asia was limited by the **War Powers Act,** which Congress had passed to curtail the power of the President to involve the United States in foreign conflicts. When he asked for aid for South Vietnam, Congress refused, and in 1975 South Vietnam finally fell to North Vietnam.

On the European front, Ford signed the **Helsinki Accords,** agreements with 30 European nations, Canada, and the Soviet Union to cooperate economically and promote human rights. He also continued the SALT talks with the Soviet Union to limit nuclear weapons.

Near the end of Ford's term, the nation celebrated its **bicentennial,** or 200th birthday, and the festivities seemed to revive the nation's sense of optimism.

## GRAPHIC SUMMARY: *The War Powers Act*

**After the Vietnam War, Congress decided to limit the President's power to send American troops overseas.**

**Passed over President Nixon's veto in 1973, the War Powers Act gave Congress more power in dealing with international conflicts.**

- The President can send troops overseas, but must inform Congress within 48 hours.
- Troops may not stay overseas more than 60 days without approval of Congress.
- Congress has the power to force the President to bring the troops home.

## REVIEW QUESTIONS

**1.** Why did the public see Ford's pardoning of Nixon as unfair?

**2. Diagram Skills** According to the War Powers Act, how long can American troops stay overseas without the approval of Congress?

# *The Carter Administration*

SECTION 5

## TEXT SUMMARY

Even though President Ford was the **incumbent,** the current office holder, he was defeated by Democrat Jimmy Carter, the former governor of Georgia, in 1976. A newcomer to national politics, Carter was also a deeply religious man. Once in office, his lack of experience in national politics caused him trouble with Congress and often with his own party.

To improve the economy, Carter supported deficit spending, which angered Congress. When inflation still rose, he cut spending on social programs, which cost him Democratic support. He had more success with **deregulation,** the removal of government controls on certain industries to stimulate the economy.

Deeply concerned with civil rights, Carter promoted many African Americans to government posts. (**Affirmative action,** policies that increase job and education opportunities for minorities, was, however, set back by the *Bakke* decision in 1978.) Carter granted **amnesty,** a general pardon, to those who had evaded the Vietnam War draft.

Human rights were a cornerstone of Carter's foreign policy. In 1978 he acted as peacemaker between Israel and Egypt with the **Camp David Accords.** Carter promoted détente with the Soviet Union, but his support of **dissidents,** Soviet activists who criticized their government, undermined this.

Carter concluded a SALT II treaty with the Soviet Union, but he withdrew it and enacted a boycott of the 1980 Moscow Olympics after they invaded Afghanistan.

Carter's most serious foreign policy crisis occurred in 1979 when 52 Americans at the U.S. embassy in Iran were seized and held for more than a year. The Iran hostage crisis and rising inflation lost Carter the 1980 election to Republican Ronald Reagan.

**THE BIG IDEA**

**Democrat Jimmy Carter won the 1976 presidential election by stressing trust and honesty.**

## GRAPHIC SUMMARY: *Presidential Election of 1976*

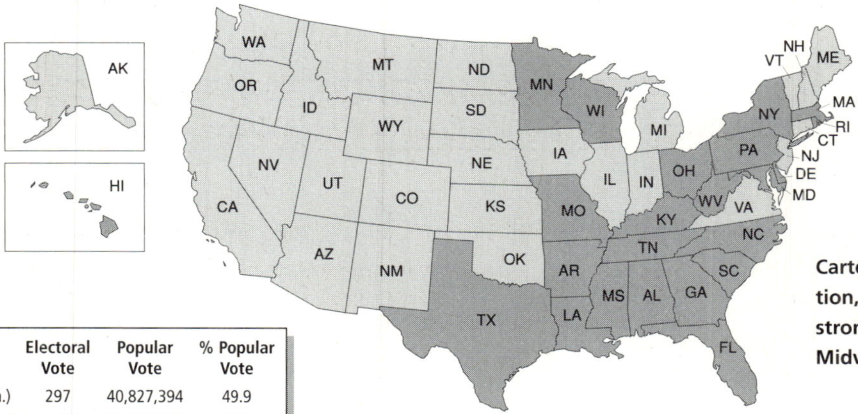


Carter won a close election, in spite of Ford's strong support in the Midwest and West.

| Candidate/Party | Electoral Vote | Popular Vote | % Popular Vote |
|---|---|---|---|
| Jimmy Carter (Dem.) | 297 | 40,827,394 | 49.9 |
| Gerald R. Ford (Rep.) | 240 | 39,145,977 | 47.9 |

## REVIEW QUESTIONS

1. How did Carter support human rights in his foreign policy?

2. **Map Skills** Which candidate won more votes in the South?

Name ______________________ Class ______________ Date __________

# CHAPTER 32 Test

## IDENTIFYING MAIN IDEAS

Write the letter of the correct answer in the blank provided. (10 points each)

____ **1.** Which of the following best describes Richard Nixon's policy concerning the federal government and the states?
**A.** deficit spending
**B.** New Federalism
**C.** wage and price controls
**D.** Keynesian economics

____ **2.** Nixon's ideas about advancing civil rights were reflected in his
**A.** appointments of advisers.
**B.** appeals to black voters.
**C.** cut backs in social programs.
**D.** southern strategy.

____ **3.** To improve relations with China and the Soviet Union, Nixon followed the policy of
**A.** *realpolitik*.
**B.** confrontation.
**C.** détente.
**D.** lifting all trade barriers.

____ **4.** The purpose of the SALT I treaty with the Soviet Union was to
**A.** limit nuclear weapons.
**B.** join in exploring space.
**C.** increase trade.
**D.** build new submarines.

____ **5.** The Watergate scandal developed into a crisis for Nixon when he
**A.** made up an enemies list.
**B.** installed wiretaps.
**C.** tried to cover up his involvement.
**D.** dismissed his advisers.

____ **6.** Because of the Watergate scandal, Nixon became the first American President to
**A.** be impeached.
**B.** resign from office.
**C.** appoint a special prosecutor.
**D.** disobey a Supreme Court ruling.

____ **7.** When Gerald Ford became President, the U.S. economy was
**A.** in a recession.
**B.** growing slowly.
**C.** growing rapidly.
**D.** stable.

____ **8.** President Ford and Congress were often in conflict because Ford
**A.** refused to balance the budget.
**B.** favored limited government while Congress supported a more active government.
**C.** favored an active government while Congress wanted a limited government.
**D.** raised taxes over Congress's objections.

____ **9.** President Jimmy Carter had trouble dealing with Congress because he was
**A.** dishonest.
**B.** highly skilled.
**C.** politically inexperienced.
**D.** too open and honest.

____ **10.** One of Carter's great foreign policy successes was helping to negotiate peace between
**A.** the Soviet Union and Afghanistan.
**B.** Israel and Egypt.
**C.** China and the Soviet Union.
**D.** the United States and Cuba.

# The Conservative Revolution (1980–1992)

CHAPTER 33

## SECTION 1 Roots of the New Conservatism

### TEXT SUMMARY

Ronald Reagan's election as President in 1980 marked a major shift in American politics. Reagan's idea that government was simply too big reflected the growing popularity of conservative beliefs among many Americans. Reagan, once a Democrat, had now joined the Republican party, and as a spokesman for business, he attacked communism and praised the capitalist system. He won national political recognition for his conservative policies as governor of California in the 1960s.

For decades conservatives had opposed New Deal social programs, and during the turbulent 1960s and 1970s were troubled by the cultural changes. When Richard Nixon became President, he wanted to trim social programs, but in fact, the government grew in size with further programs to protect the environment and regulate conditions in the workplace.

By 1980, however, conservatives had formed a powerful political coalition called the **New Right.** This coalition was determined to decrease the size of government by cutting government-funded social programs. A subset of this coalition, the Moral Majority, was led by evangelists who used the format of **televangelism** to appeal to viewers to contribute money to the New Right. In the 1980 presidential election, Ronald Reagan won by a landslide, and Republicans gained control of the Senate for the first time in 25 years. Conservatives now controlled the nation's agenda.

**THE BIG IDEA**

**Ronald Reagan's rise to the presidency reflected a growing belief that government had grown too large.**

### GRAPHIC SUMMARY: *The Rise of Conservatism*

| | |
|---|---|
| 1934 | • American Liberty League established in opposition to New Deal. |
| 1952 | • Dwight Eisenhower elected President, begins eight years of Republican rule. |
| 1964 | • Senator Barry Goldwater runs for President on conservative platform, loses to Lyndon Johnson. |
| 1968 | • Richard Nixon wins the presidency, bringing Republicans back into power. |
| 1970s | • Conservative groups form the New Right, a powerful political coalition. |
| 1980 | • Ronald Reagan elected President, brings conservative policies to the White House. |

Support for conservative ideas grew, leading to the election of Ronald Reagan as President.

### REVIEW QUESTIONS

1. Summarize the beliefs of the New Right.
2. **Chart Skills** What year was Reagan elected President?

# SECTION 2 THE REAGAN REVOLUTION

## TEXT SUMMARY

President Reagan's overall goals were to restore America's strength, reshape the federal government, and bring prosperity to the nation. He began with a program to spur economic growth through **supply-side economics,** a policy that focused on cutting taxes and putting more money into the hands of businesses, which would then hire more people and produce more goods, making the economy grow faster.

### THE BIG IDEA

**Under President Reagan, the government lowered taxes, cut spending on social programs, and increased military spending.**

To limit both the size and role of the federal government, Reagan began to eliminate government regulations that he believed stifled business growth. He also challenged the power of labor unions. Believing that government intruded too much into people's lives, Reagan cut back the role of the federal government in public programs. He promoted a policy called the **New Federalism,** which gave more responsibility to state and local governments to create and pay for social programs. New Federalism did not work as planned, however, because the state and local governments, while having more responsibility, did not have enough money to continue most of the programs previously funded by the federal government.

Reagan also began a military buildup to defend American interests in the Cold War, announcing a **Strategic Defense Initiative (SDI)** that would provide a missile shield in space to counter any Soviet aggression. The President also fought terrorism in the Middle East and communism in Central and South America by aiding anti-Communist forces.

Despite a deep recession, high inflation and unemployment, and an increase in the federal deficit in Reagan's first two years in office, the conservative movement thrived. Toward the end of Reagan's first term, the economy began to recover, and in 1984 he was reelected.

## GRAPHIC SUMMARY: *Federal Budget Deficit, 1980–1992*

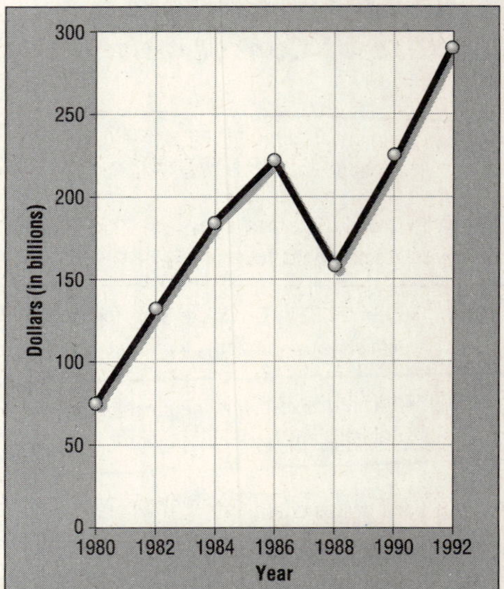

Source: *Statistical Abstract of the United States*

**By the end of the 1980s the United States government was over $3 trillion in debt.**

## REVIEW QUESTIONS

1. Describe supply-side economics.
2. **Graph Skills** In what year did the federal budget deficit first exceed $200 billion?

SECTION 3

# Reagan's Second Term

## TEXT SUMMARY

President Reagan's optimism and a recovering economy gave him a landslide victory in the 1984 election. For many Americans it was a time of patriotic renewal as the Olympic games were held in Los Angeles and Americans celebrated the 200th anniversary of the Constitution in 1987.

Social debates continued, however. Although African Americans were gaining more influence and higher political offices, resistance to civil rights initiatives grew. The nation became polarized as the extension of women's and homosexuals' rights were hotly debated. Many of these issues ended up in the Supreme Court, where conservative justices, appointed by Reagan, ruled in favor of the status quo. However, Reagan did appoint the first woman to the Supreme Court, Sandra Day O'Connor.

Prosperity around the nation was uneven. Farmers suffered from falling prices and industries shifted away from manufacturing, causing unemployment and factory closings. Wealth was also unevenly distributed, and the wealthy grew richer under Reagan's economic policies.

Ronald Reagan took a hands-off policy as a leader, delegating much of his authority to those who worked for him. When scandals erupted over corruption in some Savings and Loan banks, and some government officials committed illegal activities and secret dealings in the **Iran-Contra affair,** the President's reputation remained unscathed.

Reagan improved relations with the Soviet Union, signing the **INF Treaty** in 1987. This treaty provided for the destruction of about 2,500 Soviet and American missiles in Europe.

Reagan's presidency is marked by his emphasis on restoring national pride and his own charismatic personality. He made Americans feel confident in the United States for the first time in decades.

**THE BIG IDEA**

**During his second term, Reagan remained popular and the economy grew, though not everyone shared in the prosperity.**

## GRAPHIC SUMMARY: *The Savings and Loan Scandal of the 1980s*

Savings and loan banks, or S & Ls, make loans to individuals

↓

Reagan administration deregulates S & Ls, allowing them to make riskier investments

↓

Officials at some S & Ls take advantage of new laws by making risky real estate investments, hoping for huge profits

↓

Real estate markets cool down in late 1980s, S & Ls lose $2.6 billion from people's savings accounts

↓

Because bank accounts are insured by the government, taxpayers have to make up for the billions of dollars lost

↓

Several S & L officials are prosecuted for their role in the scandal and their efforts to cover it up

**Reagan's hands-off approach led to several problems, including the S & L scandal.**

## REVIEW QUESTIONS

1. What did the INF Treaty do?

2. **Diagram Skills** When the S & Ls lost billions of dollars, who had to make up for the lost money?

SECTION 4

# The George H. W. Bush Presidency

## TEXT SUMMARY

The 1988 election brought Vice President George H. W. Bush into the White House. Bush promised "no new taxes" in his 1988 campaign and had served as a loyal Vice President, but he failed to gain Reagan's widespread popular support.

**THE BIG IDEA**

**As President, George Bush won major foreign policy victories, but was unsuccessful in dealing with domestic issues.**

Bush did, however, achieve successes in foreign policy, benefiting from tremendous changes in the Communist world. During his presidency the Cold War ended and Soviet Bloc countries revolted against Communist rule. In Germany, East German residents destroyed the Berlin Wall, and Germany was reunited in 1990. As the Soviet Union began breaking up, Bush negotiated a **Strategic Arms Reduction Treaty** with the new Soviet leader, Boris Yeltsin, drastically reducing long-range nuclear missile stockpiles. When a movement for democratic reforms broke out in China's Tiananmen Square and was harshly suppressed, Bush was nonconfrontational. Valuing trade with China, he preferred to negotiate quietly rather than cause an international incident. This action angered the American public.

Bush did, however, exhibit strong leadership in the Middle East. When diplomatic efforts failed to persuade Iraq to withdraw from Kuwait, America's ally, Bush launched the **Persian Gulf War.** With massive air strikes, U.S. forces, in conjunction with UN forces, liberated Kuwait in just 42 days.

President Bush's foreign policy was applauded, but he raised taxes and infuriated many. This broken promise, combined with a recession and business **downsizing** in the early 1990s, made it unlikely Bush would be elected for a second term.

## GRAPHIC SUMMARY: *The End of the Cold War*

- Anti-Communist movements gain force in Eastern Europe
- Soviet leader Mikhail Gorbachev encourages Eastern European leaders to adopt more open policies

→

- Reform leaders come to power after free elections in Poland and Czechoslovakia
- New governments take charge in Bulgaria, Hungary, Romania, and Albania
- Berlin Wall falls, East and West Germany are reunified
- Soviet Union breaks apart

**By 1991 the Soviet empire had crumbled, leaving the United States as the world's only superpower.**

## REVIEW QUESTIONS

1. What promise did George Bush make during his 1988 presidential campaign?
2. **Diagram Skills** Who was the leader of the Soviet Union when the Cold War ended?

Name ______________________ Class ______________ Date ________

# CHAPTER 33 *Test*

## IDENTIFYING MAIN IDEAS

Write the letter of the correct answer in the blank provided. (10 points each)

____ **1.** During the 1960s conservatives opposed
- **A.** the large social programs funded by the federal government.
- **B.** tax cuts.
- **C.** anti-Communist campaigns in the United States.
- **D.** the New Deal.

____ **2.** In 1980 conservative groups joined to form the
- **A.** American Liberty League.
- **B.** New Right.
- **C.** New Left.
- **D.** Committee to Reelect the President.

____ **3.** Which best describes the outcome of the 1980 presidential election?
- **A.** Carter defeated Reagan by a large margin.
- **B.** Carter defeated Reagan by a slim margin.
- **C.** Reagan defeated Carter by a large margin.
- **D.** Reagan defeated Carter by a slim margin.

____ **4.** Reagan hoped to encourage economic growth by
- **A.** lowering the national debt.
- **B.** cutting defense spending.
- **C.** increasing funding for social programs.
- **D.** cutting taxes.

____ **5.** Reagan's policy toward Central and South America called for
- **A.** supporting human rights.
- **B.** sending military aid to anti-Communist governments.
- **C.** establishing diplomatic relations with Cuba.
- **D.** placing nuclear missiles in Central America.

____ **6.** During the Reagan administration, the national debt
- **A.** disappeared.
- **B.** rose sharply.
- **C.** fell slowly.
- **D.** remained approximately the same.

____ **7.** Reagan appointed Sandra Day O'Connor as the first female
- **A.** Secretary of State.
- **B.** Ambassador to France.
- **C.** Supreme Court justice.
- **D.** Vice President.

____ **8.** During Reagan's second term, American relations with the Soviet Union
- **A.** improved.
- **B.** led to war in Europe.
- **C.** grew more tense.
- **D.** remained cold.

____ **9.** In the late 1980s and early 1990s, the Cold War
- **A.** spread in Africa and Asia.
- **B.** led to the building of the Berlin Wall.
- **C.** ended with the collapse of communism in Europe.
- **D.** ended, leaving the Soviet Union as the world's most powerful nation.

____ **10.** President Bush angered many Americans when he broke his promise not to
- **A.** create new taxes.
- **B.** support deregulation.
- **C.** protect the environment.
- **D.** run for reelection.

CHAPTER 34

# Entering a New Era (1992 to the Present)

## SECTION 1 Politics in Recent Years

### TEXT SUMMARY

When Democrat Bill Clinton won the White House in 1992, he proposed a far-reaching government health care plan. But opposition in Congress doomed the health plan.

**THE BIG IDEA**

**Voters elected Bill Clinton President in 1992 and 1996. The economy improved, but Clinton faced growing charges of scandal during his second term.**

Clinton did reduce the federal budget, but in 1994 Republicans endorsed a **Contract with America,** pledging to balance the budget, reduce taxes, cut back government, and eliminate many regulations. For a time, the clash shut down the government. Eventually, they compromised on a balanced budget. Clinton also compromised on a welfare-reform program. Near the end of his second term, the economy showed a budget surplus for the first time since 1962.

Clinton's second term was marked by scandal. In the **Whitewater affair,** he was accused of taking part in fraudulent loan schemes in Arkansas and of taking illegal campaign contributions. Another scandal erupted when his inappropriate relationship with a White House intern led to a grand jury investigation and an impeachment trial. Despite all this, the economy continued to grow.

The 2000 election between Vice President Al Gore and Governor George W. Bush was very close and became a battleground over recounting votes. The outcome was decided by the Supreme Court, which gave the election to Bush. The new President focused on a major tax cut and education reform, but other issues were put aside when on September 11, 2001, terrorist attacks on New York City and Washington, D.C., killed thousands of people. The President and the American people now had a new challenge: defeating terrorism.

### GRAPHIC SUMMARY: *Clinton's Path to the Presidency*

**1976** Elected Arkansas Attorney General just three years after graduating from law school.

**1978** Elected governor of Arkansas at age 32.

**1980** Runs for reelection, loses.

**1982** Runs again for governor, wins.

**1992** Runs for President, defeats incumbent George Bush and independent candidate Ross Perot.

1976 | 1978 | 1980 | 1982 | 1984 | 1986 | 1988 | 1990 | 1992

**Bill Clinton achieved political success as a relatively young man.**

### REVIEW QUESTIONS

1. Why did the government shut down in 1995?
2. **Time Line Skills** How old was Bill Clinton when he first become governor of Arkansas?

# SECTION 2 *THE UNITED STATES IN A NEW WORLD*

## TEXT SUMMARY

The 1990s saw historic changes. The Soviet Union collapsed and Eastern European nations' economies rebounded.

In South Africa, **apartheid,** the separation of people of different racial backgrounds, came to an end. By 1994, under Nelson Mandela, South Africa made a peaceful transition to black majority rule. In Northern Ireland, all parties signed the Good Friday Peace Accords, agreeing to major reforms and an end to the fighting. Other nations, however, were still torn by conflict. A lasting peace between Israel and the Palestinians was not achieved, and violence broke out in the Balkans among religious and ethnic minorities.

The United States continued to improve relations with China, but the issue of Chinese control over Taiwan remained a source of conflict.

The continuing growth of global trade and world economy encouraged the nations of Europe to form the European Union (EU) economic unit. The United States supported this and worked to promote greater economic opportunities around the world through the **North American Free Trade Agreement (NAFTA),** which would gradually remove trade restrictions among the United States, Canada, and Mexico. Clinton also expanded U.S. trade through the **World Trade Organization (WTO),** formed to resolve trade disputes and negotiate trade agreements.

Global economics also saw the rise of **multinational corporations,** businesses that operate in more than one nation. Opponents of NAFTA, WTO, and these corporations criticized the control of such groups over the economies of nations.

**THE BIG IDEA**

**After the Cold War ended, the United States worked to promote democracy, end conflicts, and expand international trade.**

## GRAPHIC SUMMARY: *U.S. Foreign Policy After the Cold War*

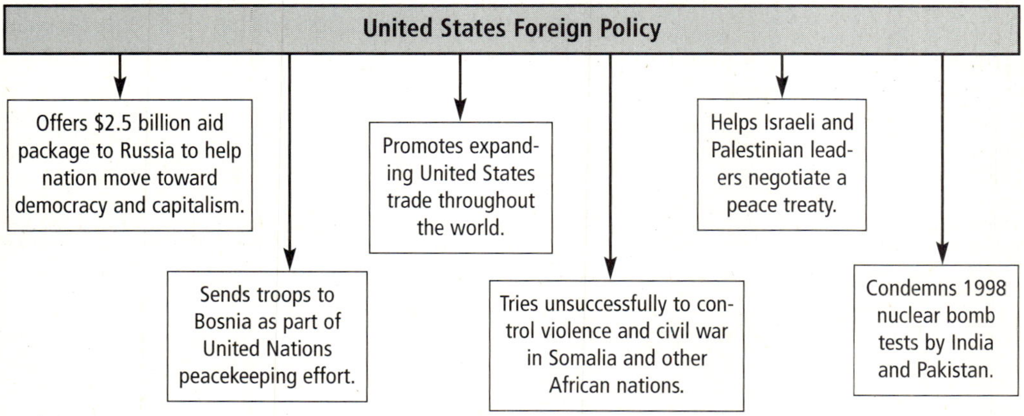


The United States continued to pursue an active foreign policy after the Cold War.

## REVIEW QUESTIONS

1. What major development took place in South Africa in the 1990s?
2. **Diagram Skills** Which two nations tested nuclear bombs in 1998?

# SECTION 3 AMERICANS IN THE NEW MILLENNIUM

## TEXT SUMMARY

**THE BIG IDEA**

**The American population grew older and more diverse during the 1990s.**

In the 1800s and the early 1900s, most immigrants to the United States came from Europe. By the 1990s close to 80 percent of all legal immigrants came from Latin America and Asia. African American populations are growing, and all groups are gaining more political power.

As diversity grows, Americans debate how to deal with the changes. Some Americans fear a breakdown of American society; others argue that immigration gives the nation a prosperous future. One issue concerns **bilingual education,** teaching children in their native language as well as in English. Debate over the validity of affirmative action continues.

Another issue is **multiculturalism,** the movement to give greater attention to non-European cultures in education. Opponents argue that multiculturalism emphasizes differences rather than shared values. Supporters believe that attention should be paid to the contributions of many different groups.

An aging population presents challenges economically, putting pressure on health-care programs and social security as older people begin entering retirement age.

The technological revolution of the late 20th century created a new information age. Computers continue to link people around the world via the **Internet,** a worldwide information network. This new technology is changing the face of government, business, education, foreign affairs, and daily life. These changes have occurred quickly, and bring advances and progress as well as challenges. Americans must commit themselves to maintaining and preserving freedom by working to understand and participate in the events that surround them.

## GRAPHIC SUMMARY: *Diversity in the United States*

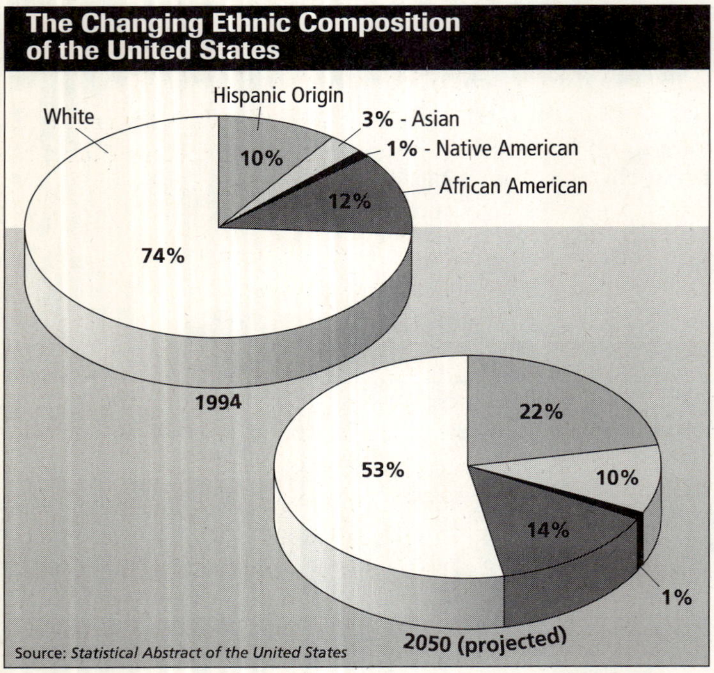


The United States will continue to grow more diverse during the twenty-first century.

## REVIEW QUESTIONS

1. What is multiculturalism?
2. **Graph Skills** Which group is expected to grow to 22 percent of the American population by 2050?

Name ____________________ Class ______________ Date ________

# CHAPTER 34 Test

## IDENTIFYING MAIN IDEAS

Write the letter of the correct answer in the blank provided. (10 points each)

____ **1.** To try to reduce the federal budget deficit, Clinton supported
- **A.** eliminating the Social Security program.
- **B.** lowering taxes on the wealthy.
- **C.** increasing government spending.
- **D.** cutting spending and raising taxes.

____ **2.** Clinton won reelection in 1996, helped by
- **A.** his support of the Contract with America.
- **B.** a steadily improving economy.
- **C.** victory in the Persian Gulf War.
- **D.** strong support from Republicans.

____ **3.** Which of these caused problems for Clinton during his second term?
- **A.** economic recession
- **B.** high unemployment
- **C.** scandals
- **D.** huge budget deficits

____ **4.** Who decided the outcome of the 2000 presidential election?
- **A.** the people
- **B.** the candidates
- **C.** the Supreme Court
- **D.** the Senate

____ **5.** In Russia and Eastern Europe during the 1990s, the United States promoted
- **A.** a return to communism.
- **B.** a military build-up.
- **C.** democracy and free enterprise.
- **D.** isolationism.

____ **6.** Which European nation broke apart, leading to ethnic and religious conflicts in the 1990s?
- **A.** Italy.
- **B.** Somalia.
- **C.** Pakistan.
- **D.** Yugoslavia.

____ **7.** The goal of the North American Free Trade Agreement was to
- **A.** increase trade with Europe.
- **B.** block imports from Latin America.
- **C.** eliminate trade barriers between the United States, Canada, and Mexico.
- **D.** raise tariffs on products from Canada and Mexico.

____ **8.** In the 1990s most immigrants to the United States came from
- **A.** Europe and Asia.
- **B.** Africa and Asia.
- **C.** Asia and Latin America.
- **D.** Europe and Latin America.

____ **9.** The movement that calls for greater attention to non-European cultures in such areas as education is called
- **A.** immigration.
- **B.** affirmative action.
- **C.** multiculturalism.
- **D.** nativism.

____ **10.** As the United States approached the twenty-first century, the number of Americans over 65 was
- **A.** growing rapidly.
- **B.** falling slowly.
- **C.** falling rapidly.
- **D.** remaining stable.

# GLOSSARY

## A

**abolitionist movement** the movement to end slavery (p. 48)

**abstinence** refraining from doing something (p. 47)

**Adams-Onís Treaty** the treaty in which Spain ceded Florida to the United States (p. 38)

**administration** term of office (p. 29)

**Affirmative action** a United States policy that seeks to end discrimination by assuring equal opportunities in education and employment (p. 165)

**Agent Orange** a herbicide used in the Vietnam War (p. 157)

**Albany Plan of Union** a union of colonies to help the war effort during the French and Indian War (p. 20)

**alien** noncitizen (p. 79)

**Alien and Sedition Acts** acts that gave the President the power to imprison or deport aliens or to fine or imprison citizens who criticized the government (p. 32)

**Alliance for Progress** Kennedy's program calling on all nations of the Western Hemisphere to work together to satisfy the basic needs of people in North, Central, and South America (p. 149)

**Allies** Britain, France, Russia, and Serbia (p. 98)

**amend** revise (p. 27)

**America First Committee** a group of isolationists that lobbied to block any U.S. aid to Britain (p. 124)

**American Expeditionary Force (AEF)** a special group of men selected to serve in WWI (p. 100)

**American Indian Movement (AIM)** a movement that confronted the federal government over land rights and broken treaties against Native Americans (p. 152)

**American Liberty League** a group that claimed the New Deal programs were un-American and limited individual freedoms (p. 118)

**amnesty** a general pardon (p. 165)

**annex** to join (pp. 53, 88)

**anti-Federalists** people who opposed the U.S. Constitution (p. 28)

**anti-Semitism** discrimination or violent hostility directed at Jews (p. 128)

**apartheid** the separation of people of different racial backgrounds in South Africa (p. 173)

**appeasement** giving in to a competitor's demands in order to keep peace (p. 121)

**apportionment** redrawing state electoral districts to give Americans in urban and rural areas equal power in state legislatures (p. 148)

**apprentices** people placed under legal contract to work for another person in exchange for learning a trade (p. 16)

**armistice** a ceasefire (p. 100)

**arms** race the struggle to gain weapons superiority (p. 135)

**arsenal** place where weapons are stored (p. 55)

**Articles of Confederation** the first set of laws adopted to govern the United States (p. 26)

**assembly line** the process in which each worker does one special task to make production more efficient (p. 109)

**assimilation** the process by which one society becomes part of another (pp. 74, 83)

**autocrat** a ruler with unlimited power (p. 98)

**autonomy** self-government (p. 152)

## B

**baby boom** an increase in the birthrate (p. 137)

**Bacon's Rebellion** an attack on the colonial government of Jamestown (p. 11)

**balance of trade** the difference in value between a country's imports and exports (p. 15)

**bank notes** form of money (p. 41)

**barrios** Spanish-speaking neighborhoods (p. 130)

**barter** trade (p. 5)

**Bataan Death March** the march of prisoners of Japan across the Bataan Peninsula (p. 129)

**Battle of the Alamo** a major victory for Mexico in the Texas War for Independence (p. 39)

**Battle of Antietam** Civil War battle in Maryland in 1862 (p. 58)

**Battle of Bunker Hill** Revolutionary War battle outside of Boston (p. 23)

**Battle of Chancellorsville** a major victory for the South during the Civil War (p. 60)

**Battle of Cold Harbor** third of three brutal Civil War battles in Virginia that forced the Confederate Army to retreat (p. 61)

**Battle of the Coral Sea** battle of WWII where U.S. naval forces prevented Japan from establishing bases from which to attack Australia (p. 129)

**Battle of Fallen Timbers** Native Americans defeated by the American army (p. 34)

**Battle of Fredericksburg** a major victory for the South during the Civil War (p. 60)

**Battle of Gettysburg** the bloodiest battle of the Civil War and a Union victory (p. 60)

**Battle of Guadalcanal** WWII battle where U.S. Marines gained control of the first piece of Japanese-held territory (p. 129)

**Battle of Iwo Jima** WWII battle of extremely high casualties (p. 129)

**Battle of Leyte Gulf** WWII battle where the United States was victorious (p. 129)

**Battle of Little Big Horn** battle between General Custer's troops and the Sioux (p. 74)

**Battle of Midway** turning point in the war in the Pacific (p. 129)

**Battle of New Orleans** fought after the War of 1812 had ended and made Andrew Jackson a hero (p. 35)

**Battle of Okinawa** WWII battle of extremely high casualties (p. 129)

**Battle of Saratoga** turning point in the Revolutionary War (p. 23)

**Battle of Shiloh** an important Union victory in the West during the Civil War (p. 58)

**Battle of Spotsylvania** second of three brutal Civil War battles in Virginia that forced the Confederate Army to retreat (p. 61)

**Battle of Tippecanoe** Native Americans were defeated by the United States Army (p. 34)

**Battle of Trenton** major victory for the Continental Army and Washington during the Revolutionary War (p. 23)

**Battle of the Wilderness** first of three brutal Civil War battles in Virginia that forced the Confederate Army to retreat (p. 61)

**Battle of Yorktown** ended the Revolutionary war; Britain surrendered (p. 24)

**Battles of Lexington and Concord** first battles of the Revolutionary War (p. 21)

**Bay of Pigs** a failed invasion of Cuba in 1961 (p. 149)

**beatniks** a group of artists and writers who tried to shock the mainstream culture (p. 138)

**Berlin Wall** the border between East and West Germany put up by the Soviet Union (p. 149)

**Bessemer Process** an easier and cheaper way of turning iron into steel (p. 68)

**bicentennial** 200th anniversary (p. 164)

**bilingual education** the teaching of children in their native language as well as in English (p. 174)

**Bill of Rights** the first ten amendments to the U.S. Constitution that protect citizens' rights (p. 28)

**bimetallic standard** when money is backed by gold or silver (p. 76)

**black codes** laws in the South restricting the rights of African Americans (p. 64)

**black nationalism** the separate identity and racial unity of African Americans (p. 145)

**black power** a movement that called for African Americans to unite, to recognize their heritage, and to build a sense of community (p. 145)

**Black Tuesday** the day the stock market collapsed (p. 112)

**blacklist** list of names of people who were suspected Communists (p. 133)

***blitzkrieg*** a lightning-quick land and air assault (p. 122)

**blockade** isolation of a nation's city or harbor to prevent trade (p. 24)

**bonanza farms** vast estates devoted to a single cash crop (p. 75)

**Bonus Army** jobless veterans and their families who marched on Washington, D.C., demanding payment of a promised war bonus (p. 115)

**boomers** settlers who ran in land races to claim land upon the 1889 opening of Indian Territory for settlement (p. 74)

**bootlegger** a person who sold alcohol illegally during Prohibition (p. 106)

**Border States** Delaware, Maryland, Kentucky, and Mississippi (p. 56)

**Boston Massacre** a violent encounter between British troops and a Boston crowd in which five colonists were killed (p. 21)

**Boston Tea Party** colonists dressed as Native Americans dumped British tea into the Boston Harbor in protest of the Tea Act (p. 21)

**boycott** a refusal to buy certain goods or use certain services (p. 21)

***braceros*** farm laborers from Mexico (p. 130)

**brinkmanship** going right to the edge of war to protect interests (p. 135)

***Brown* v. *Board of Education of Topeka, Kansas*** Supreme Court ruling that segregation in public schools was unconstitutional (p. 141)

**Bull Moose Party** nickname for the Progressive Party (p. 95)

**bureaucracy** departments and workers that make up the federal government (p. 33)

**business cycle** periods in which a nation's economy grows, then contracts (p. 112)

**buying on margin** when investors buy stock for a fraction of its price and borrow the rest (p. 110)

## C

**Cabinet** officials to head the departments of the executive branch (p. 29)

**Camp David Accords** the framework for peace in the Middle East brought about by President Carter (p. 165)

**carpet bombing** attack in which planes scatter large numbers of bombs over a wide area (p. 127)

**carpetbaggers** white northerners who settled in the South after the Civil War (p. 64)

**cash and carry** a U.S. foreign policy that required warring nations to pay cash for all nonmilitary goods and their transport from the United States (p. 124)

**cash crops** crops planted not for the plantation's use, but to sell for profit (p. 8)

**casualties** persons killed, wounded, or missing in battle (p. 23)

**cede** to give up (p. 38)

**Central Powers** Germany and Austria-Hungary (p. 98)

**centralized** when one place performs all the tasks needed to create a product (p. 41)

**charter** legal document to establish a colony (p. 11)

**checks and balances** a system among the three branches of the government allowing them to check each other so that no one branch gains too much power (p. 27)

**Chinese Exclusion Act** an act prohibiting Chinese laborers from entering the country (p. 79)

**civil disobedience** the nonviolent refusal to obey a law in order to change it (p. 96)

**civil rights** citizens' personal liberties guaranteed by law (p. 64)

**Civil Rights Act of 1964** an act that expanded civil rights by prohibiting discrimination in jobs, schools, and voting (p. 144)

**civil service** jobs in government held by nonelected people (p. 78)

**Civil War** the war between the North and the South over slavery (p. 58)

**Civilian Conservation Corps (CCC)** a New Deal program that paid young men to restore parks and forests (p. 117)

**clans** groups of families descended from a common ancestor (p. 5)

**Clayton Antitrust Act** strengthened the Sherman Antitrust Act by legalizing unions and preventing courts from issuing injunctions against them (p. 95)

**Clean Air Act** an act to control air pollution (p. 154)

**Clean Water Act** an act to control water pollution (p. 154)

**coalition** an alliance of groups with the same goals (p. 119)

**Cold War** the competition for world power and influence between the United States and the Soviet Union (p. 132)

**collaboration** close cooperation (p. 122)

**collective bargaining** a process in which workers negotiate as a group with employers (p. 71)

**colonies** areas settled by immigrants who continue to be ruled by their parent country (p. 10)

**Columbian Exchange** the transatlantic trade through which Europeans exchanged food, goods, and technologies with the people of the Americas (p. 7)

***Common Sense*** pamphlet written by Thomas Paine arguing for independence from Britain (p. 22)

**communism** an economic, social, and political theory that states that the government controls all property, that a single political party controls the government, and that the needs of the country always take priority over the rights of individuals (p. 108)

 

**Compromise of 1850** a compromise that brought California into the United States as a free state and allowed the territories of New Mexico and Utah to decide for themselves whether to become free or slave states (p. 54)

**Compromise of 1877** a compromise in which the Democrats agreed to give the election to Hayes in exchange for the removal of federal troops from the South, officially ending Reconstruction (p. 66)

**compulsory** required (p. 91)

**concession** a grant for a piece of land in exchange for a promise to use that land for a specific purpose (p. 90)

**Confederate States of America** the nation created when the South seceded from the United States (p. 56)

**conglomerates** corporations of smaller unrelated businesses (p. 137)

**congregation** members of a church (p. 37)

**Congress of Racial Equality (CORE)** a group that protested and demonstrated against the segregation of the armed forces using nonviolent techniques (pp. 130, 142)

**Congressional Union (CU)** group formed by women suffragists calling for radical change and staging military protests for a suffrage amendment (p. 96)

**conquistadors** Spanish conquerors (p. 10)

**conservationists** people who work to protect natural resources (p. 95)

**constitution** a plan of government (p. 26)

**Constitutional Convention** where delegates gathered from the states to revise the national government (p. 27)

**consumer economy** an economy that depends on people spending large amounts of money (p. 109)

**containment** U.S. foreign policy that called for the United States to resist Soviet attempts to form Communist governments anywhere else in the world (p. 132)

**Contract with America** a pledge by the Republican Party to balance the budget, reduce taxes, cut back the role of the federal government, and eliminate many government regulations (p. 172)

**convoy** a system in which troop and merchant ships sailed to Europe surrounded by armed warships (p. 100)

**Copperheads** Democrats who protested the Civil War (p. 59)

**cotton belt** area from South Carolina to Texas (p. 43)

**counterculture** youth of the 1960s and 1970s who ran counter to the culture of the time promoting freedom and individuality and challenging the authority of the mainstream (p. 153)

**craft union** a union of skilled workers (p. 71)

**Cross of Gold Speech** the speech given by William Jennings Bryan when he ran for President in 1896 (p. 76)

**Crusades** military campaigns by Christians to take Jerusalem from the Muslims (p. 6)

**Cuban Missile Crisis** the most dangerous event of the Cold War, when the Soviet Union attempted to place nuclear missiles in Cuba, almost leading to a nuclear war with the United States (p. 149)

## D

**Dawes Act** an act that divided reservation lands into plots (p. 74)

**daylight saving time** turning the clocks ahead one hour for the summer (p. 101)

**D-Day** the day the invasion of Western Europe began (p. 127)

***de facto* segregation** racial separation caused by social and economic conditions (p. 145)

***de jure* segregation** racial separation created by law (p. 145)

**death camps** concentration camps where the mass murders of hundreds of Jews across Eastern Europe occurred (p. 128)

**Declaration of Independence** document written by Thomas Jefferson declaring the colonies' independence from Britain (p. 22)

**deficit** spending more money in a year than the government receives in revenues (pp. 118, 161)

**demagogues** leaders who manipulate people by scaring them with half-truths and deceptive programs (p. 118)

**demographics** statistics that describe a population (p. 104)

**denominations** religious subgroups (p. 37)

**department store** a large retail establishment that carries a wide variety of goods (p. 86)

**depression** an economic downturn (p. 35)

**deregulation** the removal of government controls on a certain industry to stimulate the economy (p. 165)

**détente** a relaxing of tensions (p. 162)

**deterrence** making a country so powerful that no enemy would dare attack (p. 135)

**direct primary** election in which citizens, rather than political leaders, choose political candidates (p. 94)

**disarmament** when nations voluntarily give up their weapons (p. 108)

**discrimination** the unequal treatment of a group of people because of their nationality, race, sex, or religion (p. 50)

**dissent** differences of opinion (p. 18)

**dissidents** Soviet activists who criticized their government (p. 165)

**diversity** variety (p. 13)

**division of labor** a system in which workers make only one part of a product and never see the finished item (p. 70)

**dollar diplomacy** Taft's foreign policy of relying on economic rather than military force to expand American power (p. 90)

**domestic affairs** the nation's internal matters (p. 29)

**domino theory** the theory that if one nation fell to communism then its neighbors would soon follow (p. 156)

**doves** Americans who criticized the Vietnam War (p. 157)

**Dow Jones Industrial Average** an average of the stock prices of major industries (p. 112)

**downsizing** to reduce a business in size by cutting jobs and production (p. 170)

**draft** a law requiring men to serve in the military (p. 59)

***Dred Scott* v. *Sandford*** Supreme Court ruling that slaves are not citizens and are the property of their owners (p. 55)

**Dust Bowl** the name for the Midwest after prolonged drought and dust storms (p. 113)

**duty** tax (p. 15)

## E

**Electoral College** the group who elects the President (p. 27)

**emancipation** freedom (p. 48)

**Emancipation Proclamation** the declaration that freed slaves only in areas under Confederate control (p. 59)

**embargo** a restriction on trade (p. 33); a ban (p. 161)

**Enforcement Act of 1870** an act banning the use of terror, force, or bribery to prevent people from voting based on their race (p. 66)

**Enlightenment** European intellectual movement that emphasized science and reason as the key to improving society (p. 22)

**Environmental Protection Agency (EPA)** a government agency to set and enforce national pollution standards (p. 154)

**Equal Rights Amendment (ERA)** a proposed amendment to the Constitution to prohibit discrimination based on gender (p. 151)

**escalation** expansion by stages, as from a local to national conflict (p. 157)

**evangelical** emphasis on the Bible as the final authority (p. 37)

**Exodusters** a group of southern blacks who migrated west on a mass "Exodus" (p. 73)

## F

**faction** group with special interests (p. 28)

**fascism** a philosophy that stresses nationalism and the supreme authority of the leader (p. 121)

**Federal Reserve System** a network of federal banks that hold money deposits from national banks and use the money to increase the credit supply when necessary (p. 95)

**federal system of government** a system of government under which powers are shared among the states and a central government (p. 27)

**Federal Trade Commission (FTC)** enforces regulation of businesses (p. 95)

**Federalists** people who supported the U.S. Constitution (p. 28)

**feminism** theory favoring the political, economic, and social equality of men and women (p. 151)

**feudalism** an economic and political system under which a powerful noble, or lord, divided his large land holdings among lesser lords, who hired peasants, called serfs, to farm the land in exchange for a share of the harvest, shelter, and protection (p. 6)

**Fifteenth Amendment** law stating that "no citizen could be denied the right to vote on account of race, color, or previous condition" (p. 64)

**First Battle of Bull Run** the first major battle of the Civil War (p. 58)

**First Continental Congress** a meeting of delegates from several colonies to plan a united resistance against Britain (pp. 21, 22)

**flapper** a rebellious, fun-loving, bold young woman who wore short dresses and cut her hair (p. 104)

**Fort Sumter, South Carolina** fort where the first shots of the Civil War were fired (p. 56)

**Fourteen Points** President Wilson's program for reconstruction after WWI (p. 102)

**Fourteenth Amendment** law that refined citizenship to include African Americans and granted equal protection under the law to all citizens (p. 64)

**fragmentation bombs** bombs that throw thick metal casings in all directions when they explode (p. 157)

**franchise** a business opened under the name of a parent company (p. 137)

**free enterprise system** an economic system in which goods are privately owned and investments are made by private decision rather than state control (p. 41)

**free silver** the unlimited coining of silver to increase the money supply (p. 76)

**free soilers** people who fight slavery (p. 55)

**Freedman's Bureau** organization established by Congress to set up schools and give clothing, meals, and medical help to thousands of black and white war refugees (p. 63)

**Freedom Rides** term to describe when the youth of the civil rights movement rode buses south to test the Supreme Court's ruling that segregation on interstate buses was illegal (p. 143)

**French and Indian War** a war between Britain and France for control of land in North America (p. 20)

**Fugitive Slave Act** ordered all United States citizens to assist in the capture of runaway slaves (p. 54)

**fundamentalism** support of traditional Christian views (p. 106)

## G

**Gadsden Purchase** when the United States bought the land of New Mexico and Arizona from Mexico for $10 million (p. 53)

**gag rule** prohibiting antislavery petitions from being read or acted on in the House of Representatives (p. 48)

**generation gap** a difference in values and attitudes between one generation and another (p. 158)

**Geneva Accords** conference that divided Vietnam into two nations at the 17th parallel (p. 156)

**Geneva Convention** convention that established the standards for treatment of prisoners of war (p. 129)

**genocide** the deliberate killing of a group of people (pp. 100, 128)

**gentry** the wealthy (p. 16)

**Gettysburg Address** speech by Lincoln explaining that the Union's purpose in the Civil War was to protect and expand freedom (p. 60)

**ghettos** places where one racial or ethnic group dominates (p. 79)

**ghost towns** abandoned mining communities (p. 38)

**GI** abbreviation for "Government Issue" (p. 126)

**GI Bill of Rights** a bill that gave veterans low-interest loans so they could purchase homes and provided educational stipends to attend college or graduate school (p. 137)

**Gilded Age** the period following Reconstruction (p. 78)

**graft** using one's job to gain profit (p. 80)

**Grange** an organized protest group of farmers to pressure lawmakers to regulate businesses that farmers depended on (p. 76)

**Great Awakening** a movement to renew religious faith and enthusiasm (p.18)

**Great Compromise** the compromise reached on how representation would work in the federal government; it set up a bicameral legislature with one house based on population, and the other with an even number of representatives (p. 27)

**Great Crash** the collapse of the stock market in 1929 (p. 112)

**Great Depression** the most severe economic downturn in the nation's history, which lasted from 1929 to 1941 (p. 112)

**Great Migration** the movement of people to the New England colonies (p. 12)

**Great Plains** grassland between the Mississippi River and the Rocky Mountains (p. 39)

**Great Society** term used to describe President Johnson's sweeping domestic reforms in the 1960s (p. 148)

**Great White Fleet** the new American naval force (p. 91)

**Greater East Asia Co-Prosperity Sphere** a group dedicated to liberating Asia from European colonizers (p. 123)

**greenbacks** the nation's first official currency (p. 59)

**Gross National Product (GNP)** the total value of goods and services a country produces annually (p. 109)

**Gulf of Tonkin Resolution** act that gave President Johnson the power to take whatever action he deemed necessary to prevent aggression against U.S. forces in Vietnam without an official declaration of war (p. 156)

## H

**Harlem Renaissance** the time period when Harlem became the cultural center for African American writers, artists, and poets (p. 105)

**haven** safe place (p. 13)

**hawks** Americans who supported the Vietnam War (p. 157)

**Hawley-Smoot Tariff** the highest import tax in history (p. 115)

**Head Start** a preschool program for children from low-income families (p. 148)

**Helsinki Accords** agreements with 70 European nations, Canada, and the Soviet Union to cooperate economically and promote human rights (p. 164)

**Ho Chi Minh Trail** a supply route through Laos and Cambodia used by the Viet Cong (p. 157)

**Holocaust** the systematic murder of European Jews (p. 128)

**Homestead Act** an act in 1862 that sold public land very cheaply (p. 73)

**homesteaders** people who farmed claims under the Homestead Act (p. 75)

**Hoovervilles** shantytowns built by homeless people during the Depression (p. 113)

**horizontal consolidation** when a company brings together many firms of the same business into one (p. 69)

**House of Burgesses** legislature of the Jamestown colony (p. 11)

**House Un-American Activities Committee (HUAC)** government agency that relentlessly pursued anyone it suspected of supporting Communist ideas (p. 133)

**hundred days** refers to FDR's first one hundred days in office (p. 117)

## I

**ICBMs** intercontinental ballistic missiles (p. 135)

**immigrants** people who enter a new country to settle (p. 18)

**impeach** charge a government official with wrongdoing in office (pp. 64, 163)

**imperialism** a foreign policy in which stronger nations attempt to create empires by dominating weaker nations economically, politically, culturally, or militarily (p. 88)

**impressment** British policy of stopping American ships at sea and forcing the people into the British navy (p. 35)

**inauguration** official swearing-in ceremony (p. 29)

**incumbent** the current officeholder (p. 165)

**indentured servants** men and women who worked for seven years in exchange for their passage to the Americas (p. 11)

**Indian Removal Act** allowed the government to remove thousands of Cherokees from their homelands (p. 45)

**Industrial Revolution** the ongoing process to increase production of goods through machines (p. 41)

**industrialization** the growth of industry (p. 42)

**industrialized union** a union that organizes workers from all crafts in a particular industry (p. 71)

**INF Treaty** treaty between the United States and the Soviet Union that provided for the destruction of about 2,500 Soviet and American missiles in Europe (p. 169)

**inflation** a steady increase of prices over time (p. 24)

**infrastructure** the public property and public services of an area (p. 65)

**initiative** allows voters to put a law they want on the ballot (p. 94)

**installment plan** a system of payment that allows people to pay for things over a period of time (p. 109)

**integration** the bringing together of different races (p. 141)

**interchangeable parts** the system in which all parts are made to an exact standard (p. 41)

**interned** confined (p. 130)

**Internet** a worldwide information network (p. 174)

**interracial** made up of different races (p. 142)

**investment capital** money a business spends in the hope of future gain (p. 41)

**Iran-Contra affair** refers to the scandal of the Reagan administration when some government officials carried on illegal activities and secret dealings with Iran (p. 169)

**Irish Potato Famine** when disease ruined the Irish potato crop and caused massive starvation (p. 50)

**iron curtain** name given by Churchill to Communist domination and oppression in Asia and Europe (p. 132)

**island hopping** U.S. military offensive strategy in the Pacific during WWII (p. 129)

**isolationism** avoiding political alliances with foreign countries (p. 108)

**itinerant** traveling (p. 18)

## J

**Japanese American Citizens League (JACL)** an organization of Japanese Americans who sought compensation for their losses because of internment during WWII (p. 152)

**Jay's Treaty** a treaty between Britain and the United States in which the British left the Northwest Territory in exchange for better trading rights (p. 31)

**Jazz Age** name given to the 1920s (p. 105)

**Jim Crow** laws designed to prevent African Americans from exercising their equal rights (p. 85)

**jingoism** intense national pride (p. 89)

**joint stock company** companies formed by investors to found colonies (p. 11)

**judicial review** the power of the Supreme Court to decide if laws made by Congress are constitutional (p. 33)

## K

***kamikazes*** Japanese suicide planes (p. 129)

**Kansas-Nebraska Act** an act that created two new territories, Kansas and Nebraska, whose residents could decide for themselves whether or not they wanted slavery (pp. 54, 55)

**King Philip's War** war between English settlers and Native Americans over land (p. 12)

**kinship** family relationships (p. 5)

## L

**labor union** an organization of workers formed to protect their interests, usually by negotiating to resolve issues such as wages and working conditions (p. 42)

**land mine** an explosive device planted in the ground (p. 157)

**land speculators** people who bought land cheaply from the government to resell to settlers at a large profit (p. 73)

**laissez-faire** hands off (p. 78)

**Latinos** people whose origins are in Spanish-speaking Latin America (p. 152)

**League of Nations** an organization of all the nations to work for worldwide security and peace (p. 102)

**legislature** lawmaking assembly (p. 11)

**Lend-Lease Act** an act giving the President the authority to aid any nation whose defense he believed was vital to the security of the United States (p. 124)

**Liberty Bonds** special war bonds sold to Americans during WWI (p. 101)

**Limited Test Ban Treaty** a treaty between the United States and the Soviet Union prohibiting nuclear testing above ground (p. 149)

**Lincoln-Douglas Debates** senatorial debates between Abraham Lincoln and Stephen Douglas where slavery was a major issue (p. 55)

**lineage** tracing origins to a common ancestor (p. 7)

**literacy** the ability to read and write (p. 83)

**long drive** the herding of thousands of cattle to railway centers scattered along the plains (p. 75)

**loose construction** a way to interpret the U.S. Constitution that states that the government can do anything not specifically prohibited in the U.S. Constitution (p. 31)

**Lost Generation** writers and artists who rejected the spirit of the Jazz Age and materialistic values and scorned popular American culture (p. 105)

**Louisiana Purchase** land purchased by Jefferson from France expanding the size of the United States (p. 33)

**Lower South** portion of the United States that included Texas, Louisiana, Mississippi, Alabama, Florida, Georgia, and South Carolina (p. 56)

**Loyalists** people loyal to Britain during the Revolutionary War (p. 23)

**lynching** the unlawful killing of a person at the hands of a mob (p. 85)

## M

**Magna Carta** document granting nobles various legal rights (p. 6)

**mail-order catalog** printed material that advertises a wide range of goods that can be purchased by mail (p. 86)

**Manchurian Incident** when the Japanese army seized Manchuria from Chinese troops (p. 123)

**mandate** a public endorsement of ideas (p. 147)

**Manhattan Project** the name given to the research project to develop the atomic bomb in the United States (p. 129)

**manifest destiny** an undeniable fate (p. 38, 53)

**manufacturing** production of goods by machinery (p. 41)

**March on Washington** a civil rights march on Washington in 1963 to call for jobs and freedom for African Americans (p. 144)

**Market Revolution** the change in the way Americans made, bought, and sold goods (p. 41)

**Marshall Plan** the plan in which the United States gave financial aid to Europe and at the same time gained allies and trading partners (p. 133)

**martial law** emergency rule by the military (p. 59)

**mass media** the use of print and broadcast methods to communicate to large numbers of people (p. 105)

**mass production** production in great amounts (p. 68)

**Massacre at Wounded Knee** when American troops killed 200 unarmed Sioux men, women, and children (p. 74)

**Mayflower Compact** an agreement made by the English Puritans of the Plymouth Colony to obey all the laws set out by the government of the colony (p. 12)

**McCarthyism** engaging in smear tactics and baseless accusations to find Communists in the government (p. 135)

**Medicaid** medical coverage for low-income Americans (p. 148)

**Medicare** medical insurance for Americans 65 and older (p. 148)

**mercantilism** the theory that a nation should try and keep as much bullion, or uncoined gold and silver, as possible (p. 15)

**mercenaries** foreign soldiers who fight for pay (p. 23)

**MIA** missing in action (p. 159)

**Middle Ages** time period from around 500–1300 A.D. (p. 6)

**Middle America** mainstream Americans (p. 158)

**middle class** class of people that arose in Europe in the Middle Ages consisting of merchants, traders, and artisans (p. 6)

**Middle Colonies** New York, New Jersey, Pennsylvania, and Delaware (p. 13)

**Middle Passage** the route that brought enslaved Africans to the American colonies (p. 17)

**migrant farm workers** the people who moved around the country to plant and harvest crops under backbreaking conditions (p. 152)

**migrate** to move (p. 18)

**migration** the movement of people to settle in a new place (p. 5)

**militarism** the aggressive buildup of armed forces (p. 98)

**military-industrial complex** permanent mobilization of the military and its ties to business and industry (p. 134)

**militia** armed citizens who serve as soldiers in an emergency (p. 20)

**Miranda rule** states that police must inform criminal suspects of their rights before questioning (p. 148)

**missions** settlements of Catholic priests established to preach, teach, and convert Native Americans to Christianity (p. 10)

**Missouri Compromise** a compromise in 1820 that admitted Missouri as a slave state and Maine as a free state, ensuring slave and free states equal power in the Senate (p. 35)

**mobile society** society where people continually move from place to place (p. 37)

**mobilization** getting military forces ready for war (p. 98)

**Modern Republicanism** Eisenhower's program to slow the growth of the federal government and limit presidential power (p. 139)

**monarchs** rulers of territories or states (p. 6)

**money supply** the amount of money in the national economy (p. 76)

**monopoly** complete control over one product or service (p. 69)

**Monroe Doctrine** foreign policy that warned foreign nations not to interfere in the nations of the Western Hemisphere and closed the Western Hemisphere to colonization (p. 44)

**Montgomery bus boycott** a boycott during which African Americans refused to ride the public buses until they were integrated (p. 141)

**muckrakers** journalists who uncovered wrongdoings among businesses and politicians (p. 93)

**multiculturalism** the movement to give greater attention to non-European culture in education (p. 174)

**multinational corporations** businesses that operate in more than one nation (p. 173)

**municipal** city (p. 94)

**mutiny** revolt (p. 17)

## N

**napalm** a jellylike substance that burns uncontrollably (p. 157)

**Nation of Islam** a religious movement, also known as Black Muslims, which opposes integration and preaches self-help (p. 145)

**National Aeronautics and Space Administration (NASA)** an independent agency for space exploration (p. 139)

**National American Woman Suffrage Association (NAWSA)** an association that fought for women's suffrage (p. 96)

**National Association for the Advancement of Colored People (NAACP)** an organization that fought for African American rights through the courts (p. 85)

**national debt** the amount of money the government borrowed that had to be paid back (p. 119)

**National Defense Education Act** an act giving money to schools to improve education in science and mathematics (p. 139)

**National Organization for Women (NOW)** women's organization founded in 1966 to bring women into full participation in American society (p. 151)

**nationalism** the belief that one nation's goals are superior to those of other nations (p. 88)

**nativism** a policy that favored native-born Americans over immigrants (pp. 54, 81)

**natural rights** rights of people because they are human beings (p. 22)

**Nazism** a philosophy that includes fanatical ideas of nationalism and racial superiority (p. 121)

**neutral** not taking either side (p. 31)

**Neutrality Acts acts** passed by FDR to help the United States maintain neutrality in WWII (p. 124)

**New Deal** FDR's program to help the nation deal with the Great Depression (p. 117)

**New England Colonies** Massachusetts, New Hampshire, Connecticut, Rhode Island, Maine, and Vermont (p. 12)

**New Federalism** Nixon's policy of calling for a new partnership between the federal government and the state governments (p. 161); Reagan's policy that gave more power to the state and local governments to create and pay for social programs (p. 168)

**"New Frontier"** Kennedy's programs and policies to improve the economy, fight poverty and inequality, and develop a space program (p. 147)

**New Left** an anti–Vietnam War political movement that demanded radical change to cure the ills of poverty and racism (p. 158)

**New Nationalism** FDR's policy calling for reforms in business, welfare, and the workplace (p. 95)

**New Right** a powerful conservative coalition (p. 167)

**Niagara Movement** a movement that called for full civil liberties for African Americans, an end to racial discrimination, and a recognition of human brotherhood (p. 83)

**nomads** people who roam from place to place (pp. 39, 74)

**North American Free Trade Agreement (NAFTA)** agreement that would gradually reduce the trade restrictions among the United States, Canada, and Mexico (p. 173)

**North Atlantic Treaty Organization (NATO)** an alliance of mutual military assistance (p. 133)

**Nuclear Regulatory Commission (NRC)** a government agency to oversee the safety of nuclear power plants (p. 154)

**nullification** rejection (p. 32)

**nullified** rejected (p. 45)

**Nuremberg Trials** the prosecution of top Nazi leaders for crimes against humanity (p. 128)

## O

**obsolete** outdated (p. 52)

**Office of War Mobilization** government superagency that served to centralize the nation's resources and maximize production (p. 126)

**Olive Branch Petition** American colonists asking the king for peace (p. 22)

**Open Door Policy** United States' foreign policy toward China with the goal of gaining access to China's huge markets (p. 89)

**oral histories** the passing down of customs and traditions from one generation to another by word of mouth (p. 5)

**Oregon Trail** main route across the Plains and the Rockies (p. 38)

**Organization of Petroleum Exporting Countries (OPEC)** a group of nations in the Middle East that control the export of oil from that area (p. 161)

## P

**pardon** forgiveness for a crime (p. 63)

**Paris peace talks** President Johnson's failed attempt to reach a peace settlement in Vietnam (p. 159)

**patent** grant from the government giving an inventor the sole right to use, make, and sell a product for a certain period of time (p. 41)

**patriotism** love of one's country (p. 24)

**patronage** the system of giving government jobs to friends and supporters (p. 45)

**Peace Corps** a program that sends volunteers around the world as health workers, educators, and technicians (p. 149)

**Pendleton Civil Service Act** an act in 1883 that created the Civil Service Commission to test employees (p. 78)

**penny auctions** auctions where farmers would bid pennies on land and machines auctioned off by banks to help out their neighbors (p. 114)

**Pequot War** a war fought between Connecticut settlers and the Pequot people (p. 12)

**per capita income** the average annual income per person (p. 137)

**persecuted** attacked for religious beliefs (p. 12)

**Persian Gulf War** a war between the United States and Iraq over the Iraqi invasion of Kuwait (p. 170)

**philanthropists** people who give donations to worthy causes (p. 83)

**piecework** a system in which workers get paid a fixed amount for each piece they produce (p. 70)

**plantations** large farms (p. 8)

**Platt Amendment** law giving Cuba limited independence from the United States (p. 89)

***Plessy* v. *Ferguson*** Supreme Court case establishing the "separate but equal" doctrine, which legalized segregation (p. 85)

**pogroms** violent massacres of Jews (p. 79)

**political machines** groups run by "bosses" that controlled city government (p. 80)

**political party** a group that seeks to win elections and hold public office (p. 31)

**poll tax** a special fee paid to vote (p. 85)

**Pontiac's Rebellion** a rebellion of Native Americans against the British (p. 21)

**popular sovereignty** allowing people to choose for themselves if their state is free or slave (p. 54)

**Populists** another name for the People's Party (p. 76)

**POWs** prisoners of war (p. 159)

**preamble** introduction (p. 22)

**precedents** rules, examples, or traditions to be followed by others (p. 29)

**presidios** Spanish forts (pp. 10, 39)

**price controls** a system of pricing determined by the government (p. 101)

**privateer** English adventurer (p. 11)

**Proclamation of 1763** when the British government declared all land west of the Appalachian Mountains closed to settlement (p. 21)

**Progressive Era** the period from about 1890 to 1920 (p. 93)

**Prohibition** a ban on the manufacture and sale of alcohol (p. 81)

**propaganda** information intended to sway public opinion (p. 98)

**proprietary colony** a colony granted by a monarch to an individual or group to govern (p. 13)

**public works programs** government-funded projects to build public facilities (p. 117)

**Pueblo Revolt of 1680** Native American revolt against the Spanish colonization in Florida (p. 10)

**puppet state** a supposedly independent country under the control of a powerful neighbor (p. 123)

**purges** the process of removing enemies and undesirable individuals from power (p. 121)

**Puritans** settlers in New England who wanted a "purer" religion (p. 12)

**push-pull factors** events and conditions that drove Americans and immigrants west (p. 73)

## Q

**Quakers** Protestants who suffered religious persecution in England (p. 13)

**quota** numerical limit (p. 108)

## R

**racism** the idea that a person's intelligence and character are based on race (p. 91)

**Radical Republicans** members of Congress who opposed Lincoln's Reconstruction plan because they felt it was too lenient (p. 63)

**ragtime** a melody imposed over a marching-band beat (p. 84)

**ratify** approve (p. 28)

**rationing** distributing goods to consumers in a fixed amount (p. 101)

***realpolitik*** Kissinger's policy in which a nation makes decisions based on maintaining its own strength rather than following moral principles (p. 162)

**recall** allows citizens to remove public officials from office before an election (p. 94)

**recession** a period of slow business activity (p. 119)

**Reconstruction** the period of rebuilding the South and restoring the southern states to the Union after the Civil War (p. 63)

**Reconstruction Finance Corporation (RFC)** an organization that gave government credits to large industries and lent money to banks (p. 115)

**reconversion** the social and economic transition from a wartime economy to a peacetime economy (p. 139)

**red scare** an intense fear of communism and other politically radical ideas (p. 108)

**referendum** allows citizens to approve or reject a state law (p. 94)

**Reformation** revolt led by Martin Luther against the Catholic Church (p. 6)

**religious tolerance** the idea that people of different religions should live in peace together (p. 12)

**Renaissance** a movement of artists, writers, and scholars who sought knowledge in all fields of study (p. 6)

**reparations** payment for economic injury suffered during a war (p. 102)

**republic** a government run by the people through representatives (p. 26)

**republican virtues** virtues such as self-reliance, industry, frugality, harmony, and sacrifice of individual needs for the good of the community that were promoted to develop character in the new republic (p. 37)

**reservations** lands set aside by the government for Native Americans (pp. 34, 74)

**revival** meeting during which people are brought back to religious life by listening to preaching (p. 37)

**Revolutionary War** the war for American independence (p. 21)

**rock-and-roll** a new style of music that developed in the 1950s (p. 138)

***Roe* v. *Wade*** Supreme Court decision that legalized abortion (p. 151)

**Roosevelt Corollary** an extension of the Monroe Doctrine stating that the United States could intervene in any international affair to prevent intervention from other powers (p. 90)

**royal colony** a colony with a royal governor appointed by the king (p. 11)

**rule of law** public officials must make decisions based on law not on personal wishes (p. 22)

**rural** farm areas and countryside (p. 42)

**rural free delivery (RFD)** free mail delivery of goods to people on farms (p. 86)

**Russian Revolution** a revolution in Russia in which the people overthrew the Czar (p. 99)

## S

**SALT I** the Strategic Arms Limitation Treaty that froze intercontinental ballistic missiles at the 1972 level (p. 162)

**salutary neglect** when England did not enforce trade regulations with the colonies (p. 15)

**Sand Creek Massacre** battle between the United States and the Cheyenne (p. 74)

**Santa Fe Trail** trail that veered southwest into New Mexico (p. 38)

**satellite nations** countries dominated by a more powerful neighbor (p. 132)

**saturation bombing** military strategy that calls for the dropping of thousands of tons of explosives over wide areas (p. 157)

**savanna** grasslands (p. 7)

**scalawags** white Southern Republicans (p. 64)

**scarce** in short supply (p. 7)

**Scopes trial** the trial of a science teacher who challenged a state law prohibiting the teaching of evolution (p. 106)

**secede** to withdraw formally from membership in a group or organization (p. 45)

**secessionists** people who wanted to leave the Union (p. 56)

**Second Continental Congress** a gathering that took place in the summer of 1775 during which delegates from the colonies met in Philadelphia to discuss the independence of the United States (p. 22)

**Second Great Awakening** a religious movement among Protestants to revive religion in people's lives, resulting in the rapid growth of new Protestant denominations and the Mormons (p. 37)

**Second New Deal** refers to FDR's second round of programs to aid the nation during the Great Depression (p. 117)

**sections** distinct regions (p. 42)

**sedition** any speech or action that encouraged rebellion (p. 101)

**segregation** the separation of people by race (p. 85)

**Selective Service Act** an act that authorized a draft (p. 100)

**Selective Training and Services Act** a draft that required all men from ages 61 to 76 to register for military service (p. 126)

**self-determination** the power to make decisions about one's own future (p. 102)

**self-sufficient** making or having what is necessary to maintain survival (p. 16)

**Seneca Falls Convention** a convention in 1848 of women activists to protest their lack of social and political rights, including suffrage (p. 49)

**separation of powers** giving each branch of government its own area of authority (p. 27)

**settlement houses** community centers that offered social services (p. 81)

**sharecropping** a system of farming in which the people farm land for a share of the crop (p. 65)

**Shays' Rebellion** a revolt of Massachusetts farmers against an unfair tax (p. 26)

**Sherman Antitrust Act** an act passed in 1890 outlawing trusts and restraining interstate trade (p. 69)

**Sherman Silver Purchase Act** law passed by Congress in 1890 to increase the amount of silver the government was required to purchase every month (p. 76)

**siege** military strategy of surrounding a city and starving it into surrender (p. 60)

**silent majority** those who opposed the anti–Vietnam War protesters and radical change (p. 159)

**sit-down strikes** strikes in which laborers stopped work but refused to leave the workplace (p. 119)

**sit-ins** a form of protest in which groups sat down in segregated public places and refused to move (p. 143)

**social Darwinism** the theory that argued that the government should not interfere in business practices so that those most "fit" would rise to the top and everyone would benefit (p. 69)

**social gospel movement** a movement among religious institutions seeking to apply the Gospel teachings directly to society (p. 81)

**Social Security system** a New Deal program to provide financial security, in the form of regular payments, for retirees, unemployed people, and the disabled (p. 117)

**social welfare programs** programs such as unemployment benefits, health benefits, and social security (p. 94)

**socialism** an economic and political philosophy that favors public rather than private control of property (p. 71)

**sociology** the study of how people interact with society (p. 81)

**soddie** a house made of tough prairie soil (p. 75)

**solid South** new bloc of southern Democrats in Congress (p. 66)

**sooners** in 1889, people who illegally claimed land by sneaking past government officials before the land races began (p. 74)

**Southern Christian Leadership Conference (SCLC)** a group founded by Martin Luther King, Jr., that focused on the civil rights movement in the South using nonviolent protests (p. 142)

**speakeasies** illegal bars during Prohibition (p. 106)

**special prosecutor** a prosecutor that works for the Justice Department but leads an independent investigation (p. 163)

**specialization** a system where each worker performs just one part of the entire production line (p. 41)

**speculation** the practice of making high-risk investments in the hopes of getting a huge return (p. 110)

**sphere of influence** areas of economic and political control (p. 89)

**spoils** rewards of war (p. 102)

***Sputnik*** the first artificial satellite to orbit Earth, launched by the Soviets (p. 135)

**stagflation** a stalled economy (p. 164)

**stalemate** when neither side in a conflict has an advantage (p. 98)

**Stamp Act** tax on all printed material (p. 21)

**staple crops** crops always in demand (p. 15)

**stereotypes** exaggerated or oversimplified descriptions of reality (p. 75)

**Stono Rebellion** a slave revolt in South Carolina (p. 17)

**Strategic Arms Reduction Treaty** treaty between the United States and the Soviet Union that drastically reduced the size of both nations' long-range nuclear missile stockpiles (p. 170)

**Strategic Defense Initiative (SDI)** Reagan's initiative to provide a missile shield in space to counter anti-Soviet aggression (p. 168)

**strict construction** a way to interpret the U.S. Constitution that states that the national government can only exercise powers specifically stated in the U.S. Constitution (p. 31)

**strikes** work stoppages intended to force an employer to meet certain demands, as in the demand for higher wages (p. 42)

**Student Nonviolent Coordinating Committee** founded in 1960, a student civil rights organization and an offshoot of the SCLC (p. 142)

**subsidy** a payment made by the government for the development of certain key industries (p. 78)

**suburbs** residential areas around cities (p. 80)

**suffrage** the right to vote (p. 49)

**supply-side economics** a policy that focuses on cutting taxes and putting more money in the hands of business, which would then hire more people and produce more goods, making the economy grow faster (p. 168)

**Sussex Pledge** German promise not to attack ships without warning (p. 99)

**sweatshops** factories where people worked long hours for low pay (p. 70)

**synagogue** house of Jewish worship (p. 13)

## T

**tariff tax** (p. 31)

**Tariff of 1828** heavy tax on imports (p. 45)

**teach-ins** separate classes held on college campuses across the country to discuss the Vietnam War (p. 158)

**televangelism** using the medium of television to appeal to viewers about political as well as religious issues (p. 167)

**temperance movement** the movement to eliminate alcohol consumption (pp. 47, 81)

**tenant farming** a system of farming in which a person rents land on which they grow and sell their own crops (p. 65)

**tenements** crowded apartments that lacked sanitation, safety, and comfort (p. 42)

**Tet Offensive** the name for the massive military offensive launched by the North Vietnamese army and the Viet Cong on military bases across South Vietnam (p. 157)

**Texas War for Independence** war between Texas and Mexico for Texas's independence (p. 39)

**Thirteenth Amendment** law that ended slavery in the United States (p. 61)

**Thirty-eighth (38th) parallel** the line that separates North and South Korea (p. 134)

**Three-fifths Compromise** stated that the slave population of a state could be counted as three-fifths toward representation (p. 27)

**totalitarian** governments that used terror and force to control citizens' lives and suppress opposition (p. 121)

**trans-Appalachia** area west of the Appalachian Mountains (p. 38)

**transcendentalism** the idea that human beings were essentially good and that spiritual insight would lead to truths that reason could not (p. 47)

**transcontinental railroad** a railroad line that went across the United States (p. 68)

**transistors** tiny circuit devices that amplify, control, and generate electric signals (p. 137)

**Treaty of Ghent** the treaty that ended the war of 1812 (p. 35)

**Treaty of Greenville** gave the Native Americans land in Ohio to the United States (p. 34)

**Treaty of Guadalupe Hidalgo** ended the Mexican War and gave the United States Texas, New Mexico, and California, and paid Mexico $15 million (p. 53)

**Treaty of Paris (1763)** ended the French and Indian War, giving all French land in North America to the British (p. 20)

**Treaty of Paris (1783)** ended the Revolutionary War and recognized American independence (p. 24)

**triangular trade** system of trade between the New England colonies, Africa, and the Caribbean where rum was traded for slaves (p. 15)

**Truman Doctrine** U.S. foreign policy that calls on the United States to take a leadership role in supporting free people around the world (p. 132)

**trust** when a company combines operations with other companies all run by a board of trustees (p. 69)

**trustees** people who look after a business (p. 13)

**Turner thesis** theory of historian Jackson Turner that the frontier played a key role in the shaping of American character (p. 75)

**Turner's Rebellion** violent slave rebellion in Virginia (p. 43)

**Twenty-first Amendment** law that repealed Prohibition (p. 114)

**Twenty-fourth Amendment** law that outlawed the poll tax (p. 144)

## U

**U-boat** a German submarine that changed the rules of naval warfare (p. 99)

**Underground Railroad** a network of escape routes for slaves fleeing the South (p. 48)

**Union** unified states of the nation (p. 52)

**United Farm Workers (UFW)** a union to improve conditions for migrant farm workers (p. 152)

**Upper South** Virginia, North Carolina, Tennessee, and Arkansas (p. 56)

**urban** cities and industrial areas (p. 42)

**utopian communities** small groups dedicated to perfection in social and political conditions (p. 47)

**U-2 incident** when a U.S. spy plane was shot down over Soviet territory (p. 135)

## V

**vaudeville** shows with comic skits, magic acts, songs, and dances (p. 84)

**Versailles Treaty** the treaty that officially ended WWI in 1919 (p. 102)

**vertical consolidation** when one company buys all the phases of a product's development so that it can produce things quicker and cheaper than all other competitors (p. 69)

**veto** prohibit (p. 27)

**vice** immoral or corrupt behavior (p. 81)

**victory garden** a home vegetable garden planted to add to the home food supply and replace farm produce sent to feed the soldiers (p. 126)

**Viet Cong** Communist guerrilla forces in South Vietnam (p. 156)

**Vietminh** nationalists in Vietnam (p. 156)

**Vietnamization** Nixon's plan to withdraw American forces from Vietnam and replace them with South Vietnamese soldiers (p. 159)

**vigilantes** citizens who take the law into their own hands (p. 101)

**Virginia and Kentucky Resolutions** stated that the states, not the federal government, could decide if laws were constitutional (p. 32)

**Volunteers in Service to America (VISTA)** a program that sent people to help poor communities (p. 148)

**Voting Rights Act of 1965** an act that gave federal officials the right to register voters if state officials blocked registration (p. 144)

## W

**war of attrition** an offensive strategy in which one side inflicts losses on the other until it wears it down (p. 58)

**War of 1812** war between Britain and the United States caused by British interests in the West and conflict with the Native Americans (p. 35)

**War Powers Act** an act of Congress to curtail the power of the President to involve the United States in foreign conflicts (p. 164)

**War Refugee Board (WRB)** agency created by FDR to help rescue Jews in Eastern Europe (p. 128)

**Warren Commission** the group, headed by Chief Justice Earl Warren, to investigate the assassination of President Kennedy (p. 147)

**Warsaw Ghetto** an area where Jews lived that was sealed off by Germans in order to starve the people living there (p. 128)

**Warsaw Pact** military alliance between the Soviet Union and nations of Eastern Europe, formed in 1955 (p. 133)

**Watergate scandal** during the Nixon Administration when five men were caught trying to wiretap phones in the headquarters of the Democratic National Committee at the Watergate apartment complex in Washington, D.C. (p. 163)

**welfare capitalism** when employers begin to pay better wages and provide benefits to employees (p. 110)

**Whiskey Rebellion** when farmers in Pennsylvania revolted against a new whiskey tax (p. 31)

**Whitewater affair** during the Clinton Administration when the President was charged with taking part in fraudulent loan schemes in Arkansas and of taking illegal campaign contributions in return for political favors (p. 172)

**Wilmot Proviso** addendum asking not to allow slavery in any western territory (p. 53)

**wiretaps** listening devices (p. 163)

**Woodstock festival** a gathering of counterculture youth in upstate New York to listen to music and enjoy fellowship (p. 153)

**World Trade Organization (WTO)** organization designed to help resolve trade disputes and negotiate new trade agreements (p. 173)

**writ of habeas corpus** the legal right to a trial (p. 59)

## X

**XYZ affair** when the French government tried to bribe United States officials (p. 32)

## Y

**yellow journalism** news stories about murder, scandals, and tales of vice (p. 84)

## Z

**Zimmermann Note** an intercepted communication that said Germany would give Mexico the American Southwest if they declared war on the United States (p. 99)

# INDEX